THE TIVOLI ROAD BAKER

MICHAEL JAMES
with Pippa James

Photography by Bonnie Savage and Alan Benson

For Mum, who missed all of this.

THE TIVOLI ROAD BAKER

MICHAEL JAMES
with Pippa James

Photography by Bonnie Savage and Alan Benson

Hardie Grant

BOOKS

WELCOME TO
TIVOLI ROAD BAKERY

EAT

GRANOLA, FRUIT & YOGHURT	9.5
TOAST / FRUIT TOAST	4 / 7
HAM, CHEESE & TOMATO CROISSANT	7.5
TOASTED CRUMPETS, TRB JAM & BUTTER	8.5
HEIRLOOM TOMATOES, STRACCIATELLA & VERBENA ON S/D	11.5
LOVAGE CURED SALMON ON RYE, REMOULADE & MUSTARD LEAF	12.0

FROM 11AM UNTIL SOLD OUT

SANDWICHES	10.5
SALAD	10.5
SAUSAGE ROLLS	7.0
PIES	8.0

DRINK

SODAS	4.5
ORGANIC JUICES OJ/AJ	4.0
RED HILL SPARKLING PEAR	4.5
CHAI	4.5
HOT CHOCOLATE	4.5
ICED LATTE	4.0
SMALL BATCH ESPRESSO	FROM 3.5
TEAS	4.0
COLD DRIP	4.5

WE NOW MAKE COMPOST
FREE TO GOOD HOMES

A note from Dan Lepard

To bake a great loaf of bread just needs a good recipe and a little practice, whereas to build a great bakery ... well, that takes every ounce of your drive, patience, breathtaking nerve and talent. That's just to get it off the ground and flying, let alone keep your bakery shooting forward, so polished that it looks to all a dazzling feat of dough wizardry. And if you can keep your sweetness, curiosity and family together through it all, while the path takes you through biting challenges that could sink it, but through determination and luck doesn't, then – as Kipling wrote – yours is the earth and everything in it.

The first thing you notice as you turn into Tivoli Road, hidden from the bustle of South Yarra, is how modest the building is. Much like St John Restaurant in London, it simply inhabits the site without trying to glare itself in the eyes of passers-by with a blinding razzle dazzle. Even on a beautiful Melbourne morning when the plane trees further up Tivoli Road are in vibrant leaf, flickering sunlight hitting the front of Tivoli Road Bakery and its bluestone kerb, you could almost miss it. That pungency of fresh-baked sourdough, and croissants with their burnt-butter allure, isn't quite a giveaway outside, as the inevitably blustery weather that Melbourne is known for is likely as not to blow the aroma away before you notice it. But once you step inside, you've arrived in a magical workshop full of craft, passion and the most extraordinary baking.

If you're early you'll get the first of the all-butter croissant and Danish fresh from the oven. You might find there's ruby red rhubarb sweet Danish, with a tart, bright fragrance, baked on a blob of vanilla custard inside the crisp flaky pastry. Or savoury cheese Danish topped with roasted cipollini, cheddar and sauerkraut, utterly melting, alongside a plateful of pissaladière covered with soft onions cooked to an ochre, anchovy fillets, and fleshy Mount Zero olives.

There are cakes to the left and right of you behind the serving counter glass. You might see lemon syrup cakes drizzled with icing with a jaunty twist of lemon peel on top, or raspberry financiers rich with ground almonds and flavoured with lemon thyme and tart beads from juicy Queensland finger limes. Slices of soft pound cake, made with bitter orange marmalade and grated zucchini, or mandarin and fresh blueberry teacake. Must-buys are the Tivoli doughnuts, perhaps even the famed Lamington ones, or simply filled with salted caramel and custard, or house-made strawberry jam and cream.

Of course, the bread is astounding. Not just skilfully mixed, shaped and baked, but inspired by Australian ingredients and unusual flours that lift the crust, crumb and flavour from everyday to extraordinary. Behind the counter there are shelves of bread, and through those shelves you can glimpse the oven the loaves are baked in, and often the bakers at work. Organic stoneground sourdough rounds, slashed with a deep cross in the centre and baked to the darkest bronze, sit alongside generously girthed baguettes and long Turkish loaves. But then on some days you'll find beer breads made with ale from Three Ravens Brewery, or shio koji, wakame and sesame sourdough, or crusty loaves inspired by chef Ben Shewry, flavoured with wattleseed, macadamia and redgum honey.

Michael and Pippa James are the reason Tivoli Road Bakery is so admired around the world. They share a modesty that earns respect in a world full of boastful noise and hyperbole: up high with many great bakers and chefs today. They share an unquenchable curiosity about their ingredients and craft, and inspire each other's skills and style via snaps on Instagram or abbreviated text message questions. In the old days, people revered the concept of mastery in baking. Today the emphasis is on a continuous journey of discovery, mistakes and breakthroughs, even if your answers arrive via a 70-character tweet.

Walking through the door of Tivoli Road Bakery you'll notice that the ingredients Michael and Pippa use aren't hidden away, but are stacked on display around the walls of the bakery. In part it's a canny way to make the most of a compact space, but it also celebrates the remarkable small producers they're associated with – from sacks of organic flour from Craig and Renée at Wholegrain Milling in Gunnedah in north-eastern New South Wales, Murray View Organics dried fruit, or even milk from Saint David's Dairy for the coffee. There's an honest fist-pump about it too, being in the enviable position that you do bake with some of Australia's finest ingredients and want to tell your customers, to promote these suppliers as fellow artisans.

Too often, the word 'artisan' is limited to a very selfish badge of honour bestowed by the baker upon himself, because they use sourdough or they give their loaves a charred crust. However, in the case of Tivoli it best describes their aim to be a step in the path our food takes – from the field to the table – and otherwise let their baking speak for itself. Artisan as in an action, rather than aggrandisement.

To give this room to happen, Michael James looks after the baking while his partner Pippa makes sure the rest runs smoothly: from keeping the finances in order through to running the shop, farmers' market and the team needed to support it. So yes, they're rarely out of each other's sight and space. If there's a bigger test on a relationship, I can't think of it. They work together seamlessly like a polished dance couple, at times in unison when it's hectic, say early on a weekday morning when the bread must be pulled out of the oven pronto, before it burns onto the shelves, the deliveries arrive right when you're grasping a scalding hot tray of strawberry Danish, shop staff start to arrive as bakers are ready to leave, so that person, that rock-steady partner you need to help you has to grasp your urgency without words or anger.

At other times they have to work trustingly in separation. Out at Abbotsford Convent Slowfood Market at half past seven on a Saturday morning, the last one of each month, Pippa is out wrestling with the stand, unpacking the breads, pastries and bikkies, most days with the morning light just breaking through the old gum trees. Beautiful, a joy ... except for the days it pours with rain, bitterly cold and miserable, having arrived at the bakery across town at 6 am in order to load the trailer and get moving before the traffic starts to squeeze the roads, while Pippa's dad makes breakfast for their two-year-old daughter Clover. Or those times when Michael gets halfway through the baking and suddenly the whole building loses power, with loaves rising towards their collapse point. You fix it, everything's fine, yet there's only really one unprintable word to describe those days. But close by you have your partner to reassure you, and you know, the next day it's all forgotten.

There is love at work at Tivoli, along with all the dedication and skill Michael and Pippa demonstrate, and this book is all the evidence you need. The enthusiasm that surrounds the bakery, the help that colleagues and friends are willing to give without question, all signify the admiration we have for what they've achieved.

Introduction

This book is a reflection of our bakery at a moment in time, and also of our belief that the food we eat shapes our interactions with the world and each other. My aim is for you to be able to recreate what we make at Tivoli Road and enjoy what we see and do every day. I also want to demonstrate the importance of the raw ingredients we use, and have highlighted some of the wonderful suppliers who help us in our journey. In many instances the produce that is available to us at any given time informs what we can make, and these primary producers really are heroes in our eyes.

Pippa and I met working at a restaurant in London. I had moved there from Cornwall aged eighteen after qualifying as a chef, and Pippa was doing the Aussie-on-a-working-holiday thing. I worked in all the sections of the kitchen, and found I enjoyed pastry the most. From there I started learning about different types of bread, and then Viennoiserie pastry, and I knew I had found my vocation. I gained experience in Michelin-starred kitchens, pastry shops and bakeries, picking up knowledge along the way. Pippa continued to work managing restaurants in London, Sydney and Melbourne, until we bought the bakery.

Our primary aim since day one has always been to maintain quality in the product, be that the bread we make, the pies, pastries, cakes or coffee, or the service we offer. One unexpected by-product of this is a sense of community that is truly amazing. Tivoli Road is really a network of relationships, between us and our staff, our suppliers and our loyal customers. One of our customers commented on this, noting that at the bakery he had met neighbours he'd lived beside for twenty years but hadn't known until we opened. Another couple who met at the bakery are about to get married. Something in our small space draws people in and makes them want to be part of the club.

This is an exciting time in Australian food culture, with native ingredients becoming more accessible and widely used. They haven't been used much in modern baking, and we love exploring ways to incorporate them into what we do. We talk all the time with colleagues, growers and suppliers, always wanting to find ingredients that we haven't used before so we can keep learning.

Tivoli Road Bakery is located in a rapidly developing area in Melbourne, with a seemingly endless population boom supported by multiple high-rise apartment developments. In the early days, every time a new cafe opened and we got a bit nervous about the competition, we reminded each other to focus on doing what we do to the best of our ability. Over time the white noise has faded and it's become easier to maintain that focus.

What we do isn't magic, it's the result of excellent ingredients, years of trial and error, and dedication to an ancient craft. I hope you can use our recipes and tips to create great food at home to share with the people you love.

BREAD

My thoughts on bread

There is something magical about pulling a loaf of bread out of the oven, whether at home or at the bakery. The crackling of the crust and the aroma filling the air is always exciting. To me bread is simple: flour, water and salt. The quality of these ingredients, plus time and temperature, are the important factors in making great, naturally leavened bread. My aim is to show you how to make nourishing real bread, and to give you the confidence to adapt the recipes in this book to suit your schedule.

Don't be discouraged by mistakes; use them to learn. Keep notes and make adjustments, and over time your bread will improve. It really is possible to make beautiful sourdough bread at home, mixing by hand and baking in your domestic oven.

Fermentation in sourdough

The sourdough starter that is the basis of our naturally leavened bread is a stable culture of lactic-acid bacteria and wild yeasts, whose activity works to break down the starches present in flour and turn them into sugars. Lactic-acid bacteria acidify the flour–water mixture, causing flour enzymes to break down grain proteins into peptides and amino acids, which yeast consume for growth. As the yeast grows, yeast invertase breaks down more starch, freeing up more sugar for lactic-acid bacteria. Sourdough's wild yeast Candida can survive in a low pH environment, unlike other yeast strains, and it converts the sugar it digests into carbon dioxide and ethanol. These are trapped by the elastic gluten structure formed by mixing the dough and fermentation. Fermentation involves a unique interaction between the wild yeast fungus and bacteria; the lactic-acid bacteria metabolise sugars that yeast cannot, while the yeast metabolises the by-products of lactic-acid fermentation.

Sourdough starters can vary in texture from liquid to a firm paste, and produce different flavours depending on the flour to water ratio. I prefer to use a liquid starter, as it is easy to maintain and use. A liquid starter between 20°C and 30°C (68°F and 86°F) will produce more bacterial activity and less yeast growth over time. As the yeast cells die, the bacteria takes over, producing a lactic acid flavour similar to yoghurt. A drier starter in the same temperature range will have a greater 'sweet-sour' effect on the final product, and will often smell fruitier.

Nutrition

Naturally leavened bread has been sustaining people all over the world for centuries. Real bread is a fermented-grain health food, not to be confused with the quick-risen processed loaves suffocating in plastic bags on the supermarket shelf. Even many 'sourdough' loaves these days are imposters, made with commercial yeasts, vinegar, palm oil and vital gluten.

Complex carbohydrates in the form of whole grains provide us with one of the most vital food products. Civilisations were started with grain storage and stone milling. In the old days everyone just had stone-ground whole grains that were milled in a local mill and baked in a community oven. Over time, this healthy food system became largely industrialised and the long-term costs of this are only now being counted in soil degradation, water pollution, increased wealth inequality, and the human health impacts resulting from greater consumption of processed food.

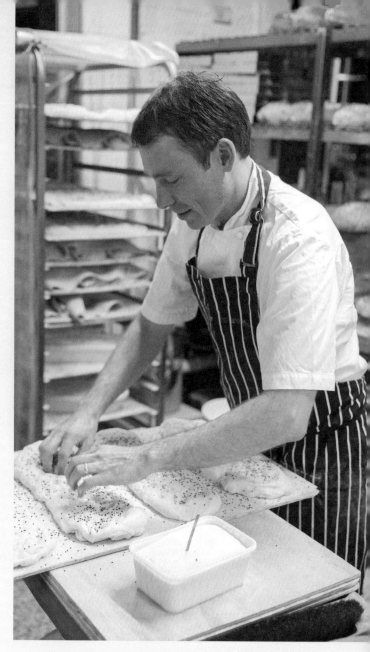

Sourdough bread is easier to digest and better for us than the highly processed, mass-produced loaves that now fill supermarkets and franchise bakeries. Proteins in the gluten complex cannot be broken down into smaller, safer peptides and amino acids without natural, slow fermentation. The exclusive use of refined flour overloads us with glucose, causing our sugar levels to spike and contributing to type 2 diabetes and other obesity-related illnesses. The bacteria present in sourdough and the lactic-acid action mean sourdough has a much lower glycemic index than processed bread, so the glucose is absorbed more slowly, stabilising blood sugar and aiding digestion.

The wheat berry is made up of the bran, germ and endosperm, each of which has different nutritional properties. *Bran* contains large quantities of vitamins B6, B5 and B3, as well as trace minerals and dietary fibre. B vitamins are beneficial for skin health, digestion, eyesight, nerve function and appetite, and fibre intake is critical to keeping the bacteria in our gut well fed. When we have too little fibre in our diet, our gut flora are actually forced to eat the mucus lining that protects our large intestine.

The *wheat germ* contains high-quality proteins, trace minerals, omega 3 fatty acids, monounsaturated and polyunsaturated fats, thiamin, vitamins C and E, zinc, phosphorous, folic acid and magnesium, iron and potassium. The *endosperm* comprises about 83 per cent of the berry and contains the carbohydrate, iron and soluble fibre. The aleurone layer is a layer of protein tissue that wraps around the endosperm and delivers vitamins, phytochemicals and minerals to us. This is most beneficial in wholegrains that have a high extraction and are stone ground.

Aside from creating good gluten structure in dough, one of the many benefits of a long fermentation process is the ability to make vital nutrients and minerals much simpler for our bodies to absorb. This is due to the lactic acid in the fermentation process, which helps to neutralise the acids that inhibit the absorption of nutrients and minerals.

Gluten sometimes gets a bad rap these days, and has been linked to many ailments, from IBS to infertility to depression. The problem with this is that it oversimplifies the issue in an attempt to find a silver bullet cure for everything, while ignoring the fact that many grain-based foods consumed today are highly processed and made from refined flour, often with added stabilisers, emulsifiers, oils and vital gluten (an additive made from wheat proteins that aids strength and elasticity in the dough, speeds up mixing, and guarantees a good rise – it basically produces bread on steroids). While arguing that 'gluten is bad for you', many people disregard the benefits of whole-grain baking in the search for an easy fix. In fact, what is needed is a balanced diet, comprised mostly of plants in an unprocessed form. And grains come from plants.

In sourdough, the process of fermentation neutralises the gluten so that, over time, your bread in effect becomes lower in gluten. A loaf of real sourdough bread made with good grains will be better for your gut than many of the processed gluten-free 'health foods' that are so widely available.

The reason we use organic whole grains and slow fermentation to make our bread is because it performs and tastes much better than highly processed flour and quick-rise methods. It is better for our environment and our health. And ultimately, it's far more fun and rewarding working with something that is alive.

Evolution of grain

There is a lot of buzz about 'ancient grains' such as einkorn, emmer and spelt. More of these grains are being planted in Australia to meet growing demand from bakers and consumers. It is very exciting to see the variety in flavours of these grains, from chocolate notes to apricot to vanilla. They are often described as being 'nutty' in flavour, but the subtleties are far more complex, as are the health benefits. These ancient grains are harder to extract and have a lower yield than modern wheat, making them more expensive to produce.

In the 1950s American biologist Norman Borlaug created high-yielding, fast-growing dwarf wheats in response to growing famine. While these varieties quickly yielded grain to feed millions, they also depended on expensive fertilisers, and required more water than traditional varieties, making them an unsustainable crop for small farms. Borlaug was credited as a humanitarian, and even won the Nobel Peace Prize, but the short-term benefits of industrial monoculture farming have only benefited large corporations in the long run, at the expense of small farmers.

This has created a huge wealth divide, and the health impacts of altering our food system so dramatically are becoming more apparent, with millions of people overweight and suffering related health issues. Soil health dramatically

declined, as dwarf wheat was short and stubby, with a short root system. There are billions of microbes in every few centimetres of soil, and the shorter the root the less we gain from it, making this wheat less nutritious, even before the bran and germ have been removed.

Using fewer varieties of grains has also led to greater dependence on pesticides, fertilisers and herbicides, resulting in weaker soil and even lower nutritional value of the produce being grown in them.

I source my grain the same way most chefs source free-range chickens or organic heirloom tomatoes. I want to know where it comes from, and its history. I don't want to support the corporations growing commodity wheat. Our local farmers' markets now have a grain grower milling to order, and there are several good small producers supplying health food shops. When sourcing your flour, ask about the growers and the millers, and support the little guys who are doing the right thing. Never forget that your dollar counts, and that in time, demand can create supply.

Milling processes

For centuries, grain was ground between two large stones to produce flour. This was part of village life; the stone mill was often set up next to a river and the force of the running water was used to turn the stones. Stone milling leaves all elements of the grain intact, but it is slow and laborious. The roller mill became popular in the 1850s as a faster alternative. A series of rollers crush and sift the grain, separating the starchy endosperm from the nutritious bran and germ and producing white flour. White flour is great for producing a fluffy white bread, but not so great for flavour or nutrition. The germ embryo is broken off, which means we lose most of the nutritional benefits. White flour became highly sought after as it made baking easier, quicker and more consistent. It also made bakers lazier; profits went up and a lot of the skills and judgement required for making real bread were lost. Manufacturers were concerned about protein content, gluten strength and yield rather than flavour or nutrition.

The local grain movement, from the farmers to the miller and then the baker, faces the mammoth task of educating the wider public about the benefits of sustainable growing methods, whole grains and quality milling processes, as well as providing quality while maintaining a profit.

I believe the solution is to buy flour from local health food shops, where the proprietors care about where it comes from. It is not always easy to find, but if you have the choice you will be rewarded. Try experimenting with the sourdough bread and wholegrain recipes in this book and enjoy discovering the different textures and flavours. They may cost a little more, but in this world, you get what you pay for.

Equipment

Below are some items of equipment that will make your bread adventures easier and ultimately more successful.

- A banneton (or proving basket) to maintain the shape of your loaf during the final prove. Bannetons are traditionally made of wound cane or terracotta, but there are also plastic versions available nowadays. You can also use a bowl or even the inside of the lid of an egg carton.

- Scales – bread recipes are based on formulae, and work better when ingredients are measured precisely. You will also be better able to identify issues in your technique if there is no variation in the recipe. It's worth investing in an inexpensive set of scales that measure to 1 gram.

- A temperature probe and an oven thermometer. Temperature is the most crucial element in developing your sourdough starter and your dough. A temperature probe will make calculations of dough temperature much easier, and an oven thermometer will give you confidence in your bake times and temperatures.

- A dough scraper, to scrape dough off a bench or to divide your dough.

- A Dutch oven, for baking in. This is my preferred method when baking at home (see page 23). A large pot made of a material that conducts heat well, such as cast-iron or clay, is perfect. Many home bakers have a dedicated pot for this purpose, as they can take quite a beating being repeatedly exposed to the highest temperature ovens can reach. Alternatively, a hearthstone and a spray bottle filled with water are useful.

A note on flour
In all of our bread recipes we use baker's flour, which typically has a protein content of at least 10 per cent. You need strong flour in order for the dough to hold up under long fermentation.

How to make and maintain a starter

One of the most important jobs at our bakery is feeding our sourdough starters. We do it twice a day; it is the first and last job, every day. We use two starters at the bakery – one wheat and one rye, which we use for different bread formulae. It is very easy to make a starter (also known as the mother, levain or biga): simply mix together flour and water, and give it time. I recommend using organic wholegrain rye or whole-wheat flour. They contain more wild yeast and bacteria than processed flour, which helps to accelerate the fermentation process.

Your choice of flour is important. While researching for this book I experimented with several different flours, including a supermarket brand 'wholemeal' flour. This flour produced no aroma or flavour, and the starter oxidised before it was able to ferment, with black spots appearing throughout the mixture. Eventually it started to ferment, but the aroma was almost non-existent, and the flavour was flat and bland.

A healthy sourdough starter contains two types of organisms: yeast and lactic-acid bacteria. The single most important factor when building or maintaining a starter, and when mixing your bread dough, is temperature. The yeast and lactic-acid bacteria are most active between 22°C and 30°C (72°F and 86°F), and the ideal temperature is around 26°C (79°F).

To achieve the desired temperature for your starter or dough, multiply your ideal temperature by two and then subtract the air temperature. The resulting number will be the temperature your water needs to be. The water temperature balances out the difference between the flour temperature (which tends to be the same as the air temperature) and your desired starter or dough temperature.

Let's say the temperature in your kitchen is 19°C (66°F). To achieve a starter or dough temperature of 26°C (79°F), do the following calculation:

$$26°C \; (desired\ temperature) \times 2$$
$$= 52$$
$$- 19°C \; (current\ air\ temperature\ in\ your\ kitchen)$$
$$= 33°C \; (the\ temperature\ of\ the\ water\ needed\ for\ your$$
$$starter,\ or\ dough)$$

To achieve the required water temperature, just run the hot tap and collect some warm water, then check the temperature and adjust as necessary by adding more cold or hot water.

It takes five to seven days to make an active starter full of good bacteria and wild yeast. You want a starter that's full of bubbles and has the characteristic smell of fermentation. That's how you know you've got a good balance of yeast and bacteria, and that they are very active. Keep your starter covered as it ferments, to allow the good bacteria and wild yeasts present in the grain to do their work without external interference.

It is a myth that using a very ancient starter is better than starting from fresh. A one-month-old starter will be very similar in character to a much older one. The main difference between any two starters will be the strains of wild yeast and bacteria present. Bread made with a hundred-year-old starter will perform and taste the same as bread made with a one-month-old starter, if they have the same feed schedule, using the same flour. But a starter made in San Francisco can never be the same as a starter made in Melbourne. The differences in the flours and environment mean that they will each contain different strains of bacteria, in effect giving bread a sense of 'terroir'.

What matters is not the amount of time the starter lasts, but how well it's taken care of. A newer starter, if properly established, will produce similar results to an older one that's been well maintained. A newer one that's been well maintained will produce better bread than an old one that's been poorly maintained.

Below, I have outlined the process for establishing your starter from scratch, and have made some notes about some of the smells you may notice as the starter gets going. These are useful to have as a guide, but are not key to describing the healthy development of a 'good' starter. You may notice 'off' smells, but don't worry. This can occur if the temperature is too low, and as you continue your feeding schedule the bacteria and yeast present will eventually balance out into a nice, healthy starter. You may find it simpler just to focus on the appearance, and get familiar with the fermentation process before trying to read too much into the characteristics of your starter.

Day 1
In a jar with a capacity of at least 330 ml (11 fl oz), mix 1 tablespoon of water at 26°C (79°F) with 1 tablespoon of wholegrain flour, then cover and leave in a warm place for 24 hours.

Day 2
When you open your jar there may be a bubble or two, but don't worry if there aren't any – they will come. You may also notice a slightly tangy smell. Add 1 tablespoon of water at 26°C (79°F) and 1 tablespoon of wholegrain flour, and stir it in until thoroughly combined. Cover and leave in a warm place for 24 hours.

Day 3
When you open the jar you should see some tiny bubbles starting to appear. You may notice a slightly grassy or sweet tangy smell, as well as a more acidic smell, like vinegar. These are good signs, and an indicator that you're on the right track. Add 1 tablespoon of water at 26°C (79°F) and 1 tablespoon of wholegrain flour, and stir to combine. Cover and leave in a warm place for 24 hours.

Day 4
By now you should have more tiny bubbles and the fermentation should be well and truly happening. You may notice stronger smells, such as bananas and wheat beer. Add 1 tablespoon of water at 26°C (79°F) and 1 tablespoon of flour, and stir to combine. (If you want to switch to a wheat or spelt starter, this is a good time to start feeding with your preferred flour.) Cover and leave in a warm place for 24 hours.

Day 5
You should see lots of tiny bubbles on the surface of your starter, and may notice quite a strong acidic scent, like vinegar, when you open the lid. The smell will be quite sweet and slightly tangy, and will disappear when you feed the starter. Add 1 tablespoon of water at 26°C (79°F) and 1 tablespoon of flour, and stir to combine. Your starter may even be ready by now or Day 6. Cover and leave in a warm place for 24 hours.

Day 6
The starter should be very bubbly and active by now, with a strong, slightly alcoholic smell of fermentation. It should be ready to use by this day; if not, add 1 tablespoon of water at 26°C (79°F) and 1 tablespoon of flour, and stir to combine. Cover and leave in a warm place for at least 12 hours. If you want to accelerate the whole process, you can feed every 12 hours instead of every 24 hours.

Day 7 onwards
The starter is now ready to use, and should have lots of tiny bubbles on the surface and throughout. And if you're not using it immediately, you can discard all but 1 tablespoon for maintenance. Feed this with 1 tablespoon of water at 26°C (79°F) and 1 tablespoon of flour, and stir to combine.

Maintenance

Proper maintenance of your starter is as important as creating one, if not more so. If you consistently refresh your starter, maintaining a temperature of around 26°C (79°F), you will always make good bread. When using your ripe starter for baking, always be sure to leave some behind to maintain a continuous fermentation cycle. Replace what you've used by feeding what's left with an equal combined weight of flour and water. This way you avoid having to start again every time you make bread.

Yeast and bacteria like a good, clean environment. Once a week, clean the container and discard all but 1 tablespoon of your starter before feeding it, as above. If you're not making bread every day, you will find that your starter grows too quickly with a daily feed. In this case, it's best to store it in the fridge, in an airtight container. It will store safely for up to a month, but if you can, refresh or feed it once a week. Before you put your starter into cold storage, give it a feed of 100% hydration. That means if your starter weight is 50 g (1¾ oz), add 50 g (1¾ oz) water and 50 g (1¾ oz) of flour, and mix it through. Leave it at room temperature for 4–6 hours to allow the yeast and bacteria to build up before transferring it to the fridge.

If storing your starter at room temperature it's better not leave it for more than 7 days between feeds. If you do, when you come to use it again it may be highly acidic and a bit mouldy. It can still be resurrected, though. Just scrape any discoloured bits off the top and take a tablespoon of clean starter from underneath. Start the fermentation process again from Day 4, and it will be good to go after being refreshed 3–4 times.

It's better not to store your starter in the freezer, as the temperature kills off too many wild yeast and bacteria. Either store it in the fridge and refresh it once in a while, or make a new starter after your baking hiatus.

To turn your existing starter into a different grain starter (rye, emmer, khorosan or spelt, for example), remove all but 1 tablespoon of the starter. Refresh it by adding 1 tablespoon of your preferred flour and 1 tablespoon of water. It will need to be refreshed about eight times before it is truly a starter of the new flour. You can refresh twice a day if you want to speed this process up.

Why an active starter is important

A healthy, active starter is the most crucial element to making good bread. No recipe, no matter how great, will make up for an underactive starter. A good, bubbly starter will result in well-fermented loaves, whereas an underactive starter will result in gummy, dense loaves. The starter that you use or create will take on whatever bacteria or wild yeast is around your environment, and will develop and change accordingly. You will get locally dominant strains of wild yeast and bacteria that will subtly alter its taste and smell.

At the bakery, we feed our wheat and rye starters twice a day with a combination of bakers flour and whole-wheat flour. The whole-wheat helps to nourish and maintain a good healthy yeast population, as well as good bacteria for flavour. Wholegrain flour, particularly when freshly milled, contains a lot of wild yeast and good bacteria, so it's very beneficial to making and maintaining a healthy starter.

Preparing the starter build

The starter build refers to the feeds you do before you mix your dough, so you have the right quantity for the recipe, and still some left over for maintenance. If your starter has been stored for a while, you'll need to feed it three times before using it in order to achieve good results and active fermentation in your dough. This is because extended cold storage below 4°C (39°F) kills off significant numbers of yeast and bacterial cells. While the remaining cells are kept in a dormant state and are still completely viable, their numbers will need to be built back up to ensure an active fermentation.

Likewise, if you're multiplying our recipes, you'll need to make 2–3 feeds over a couple of days prior to mixing, to ensure that you have enough to mix as well as some left over to maintain. If using a wheat starter and making one loaf of bread, 4–6 hours before mixing the dough, take 50 g (1¾ oz) of active starter and feed it with 50 g (1¾ oz) of water, 25 g (1 oz) bakers flour and 25 g (1 oz) whole-wheat flour. This is a 100% hydration feed; it will get the starter nice and active, and ensure that you have enough for your dough as well as for maintaining the starter.

If using a rye starter you will need a bit more, as it's not as active. Take 100 g (3½ oz) of starter and feed it with 100 g (3½ oz) of rye flour and 100 g (3½ oz) of water.

To test if the starter is ready for mixing, drop a little into a bowl of water; if it floats, it is ready to use.

Mixing the dough

Mixing is a skill that takes practice. When we mix at the bakery, we almost ignore the formula and instead judge the dough by feel, look and smell. Mixing by hand is the best way to learn how to judge variations in hydration and fermentation. As you become familiar with the texture and feel of the dough, over time you will gain confidence in handling the many variables that will inform the way your dough performs, such as humidity, outside and ambient temperature, flour quality and water temperature. No two days are the same; some days the dough will take a lot of hydration and mixing, some days less. These skills come with practice and experience, but here are some pointers to get your dough off to a good start.

Autolyse

The autolyse (pronounced *auto-leez*) is the period after the flour and water are initially mixed, before the addition of starter and salt. This hydrates the flour, and allows the amylase and protease enzymes in the grain to start the hard work of breaking down the starch and the protein. This means less work for you in mechanically mixing the dough later on.

Gluten is a type of protein that, in wheat, has two components: glutenins (responsible for elasticity and structure) and gliadins (responsible for viscosity, cohesiveness, stickiness and extensibility). Different grains contain these in differing proportions, which is why, for example, spelt flour behaves differently to wheat flour. When glutenin and gliadin mix with water, they start to build strong gluten bonds. Once the starter is added, these bonds will trap the gases created by fermentation and give the loaf its rise.

Remember that yeast and bacteria are most active between 22°C and 30°C (72°F and 86°F), and the ideal temperature for healthy growth is around 26°C (79°F). It's a good idea to get into the habit of checking the temperature of your water before you mix, as it can vary enormously depending on the day.

To start the autolyse, combine the flour and water in a large mixing bowl. Mix with your hands for a couple of minutes, until there is no dry flour visible and the flour and water have come together as one. If you're still getting the hang of bread mixing and handling wet doughs, you can hold back a little water at this point, and add more when you come to mix the dough. You can add still more if needed when you do the first couple of folds.

Cover with a damp cloth and set aside for at least 30 minutes and up to 8 hours before mixing your dough. Ideally, the temperature will sit at around 26°C (79°F). If it gets too warm, refrigerate it until it has returned to the ideal temperature. If it gets too cool, move it to a warmer spot in your kitchen.

Mixing

I like to mix my bread doughs by hand at home, but you could use a stand mixer if you prefer. In this case I recommend using the paddle attachment, and not the dough hook. In my experience the dough hook only serves to spin the dough around the bowl, and doesn't actually do the work required to develop the dough properly.

Add your starter to the flour and water after the autolyse. Rotate the bowl with one hand while using the other hand to massage or squeeze the flour, water and starter together (see Step 1, page 21). Keep turning the bowl, and use your knuckles to push all the way into the dough as it forms. Do this for a couple of minutes, until the starter is fully incorporated and the dough starts to come together. Sprinkle the salt evenly over the top, then fold the dough by lifting it up and over itself, turning the bowl between each fold, until the salt is fully incorporated. Cover the bowl with a damp cloth and rest at room temperature for around 40 minutes.

Turn and fold

Folding rather than kneading is gentler on your dough, and I find it produces a better result. Turning and folding builds strength in the dough and is easier than spending hours kneading. This is especially useful with wetter doughs, making them tighter and easier to work with. Highly hydrated doughs are usually slacker and harder to work with for a new or less experienced baker.

Before you start, wet your hands or rub them with a little oil to keep the dough from sticking to them. At the bakery we fold the dough in large containers; at home I use the same bowl I used for mixing.

Use one hand to hold and turn the bowl while you use the other hand to fold. Put the back of your folding hand flat against the inside of the bowl. With your palm facing the dough, slide it down and grab the outside edge, pull it up and fold it over onto itself (see Step 2, page 21). Rotate the bowl 90 degrees and repeat the folding action, using your hand to bring the dough up and over itself. After 6–8 turns it will be quite tight and harder to fold. Cover it with a damp cloth and leave it to rest for 30–45 minutes between each set of folds, to allow the gluten in the dough to relax and fermentation to occur.

Bread doughs usually take between 3–5 sets of folds, depending on the quality and type of flour you are using. For example, spelt contains less glutenin than wheat, so spelt dough will take more folds to build the desired elasticity. Signs that your dough needs another turn and fold include:

- a small amount of unabsorbed water sitting on the top of the dough
- the dough breaks easily
- the dough feels wet, or slack.

If you don't notice any of these signs, use the windowpane test to check the dough. Take a small ball of dough and gently stretch it between your hands. When it's ready, you will be able to stretch it very thin without it breaking.

You will start to notice bubbles late in the process, indicating that fermentation is taking place in the dough. Your bread is alive!

Bulk prove

After the final set of folds, the dough is left to ferment and gain strength, before pre-shaping. At the bakery we call this bulk proving, as it is done before the dough is cut into loaves. The bulk prove takes 2–3 hours, depending on the dough, the ambient temperature and the dough temperature. The dough will rise and feel stronger, and show signs of fermentation such as air bubbles and fermented smells. It takes time to understand these variations, but the best part is that you are always learning and no two days are the same. It's okay to make a mistake – learn from it and enjoy the process!

Pre-shaping

Despite the name, pre-shaping isn't so much about creating shape as it is about knocking out air and building strength in your dough.

Left alone, the large bubbles of air in the dough after the bulk prove will result in big caverns in your loaf. When you knock back the dough you are not destroying these bubbles, you are simply evacuating the accumulated air inside them. Imagine the dough as being filled with a million beach balls of different sizes. When you knock them back, you are simply deflating them. The balls are still present, waiting to be refilled with the carbon dioxide produced during the final prove. If the beach balls are not deflated at this point, they will fill with too much air and pop. Knocking back doesn't destroy them, but NOT knocking them back does!

If the bench has too much flour on it when pre-shaping, the dough will just slide around. You need just enough flour for the bench not to be sticky, while still allowing a bit of friction when you roll the dough. Experiment a little and you will find the amount that works for you. Lightly flour your hands before you start.

Place the dough on the bench. Pull, stretch and fold the edges of the dough over the middle until you have a roundish shape (see Step 3, page 21). Flip the dough over so that the seam is underneath. Cup your hands around the back of the dough, as if you were about to drag the dough towards you, and rotate it across the bench, using firm pressure to create tension through the dough (see Step 4, page 21). Smack out any large bubbles.

When you first roll the dough it will feel like a rare steak, very slack. Continue rotating the dough, pushing it around until it looks taut and feels firm when pressed, a bit like a well-done steak. You will know you have gone too far if the surface of your dough begins to tear or break.

You want a tight round ball of dough that sits up on the bench, rather than a saggy form. Leave the dough on your bench covered with a damp tea towel for 15–20 minutes. When the dough has visibly relaxed, it is ready for shaping.

Shaping

Now you need to shape the bread and transfer it to a banneton or bowl to support the structure during the final prove. You can purchase bannetons specifically made for proving bread, or just use a mixing bowl, basket or even the lid of an egg carton. Shaping also builds strength in the dough so it can support the air created during the final prove, giving you a nice open crumb. You need to stretch the surface of the dough very tightly and evenly all around. Imagine a piece of fabric stretched tightly around a ball and knotted at the bottom – that's what you want it to resemble.

Once again, if the bench has too much flour on it the dough will just slide around. You need just enough flour for the bench not to be sticky, while still allowing a bit of friction when you rotate the dough. Sift some flour over the proving basket, too, so the dough doesn't stick, and dust your hands with flour before you start.

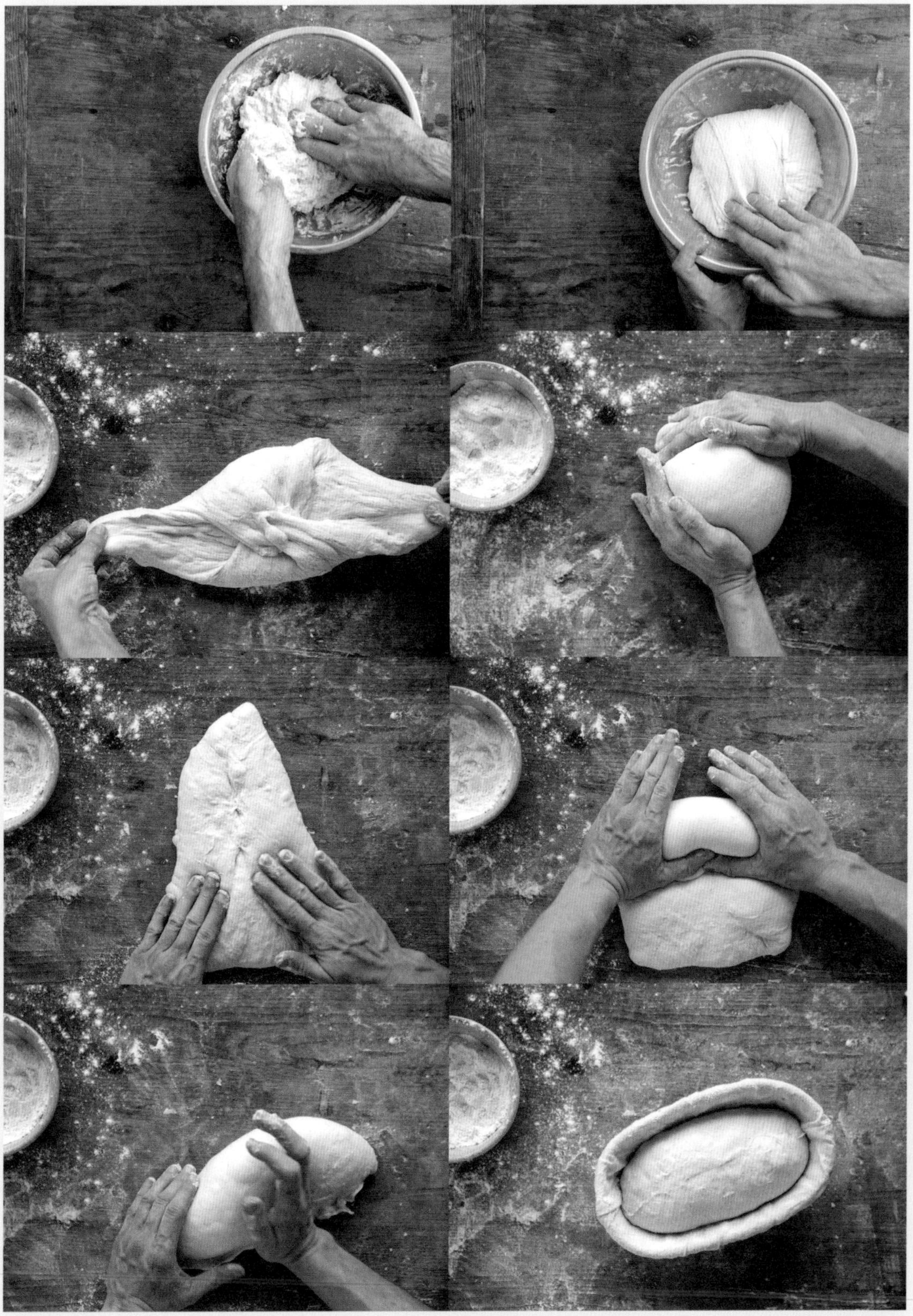

1. 2. 3. 4. 5. 6. 7. 8.

Shaping a round loaf

Flip your pre-shaped dough over onto the bench, so the seam is now on the top. Pull, stretch and fold the edges of the dough over the middle, repeatedly folding up and over the previously pulled and stretched edges about eight times, until it starts to form a tight round ball.

Flip the dough over so that the seam is underneath. Cup your hands around the back of the dough, as if you are about to drag the dough towards you, and rotate it across the bench, using firm pressure to create tension through the dough. It should catch slightly on the benchtop, stretching the surface and bulging out ahead of your hand. Don't let the dough roll over, but push it gently and let it bulge out. You know when you've perfected this action because it will result in a ball of dough that sits tight and high on the bench. It should no longer sag and spread out flat.

Smack out any large bubbles, then close the seams as much as possible by tucking them under with your fingers while moving the dough along the bench. If any seams start to open, just pinch them back together. Place the dough into the floured proving basket seam side up and lightly dust the top with flour or semolina.

Shaping a batard loaf

Flip your pre-shaped dough over onto the bench, so the seam is now on the top. Shape it into a wide rectangle, with the short edge towards you, and gently flatten it. Turn over the top corners to create a triangle (see Step 5, page 21). Roll the dough down from the top, pushing into the middle with your thumbs as your fingers pull the dough over (see Step 6, page 21). Roll tightly to create tension in the loaf, especially at the top. Use the heel of your hand to seal the seam at the bottom, knocking out any large air bubbles (see Step 7, page 21). Use a dough scraper to peel the dough off the bench, and tidy any seams by pinching them together.

Your loaf might end up looking a bit like a pasty with crimped edges – that's okay. Better that than an inconsistent and bubbly loaf. Tip the dough into your proving basket, seam side up, and dust the bottom of the loaf with flour or semolina (see Step 8, page 21).

Final prove

Once the loaf has been shaped, place it in a banneton, basket or bowl that fits the dough with room to allow it to rise. Either leave it at room temperature for a few hours before baking, or refrigerate it overnight (or for up to 48 hours), and bake when needed. If you refrigerate it, you will need to check the dough as described below before baking – it may be ready or it may need some time at room temperature to finish the final prove.

Most domestic fridges sit at around 5°C (41°F); yeast activity ceases at 8°C (46°F), and bacteria at 4°C (39°F). So when retarding the prove in the fridge, only the bacteria will continue to metabolise. They will remove the sugars and cause more enzymatic browning in the crust due to protein breakdowns caused by the acids produced. At room temperature, less overall acid is produced because the yeast is also active. The result will be a lighter and fresher tasting loaf, with the flavour of the wild yeast and the grain coming through more strongly.

What you are looking for is a loaf that has risen by half. Test it by pressing gently into the dough with your finger. When the imprint of your finger stays on the dough it is proved and ready to bake. If the dough springs back immediately, it will require more time to prove. If it deflates quickly then it is over proved and the baked loaf will have a dense crumb. In this case you can still enjoy your loaf, safe in the knowledge that next time you will test it sooner.

The bake

Dutch oven method

This is my preferred method when I make bread at home. I use a cast-iron casserole dish with a lid, which forms a Dutch oven that mimics the baker's oven beautifully. Cast iron retains the high heat needed to produce a deep golden crust and moist crumb; a clay pot with a lid would also work well.

If you are baking more than one loaf you will need to bake them one at a time, unless you have a very large oven and several suitable dishes. In this case, leave the other loaves in the fridge until ready to bake.

Preheat your oven to 250°C (480°F) for at least 30 minutes, with the Dutch oven (lid on) inside.

Once the dough is ready, boil the kettle and place a piece of baking paper on the bench, slightly longer and wider than your loaf. Sprinkle this with semolina, then tip the loaf out of the proving basket onto the paper, seam side down.

Carefully transfer the loaf to the hot Dutch oven, then slide the paper out from underneath (if using a deep pan, you can leave the paper in). Score the top of the loaf roughly 2 mm (1/10 in) deep using a razor blade or sharp knife, or cut it with a pair of scissors. This allows the loaf to expand and rise with the aid of the steam trapped inside the pot. Pour about 30 ml (1 fl oz) of boiling water around the bread, being careful of the steam and the very hot pan. Put the lid on and place it immediately into the middle of the oven.

Bake with the lid on for around 25 minutes, and then remove the lid and bake for a further 5 to 8 minutes to get a nice golden colour. Every oven is different and every baker likes a different level of colour on their loaf, so use these times as a guide and adjust until your bread is just the way you like it.

Pizza stone or hearthstone method

Before I started using the Dutch oven method, I used a pizza stone to bake my bread on. This will also retain the required heat, but will not trap the steam like a Dutch oven. In this case, the boiling water is added to a roasting tray that sits at the bottom of the oven.

This method is great for focaccia, pizza or baguettes (you can use the basic sourdough recipe to make pizza or baguettes). The stone gives the bread a nice golden finish on the bottom.

Preheat your oven to 250°C (480°F) for at least an hour, with the pizza stone inside and a roasting tray at the bottom of the oven. When the oven is very hot, boil the kettle and pour 150–200 ml (5–7 fl oz) of boiling water into the roasting tray to create a humid, steamy environment.

Use a small wooden peel or paddle to load the bread onto the stone (a sturdy, clean piece of cardboard or flat lid will also work well). Dust the peel with semolina then tip the loaf onto it, seam side down. Gently shake it to ensure it is not sticking, so you know you will be able to slide it onto the stone.

Score the top of the loaf roughly 2 mm (1/10 in) deep with a razor blade or sharp knife, or cut it with a pair of scissors, then slide the dough onto the stone. Spray the sides of the oven with a little water to maximise the steam and then shut the door. After a minute or so, open the oven door slightly and spray the sides again with more water.

Reduce the heat to 220°C (430°F) and bake for around 35 minutes, until the loaf is crusty and the colour is to your liking. Tap the bottom of the loaf; when it sounds hollow you know it's ready.

A STORY OF NATIVE GRAINS

Since we opened Tivoli Road, I have learnt more and more to appreciate and use Australian Indigenous ingredients. Local chefs such as Ben Shewry, Dan Hunter and Jock Zonfrillo have been using them in their cooking for several years now, bringing them into the general food conversation.

The Mesopotamians are widely credited with being the first to discover sourdough baking, around 10,000 BCE. However, new research is destroying the myth that Australian Aborigines were solely hunter gatherers, and is uncovering a rich agricultural heritage and evidence of breadmaking using native grains. Large stones found in New South Wales bearing traces of flour date back to over 60,000 years ago.

I was recently fortunate to spend some time with Bruce Pascoe in Mallacoota, in eastern Victoria. Bruce is an Indigenous Australian writer of the Kulin nation who has done a lot of work in preserving Aboriginal language and culture. He has started up a new project to help Indigenous communities grow, harvest and make a living from native seeds, plants and vegetables.

Recent research by Bruce and others shows that species such as kangaroo grass, native millet, wild rice and other local seeds were grown all over Australia before European settlement, mainly in dry inland areas. Much of the grain was harvested and then left to dry in big stacks before being threshed. Grain was stored in containers made from kangaroo or possum fur, sealed to stop spoilage or wastage. Seeds and grains were revered in Aboriginal cultures, and the land was very carefully looked after.

A lot of the evidence of how grains were once harvested and handled was destroyed as a result of European settlement, and much of the carefully tilled topsoil was destroyed by introduced farming methods and hooved livestock. But early European explorers in Australia described organised agriculture: fields of grains stretched out like a gentleman's farm, and locals who ground oats (likely to have been kangaroo grass) into a paste for eating.

The most common native grain used was native millet (*panicum decompositum*), ground between big stones and made into a paste to be baked on very hot stones, or in hot pit ovens. It is likely that the dough was fermented, as Aboriginal cultures were fermenting other items like cider gums, honey and coconut for food and drink.

Of course, there are varieties of grass all over the world that have been gathered or farmed, and made into a bread of some kind for thousands of years. Most civilisations use grain in some shape or form. In Mozambique, sorghum is ground on stones and then baked on hot stones to make flatbread. The native Ethiopian grain teff is also milled on stones, made into a paste and left to ferment for a few days before being baked to make injera.

It is a new field of research, trying to find out how early Indigenous Australians used the land, harvested grain, and fermented it to make bread. People like Bruce Pascoe are rediscovering ancient traditions, techniques and flavours to help the communities of today.

Basic sourdough

Makes one loaf

Ingredients

Starter build
50 g (1¾ oz) starter
25 g (1 oz) bakers flour
25 g (1 oz) whole-wheat flour
50 g (1¾ oz) water

Dough
90 g (3 oz) starter
330 g (11½ oz) bakers flour
90 g (3 oz) whole-wheat flour
290 g (10 oz) water
8 g (¼ oz) salt
semolina, for dusting

Bakery notes
This recipe makes one loaf. I like to double it when baking at home. Once I've shaped two loaves, I bake the first, leaving the other in the fridge for a day or two until I need another fresh loaf. Or you could use your second loaf to experiment with some of the flavour variations and techniques that are highlighted later in the book.

This is our 'house sourdough' recipe, and the best starting point if you're new to making bread. Many of our other recipes extend from this one, so once you've got the hang of the basic sourdough, you can start to experiment with different grains, flavour additions, hydration levels, and percentages of whole grain flours. We like to use some wholemeal in our starters and bread, for flavour and texture, as well as nutrition.

Starter build
Around 4–6 hours before you plan to mix your dough, combine the starter, flour and water for the starter build, mixing well to combine (see 'How to make and maintain a starter', page 16). You will use 90 g (3 oz) of this for the dough; retain the rest for maintaining your starter.

Build the dough
At least 30 minutes before you plan to mix the dough, combine the flours and water in a large mixing bowl. Mix them with your hands until thoroughly combined, then cover with a damp cloth and set aside for the autolyse (see 'Mixing the dough', page 19).

When the starter is ripe and bubbly, mix it with the flour and water mixture, sprinkle over the salt and finish mixing the dough. Cover with a damp cloth and set aside in a warm place for at least 30 minutes, before your first set of folds.

Complete four sets of folds, resting the dough in between each one for 30–45 minutes (see 'Turn and fold', page 20).

After your last set of folds, cover your dough with a damp cloth and leave to prove at room temperature for 2–3 hours (see 'Bulk prove', page 20).

Shape and final prove

If you have multiplied the recipe, divide the dough into individual loaves before you pre-shape. Pre-shape the dough, then cover with a damp cloth and leave it to rest on the bench for 15–20 minutes (see 'Pre-shaping', page 20).

When the dough has relaxed, shape as desired, then place it seam side up in a lightly floured proving basket (see 'Shaping', page 20). Cover with a damp cloth and set aside for a few hours, or in the fridge overnight, until ready to bake (see 'Final prove', page 22).

Bake your bread

Preheat the oven to the maximum temperature and bake according to your preferred method (see 'The bake', page 23). Once baked, tip the bread out of the pan onto a wire rack to cool.

Olive loaf

When I first made this bread I really wanted to use a mix of black and green olives, not only for appearance, but also for texture and flavour. There are a lot of olive loaves out there, but this one is different. We use a lot of olives and we marinate them first with loads of herbs. We also mix a tapenade through the dough to fully incorporate the olive flavour.

Makes one loaf

Ingredients

Marinated olives

250 g (9 oz) green olives, pitted
250 g (9 oz) black olives, pitted
1 sprig rosemary, leaves picked and coarsely chopped
5 sprigs thyme, leaves picked
2 sprigs oregano, leaves picked and roughly chopped
1 lemon, zested and quartered
1 tablespoon lemon olive oil

Starter build

50 g (1¾ oz) starter
25 g (1 oz) bakers flour
25 g (1 oz) whole-wheat flour
50 g (1¾ oz) water

Dough

90 g (3 oz) starter
330 g (11½ oz) bakers flour
90 g (3 oz) whole-wheat flour
290 g (10 oz) water
8 g (¼ oz) salt
140 g (5 oz) marinated olives
100 g (3½ oz) tapenade
30 g (1 oz/¼ cup) bakers flour
30 g (1 oz/¼ cup) semolina

Bakery notes

Make sure you use good quality olives. We use kalamata and mammoth olives from Mount Zero, in the Wimmera. They are the best I've tasted, and the flavour really comes through. The lemon olive oil we use for the marinade contains lemons pressed during extraction, which results in a true lemon flavour without any chemical notes. A high quality extra virgin olive oil would also work well. To avoid a wet, soggy dough, drain or squeeze excess brine and liquid from the olives before mixing them into the dough.

The marinade prepares more olives than you will need for one loaf, but it will keep for months in the fridge for your next loaf. You will also use some of it to make the tapenade for the dough. If using after cold storage, take the olives out of the fridge and bring up to room temperature before using. I like to keep them on hand to eat as a pre-dinner snack.

Marinated olives

The day before you mix the dough, drain the olives well and put them in a bowl with all the marinade ingredients. Mix to combine, cover and leave at room temperature to marinate overnight.

Tapenade

Before you mix the dough, place 100 g (3½ oz) of olives from the marinade in a blender and blitz until you have a coarse paste. The coarse chunks will add texture and give the bread an extra olive hit. Place in a fine sieve over the sink to drain any excess liquid, then mix to combine with 140 g (5 oz) of marinated olives.

Starter build

Around 4–6 hours before you plan to mix your dough, combine the starter, flours and water for the starter build, mixing well to combine (see 'How to make and maintain a starter', page 16). You will use 90 g (3 oz) of this for the dough; retain the rest for maintaining your starter.

Build the dough

At least 30 minutes before you plan to mix the dough, combine the flours and water in a large mixing bowl. Mix them with your hands until thoroughly combined, and then cover with a damp cloth and set aside for the autolyse (see 'Mixing the dough', page 19).

When the starter is ripe and bubbly, mix it with the flour and water, sprinkle over the salt and finish mixing the dough. Cover with a damp cloth and set aside in a warm place for at least 30 minutes, before your first set of folds.

Dust the remaining olives with the flour and semolina to coat. This will make it easier to incorporate them into the dough and distribute them evenly.

Olive loaf

Add the olives and the tapenade as you do the first turn and fold, ensuring they are evenly distributed.

Complete four sets of folds, resting the dough in between each one for 30–45 minutes (see 'Turn and fold', page 20).

After your last set of folds, cover your dough with a damp cloth and leave to prove at room temperature for 2–3 hours (see 'Bulk prove', page 20).

Shape and final prove

If you have multiplied the recipe, divide the dough into individual loaves before you pre-shape. Pre-shape the dough, cover with a damp cloth and leave it to rest on the bench for 15–20 minutes (see 'Pre-shaping', page 20).

When the dough has relaxed, shape the dough as desired, then place it seam side up in a lightly floured proving basket (see 'Shaping', page 20). Cover with a damp cloth and set aside for a few hours, or in the fridge overnight, until ready to bake (see 'Final prove', page 22).

Bake your bread

Preheat the oven to the maximum temperature and bake according to your preferred method (see 'The bake', page 23). Once baked, tip the bread out of the pan onto a wire rack to cool.

WHOLEGRAIN MILLING CO.

Craig and Renée Neale operate Wholegrain Milling in Gunnedah, New South Wales. We use their range of organic flours, grains and seeds for our bread. While more and more Australian farms are being purchased by foreign investors to produce export commodities, Craig and Renée are dedicated to growing high-quality produce and supporting the little guys, like us.

How did you become grain growers?
We both come from farming backgrounds. I was growing grain chemical-free way back before the now-recognised organic certification bodies were developed. This led to milling our own grain and creating Wholegrain Milling Co. We now have Renée's family farm certified organic to supplement our supply.

What role does soil play in growing good grain?
Good nutritious grain comes from good nutritious soil. It's like life – you only get out what you put in. We like to disturb the soil as little as possible, have good cropping rotation and keep the microorganisms active and alive.

Why is organic grain important?
Organic grain is the instigator of where artisan baking and food demands are today. Organic certification derived from some very dedicated people who were willing to work outside the realms of what were considered normal farming practices at that time. These people persisted and withstood criticism to create the food system we take for granted today.

What are the benefits of stone milling?
Our signature flour is stoneground. It's what we built our business on some thirty-eight years ago. It is the age-old method of crushing grain with stone. The health benefits are substantiated by the fact that the flour has little or no extraction compared to modern milling processes. The germ is still present for extra nutrition, colour and flavour.

SUPPLIER PROFILE

How do you store your grain? How does this differ from conventional mills?
We use temperature and humidity controlled systems to keep the grain in an environment that's unfavourable to grain-destroying insects. Conventionally grown and milled grains (95 per cent of what's now available) have gas or liquid chemicals applied to them, with residue properties so living insects are killed by coming into contact with them. These chemicals then have the potential to remain in the grain, flour and bread, and the human body.

Are you seeing a growing appetite for different grains?
A lot of our time is spent trying new grains with different characteristics in milling, baking and eating, to give the bakers the chance to be creative with new grains. We are driven by our ambition to grow and mill old-style grains and we cherish the results. We have recently been growing heritage grains like einkorn and khorosan, as well as a wheat variety called Foster wheat, bred in the 1950s specifically for Australian conditions.

Multigrain loaf

Makes one loaf

Ingredients

Starter build
30 g (1 oz) starter
15 g (½ oz) bakers flour
15 g (½ oz) whole-wheat flour
30 g (1 oz) water

Dough
55 g (2 oz) starter
235 g (8½ oz) bakers flour
45 g (1½ oz) whole-wheat flour
45 g (1½ oz) rye flour
25 g (1 oz) white spelt flour
270 g (½ oz) water
7 g salt
30 g (1 oz) kibbled rye, soaked in
   30 g (1 oz) water overnight
60 g (2 oz) pepitas (pumpkin seeds)
semolina, for dusting

Crust
sesame seeds
linseeds
sunflower seeds
poppy seeds

Bakery notes
We use a combination of seeds for the crust, but we don't weigh them. You can use whatever seeds you like, depending on your taste – about 100 g (3½ oz) in total. This is also true for the loaf, but if you do use kibbled rye, make sure you soak it overnight so the grain is softened and doesn't draw moisture from the dough.

Starter build
Around 4–6 hours before you plan to mix your dough, combine the starter, flour and water for the starter build, mixing well to combine (see 'How to make and maintain a starter', page 16). You will use 55 g (2 oz) of this for the dough; retain the rest for maintaining your starter.

Build the dough
At least 30 minutes before you plan to mix the dough, combine the flours and water in a large mixing bowl. Mix them with your hands until thoroughly combined, then cover with a damp cloth and set aside for the autolyse (see 'Mixing the dough', page 19).

When the starter is ripe and bubbly, mix it with the flour and water mixture, then sprinkle over the salt and finish mixing the dough. Cover with a damp cloth and set aside in a warm place for at least 30 minutes, before your first set of folds.

Add the soaked kibbled rye and pepitas as you do the first turn and fold, ensuring they are evenly distributed. Complete four sets of folds, resting the dough in between each one for 30–45 minutes (see 'Turn and fold', page 20).

After your last set of folds, cover your dough with a damp cloth and leave to prove at room temperature for 2–3 hours (see 'Bulk prove', page 20).

Shape and final prove
If you have multiplied the recipe, divide the dough into individual loaves before you pre-shape. Pre-shape the dough, cover with a damp cloth and leave it to rest on the bench for 15–20 minutes (see 'Pre-shaping', page 20).

Place the mixed seeds for the crust in a wide bowl. When the dough has relaxed, shape the dough as desired (see 'Shaping', page 20). Spray the top of the loaf with water or roll it over a damp tea towel, then roll it in the seeds to cover the loaf.

Place it seam side up in a proving basket. You don't need to flour the banneton for this bread, as the seeds will stop it from sticking.

Cover with a damp cloth and set aside for a few hours, or in the fridge overnight, until ready to bake (see 'Final prove', page 22).

Bake your bread
Preheat the oven to the maximum temperature and bake according to your preferred method (see 'The bake', page 23). Once baked, tip the bread out of the pan onto a wire rack to cool.

This lovely, wholesome loaf has taken many forms over the years, using different combinations of grains and seeds. Sometimes the combination of flour or seeds depended on what we had on hand, or the need to use excess flour. After years of experimentation, this is the recipe we've settled on, and it has become one of our best sellers.

Fruit sourdough

'A fruit loaf with lots of fruit' was what people asked for when we opened our bakery. People love that it is packed with fruit, and that it contains a good variety. Like the olive bread, this loaf takes a bit of extra work and practice, but I think it's worth the effort.

It is great eaten fresh, and will keep for days. It's also great toasted, with a nice spread of butter, as the spices really come through when it is warmed. I even flew home to Cornwall with a fruit loaf in my luggage once. My family and I ate it with some good Cornish butter, and it still tasted beautiful after all that time in a dry airline cabin.

Makes one loaf

Ingredients

Fruit soak
40 g (1½ oz) sultanas
40 g (1½ oz) currants
40 g (1½ oz) raisins
50 g (1¾ oz) pitted dates, halved
50 g (1¾ oz) dried figs, quartered
½ teaspoon ground ginger
1 cinnamon stick
1 star anise
5 cloves
50 g (1¾ oz) red wine
50 g (1¾ oz) water
100 g (3½ oz) dried apricots, chopped in half

Starter build
40 g (1½ oz) starter
20 g (¾ oz) bakers flour
20 g (¾ oz) whole-wheat flour
40 g (1½ oz) water

Dough
70 g (2½ oz) starter
235 g (8½ oz) bakers flour
45 g (1½ oz) whole-wheat flour
45 g (1½ oz) rye flour
25 g (1 oz) white spelt flour
270 g (9½ oz) water
zest of 1 orange
7 g (¼ oz) salt

Bakery notes
You can vary the fruit that you use depending on your tastes. You can also use different liquids for the fruit soak, such as water or juice, if you don't want to use wine. Soak the fruit for at least a day (or up to two weeks) before you plan to mix the dough.

The proving time will vary a lot depending on the temperature and humidity on the day. Throughout the winter months, we leave it out at room temperature to prove overnight. During summer, we prove for a shorter time, and leave it in the fridge overnight. After the final prove, you want the dough to reach the height of the tin and to retain the imprint of your finger when gently pressed, so test it using these methods, rather than following the times exactly.

Fruit soak
Put all the fruit, except for the dried apricots, in a large container or bowl and sprinkle the ground ginger over the top.

In a small saucepan, combine the whole spices and the liquids and bring to the boil over medium heat. Once boiled, take the saucepan off the heat and let the mixture infuse for 10 minutes, then strain the liquid over the fruit. Discard the whole spices.

Mix with a spoon until the fruit is evenly distributed and coated with liquid. Cover and leave at room temperature overnight, stirring occasionally to thoroughly distribute the liquid – you want it soaked through the fruit, not settled at the bottom. If leaving the fruit to soak longer than overnight, store it in the fridge.

Starter build
Around 4–6 hours before you plan to mix your dough, combine the starter, flours and water for the starter build, mixing well to combine (see 'How to make and maintain a starter', page 16). You will use 70 g (2½ oz) of this for the dough; retain the rest for maintaining your starter.

Build the dough
At least 30 minutes before you plan to mix the dough, combine the flours and water in a large mixing bowl. Mix them with your hands until thoroughly combined, then cover with a damp cloth and set aside for the autolyse (see 'Mixing the dough', page 19).

When the starter is ripe and bubbly, mix it with the flour and water mixture, sprinkle over the orange zest and salt, and finish mixing the dough.

→

Fruit sourdough

Cover with a damp cloth and set aside in a warm place for at least 30 minutes, before your first set of folds.

Add the fruit soak and the apricots as you do the first turn and fold, ensuring they are evenly distributed. If the fruit seems a bit wet, you can throw a little extra flour in. You want a slightly sticky dough, not a wet dough. Complete four sets of folds, resting the dough in between each one for 30–45 minutes (see 'Turn and fold', page 20).

After your last set of folds, cover your dough with a damp cloth and leave to prove at room temperature for 2–3 hours (see 'Bulk prove', page 20).

Shape and final prove

If you have multiplied the recipe, divide the dough into individual loaves before you pre-shape. Pre-shape the dough, then cover with a damp cloth and leave it to rest on the bench for 15–20 minutes (see 'Pre-shaping', page 20).

Lightly oil an 18 × 11 cm (7 × 4¼ in), 10 cm (4 in) high tin so it's ready for baking. When the dough has relaxed, shape the dough following the instructions for the batard loaf (see 'Shaping', page 20).

Place it in the tin, seam side down, then cover with a damp cloth and leave at room temperature overnight. If it's going to be a hot night and the dough is already feeling active, place it in the fridge, to be baked when needed. You want the dough to reach the height of the tin and to retain the imprint of your finger when gently pressed. If you've had the loaf in the fridge and it still looks small and feels dense, sit it in a warm place for 1–2 hours, until ready to bake.

Bake your bread

Place a baking tray at the bottom of the oven, and preheat the oven to the maximum temperature. When the oven is hot, boil the kettle and pour around 150–200 ml (5–7 fl oz) of boiling water into the baking tray.

Place the tin on the middle shelf of the oven and bake for 20 minutes, until the loaf is starting to colour, then reduce the temperature to 200°C (390°F) and bake for a further 20–25 minutes, until the top is a lovely dark brown.

Holding the tin carefully with a cloth, tip the loaf out and check that the sides are a nice golden colour and the loaf is firm to the touch. If it needs a bit longer, put it back in the tin and return to the oven for another 5 minutes before testing again. Tip the bread out of the tin onto a wire rack to cool.

Organic : Stoneground Sour

Spelt & honey $7.5 Oat $8.5 Spr
                   porridge   buck

$5 Turkish $5 Oats, treacle 100%
                & soda $7.5   rye

Butter-toasted oat porridge loaf

Makes one loaf

Ingredients

Porridge
10 g (¼ oz) butter
40 g (1½ oz/½ cup) rolled oats
80 g (2¾ oz) full-cream (whole) milk,
  or water
pinch salt

Starter build
50 g (1¾ oz) starter
25 g (1 oz) bakers flour
25 g (1 oz) whole-wheat flour
50 g (1¾ oz) water

Dough
90 g (3 oz) starter
270 g (9½ oz) bakers flour
60 g (2 oz) whole-wheat flour
260 g (9 oz) water
8 g (¼ oz) salt

100 g (3½ oz) rolled oats
semolina, for dusting

Bakery notes
We freshly roll our oats for this bread; it makes for an excellent, creamy porridge. The oat is soft and moist when freshly rolled, and the flavour is dramatically improved. Of course, not everyone has an oat roller sitting around – store-bought oats will also be fine. I always make porridge with milk, as it improves the flavour. It's true what they say: fat carries flavour. Just try porridge made with milk and porridge made with water – you'll taste the difference.

Porridge
Melt the butter in a small saucepan over low heat. Add the oats and mix to coat them in the butter, stirring until lightly toasted.

Add the milk or water and the salt, and cook over low heat, stirring, until a thick porridge consistency is achieved.

Allow the porridge to cool completely before adding it to the dough. The porridge can be stored in the fridge or frozen until needed.

Starter build
Around 4–6 hours before you plan to mix your dough, combine the starter, flour and water for the starter build, mixing well to combine (see 'How to make and maintain a starter', page 16). You will use 90 g (3 oz) of this for the dough; retain the rest for maintaining your starter.

Build the dough
At least 30 minutes before you plan to mix the dough, combine the flours and water in a large mixing bowl. Mix them with your hands until thoroughly combined, then cover with a damp cloth and set aside for the autolyse (see 'Mixing the dough', page 19).

When the starter is ripe and bubbly, mix it with the flour and water mixture, sprinkle over the salt and finish mixing the dough. Cover with a damp cloth and set aside in a warm place for at least 30 minutes, before your first set of folds.

Add the porridge as you do the first turn and fold, ensuring it is evenly distributed.

Complete four sets of folds, resting the dough in between each one for 30–45 minutes (see 'Turn and fold', page 20).

After your last set of folds, cover your dough with a damp cloth and leave to prove at room temperature for 2–3 hours (see 'Bulk prove', page 20).

Shape and final prove
If you have multiplied the recipe, divide the dough into individual loaves before you pre-shape. Pre-shape the dough, then cover with a damp cloth and leave it to rest on the bench for 15–20 minutes (see 'Pre-shaping', page 20).

Place the rolled oats in a wide bowl. When the dough has relaxed, shape the dough as desired (see 'Shaping', page 20). Spray the top of the loaf with water or roll it over a damp tea towel, then roll it in the oats to cover the loaf.

This bread was inspired by Chad Robertson and Richard Hart from Tartine Bakery in San Francisco. They spent a few days with us when they were in town for the Melbourne Food and Wine Festival, and they made an oat porridge loaf with a moist, soft, waxy crumb. It's an amazing loaf of bread, and well worth the effort of making a quick bowl of porridge.

Butter-toasted oat porridge loaf

Place it seam side up in a proving basket. You don't need to flour the banneton for this bread, as the oats will stop it from sticking. Just make sure the loaf is well covered with oats.

Cover with a damp cloth and set aside for a few hours, until ready to bake, or in the fridge overnight (see 'Final prove', page 22).

Bake your bread
This loaf is too tough to score easily, so at the bakery we use scissors to snip the dough so it rises properly. Make three or four incisions with the scissors across the top of the loaf.

Preheat the oven to the maximum temperature and bake according to your preferred method (see 'The bake', page 23). This loaf will also be a bit quicker to bake than others, as the oats will colour more quickly. If you find they are colouring too quickly, reduce the temperature for the end of the bake. Once baked, tip the bread out of the pan onto a wire rack to cool.

Spelt and honey loaf

The spelt grain is small when harvested, with a very hard husk that is difficult to remove. In the removal process a significant amount of the grain is discarded and turned into cattle feed. The resulting low yields mean that spelt is more expensive to produce than wheat.

When we opened Tivoli Road I was keen to offer a loaf made with an alternative grain. I started experimenting with spelt, and I soon realised that honey beautifully complements the nutty and hearty flavours. We freshly mill the whole grain for this dough, increasing the nutrient profile and flavour. Happily, spelt is becoming less and less 'alternative' now.

This is my favourite bread; I love the taste and texture. It's extremely versatile and will pair with anything from blue cheese to jam, but it's also really good just with butter.

Makes one loaf

Ingredients

Starter build
30 g (1 oz) rye starter
30 g (1 oz/¼ cup) wholegrain rye flour
30 g (1 oz) water

Dough
50 g (1¾ oz) starter
295 g (10½ oz) white spelt flour
100 g (3½ oz) wholegrain spelt flour
250 g (9 oz) water
40 g (1½ oz) honey
8 g (¼ oz) salt
spelt flour, for dusting

Bakery notes

Spelt is closely related to wheat, although it has a higher proportion of gliadin proteins. This makes it good for bread making, because it produces extensive rather than elastic dough. Towards the end of shaping and folding, rather than springing back, the dough will just stretch until it breaks. Because of this, the dough usually requires an extra fold or two to build up strength.

Starter build
Around 4–6 hours before you plan to mix your dough, combine the starter, flour and water for the starter build, mixing well to combine (see 'How to make and maintain a starter', page 16). You will use 50 g (1¾ oz) of this for the dough; retain the rest for maintaining your starter.

Build the dough
At least 30 minutes before you plan to mix the dough, combine the flours and water in a large mixing bowl. Mix them with your hands until thoroughly combined, then cover with a damp cloth and set aside for the autolyse (see 'Mixing the dough', page 19).

When the starter is ripe and bubbly, mix it with the flour and water mixture, then mix in the honey. Sprinkle over the salt and finish mixing the dough. Cover with a damp cloth and set aside in a warm place for at least 30 minutes, before your first set of folds.

Complete six sets of folds, resting the dough in between each one for 30 minutes (see 'Turn and fold', page 20).

After your last set of folds, cover your dough with a damp cloth and leave to prove at room temperature for 2–3 hours (see 'Bulk prove', page 20).

Shape and final prove
If you have multiplied the recipe, divide the dough into individual loaves before you pre-shape. Pre-shape the dough, cover with a damp cloth and leave it to rest on the bench for 15–20 minutes (see 'Pre-shaping', page 20).

When the dough has relaxed, shape the dough as desired, then place it seam side up in a lightly floured proving basket (see 'Shaping', page 20).

Cover with a damp cloth and set aside for a few hours, or in the fridge overnight, until ready to bake (see 'Final prove', page 22).

Bake your bread
Preheat the oven to the maximum temperature and bake according to your preferred method. If using the Dutch oven, bake for 20 minutes at maximum temperature with the lid on, then take the lid off, reduce the temperature to 200°C (390°F) and bake for another 5 minutes, or until the crust is a lovely golden brown. If using a hearthstone, reduce the oven to 200°C (390°F) after you put the bread in, and check the loaf after 20 minutes. You want a deep golden brown crust, without burning. Because this dough contains honey it will caramelise faster, so it's better finished at a slightly lower temperature.

Once baked, tip the bread out of the pan onto a wire rack to cool. This bread is very good eaten about 20 minutes after baking, so it's still warm inside (see 'The bake', page 23).

RAW HONEY

Moss MacGibbon and Andrew McCallum run this small family-operated beekeeping business, producing, packing and selling their bees' honey. We first met them at the farmers' markets, where they sell directly to their customers.

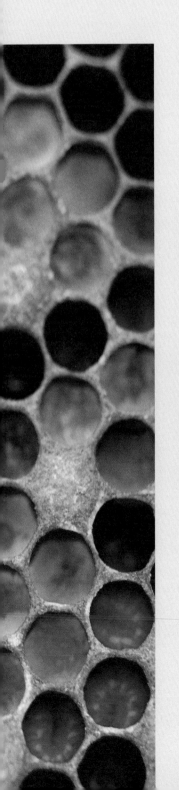

Why are bees so important?

Bees are vitally important in supporting human life. Two in every three 'mouthfuls' of food consumed are, in some way, reliant on pollination from bees. This extends beyond our consumption of nuts, fruits and vegetables; much of the meat we consume is also reliant on bees because of what the animals have been fed.

Why should people seek out good honey?

Seeking out good honey ensures that the consumer can be confident in the integrity of their purchase, and that the bees, their sources and the extraction process are being carefully managed. It also supports the best in the local beekeeping industry – those people who are prepared for the extra work to ensure the quality of their product.

What should people be aware of when selecting their honey?

As with all foods, reading the labels is important when buying honey. When looking for premium flavour and quality, as well as ethically sourced and produced foods, it is often products that are more artisan in style that provide the best options. People should be aware of any honey that is imported into Australia, particularly if it is cheap and blended. Unfortunately, there have been many cases in recent years of honey being mixed with sugar products.

Up until now, New Zealand has dominated the market in producing premium Manuka honey. Increasingly, these honeys are also being produced in Australia. Raw Honey now supplies small volumes of a couple of varieties of Tea-Tree (Australian Manuka) honeys from forests in Victoria. Consumers need to be aware of the rating systems used for this medical-grade honey.

Products that have honey as an ingredient, such as food, soaps and cosmetics, are enhanced by using good-quality honey.

Our raw honey is as it should be: cold-extracted and cold-bottled.

Are customers becoming more aware about where their honey comes from?
Consumers are becoming more aware of where all their food comes from, and this is no different for honey. Supporting good-quality local honey in turn supports the many family beekeeping businesses in Australia. Regionality is a key factor in many food purchases and has been an integral part of the success of our business. At Raw Honey we proudly extract all of our honey as small-batch single apiary extracts. Each extract is labelled to include the floral source and location.

How do you produce single flower honey?

The vast majority of the honey we produce is from eucalypts. In the native forests, different trees flower at different times in different places. This is the foundation of migratory beekeeping. Hives are moved to make the most of the floral resources available. This yields honey for harvesting and ensures the health of our bees as they are provided with a variety of pollens for their protein and nectar for their energy.

The term 'honey flow' refers to times when both nectar sources and weather conditions are favourable for bees to collect honey. When these conditions coincide there is such an abundance of nectar that the hives fill quickly. In a good honey flow some hives may have such an excess that honey can be extracted weekly. This doesn't happen every year and is a true wonder of nature. Depending on what is flowering in an area, this will produce a single-source variety of honey.

Raw Honey also embraces the unique mixed varieties of honey that migratory beekeeping can produce when hives forage in different locations or for a long period, spanning the flowering of different plants before they have enough surplus honey to extract.

How should honey be stored?

Honey is best stored at room temperature in a sealed container. The exact temperature can influence how quickly the honey may crystallise, being most rapid between 10°C and 21°C (50°F and 70°F). The crystallisation of the honey does not alter its properties. It is important to store in a sealed container as honey is hydroscopic, meaning that it will absorb moisture from the air. In extreme cases, this can cause fermentation.

SUPPLIER PROFILE

Wholegrain rye and buttermilk loaf

Our Wholegrain rye and buttermilk loaf differs from others in that it uses buttermilk instead of water. Adding a hint of molasses means the rich, deep, sweet flavour of the rye comes through strongly, with the buttermilk rounding it out nicely. It's an excellent base for the cured salmon dish on page 120.

Rye contains less gluten than wheat, so we have to use more starter to achieve a nice active dough. You can play around with adding seeds such as linseed and sunflower seeds – both lend themselves nicely to this loaf.

Makes one loaf

Ingredients

Starter build
100 g (3½ oz) rye starter
100 g (3½ oz) wholegrain rye flour
100 g (3½ oz) water

Dough
10 g molasses
300 g (10½ oz) buttermilk
200 g (7 oz) rye starter
360 g (12½ oz) wholegrain rye flour
10 g (¼ oz) salt
rye flour, for dusting

Bakery notes

Acidification can occur during sourdough fermentation or when adding an acid, such as vinegar or buttermilk. This helps to improve the crumb and adds flavour.

We use a high amount of starter in our rye dough to introduce a high level of acid. This lowers the pH level in the dough, so the starch doesn't break down into sugars during the final fermentation. This results in a loaf with more structure, and prevents a gummy and dense crumb.

There is no autolyse or pre-shaping required for this dough. This loaf can easily be made in a day, as 100% rye doughs are better baked straight after the final prove – they don't hold up well under fridge retardation.

Some whole rye flours can absorb a lot of liquid. If the dough feels too dry during mixing, you can add a bit more buttermilk.

Starter build
Around 4–6 hours before you plan to mix your dough, combine the starter, flour and water for the starter build, mixing well to combine (see 'How to make and maintain a starter', page 16). You will use 200 g (7 oz) of this for the dough; retain the rest for maintaining your starter.

Build the dough
Start mixing the dough when the starter is ripe and bubbly. Put the molasses and the buttermilk into a bowl, and stir to combine and leave at room temperature until you're ready to mix your dough.

Mix together the flour and salt in a separate, large bowl. Add the starter and the buttermilk mixture to the flour mixture, and scrunch the dough with your hands until there is no dry flour visible. Cover with a damp cloth and leave in a warm place for at least 1 hour. Mix the dough with your hands for 2–3 minutes to knock it back and thoroughly incorporate the ingredients. The dough should be tacky and slightly sticky; if it feels dry, add a little buttermilk and continue mixing until you have sticky dough. Cover with a damp cloth and leave in a warm place for 4–5 hours.

When the dough has risen a little and contains visible bubbles, press it gently to test if it's ready to shape. If the imprint of your finger stays in the dough when gently pressed, it is ready. The dough should feel light and airy, not dense and thick – if it does feel dense, it requires more time.

Shape and final prove
Lightly grease an 18 × 11 cm (7 × 4¼ in), 10 cm (4 in) high tin so it is ready for baking. Tip the dough onto a lightly floured bench, and gently flatten it into a wide rectangle, with the short edge towards you.

Roll the dough down from the top, pushing into the middle with your thumbs as your fingers pull the dough over. Roll from top to bottom using an even pressure. Turn the dough 90 degrees and gently flatten it once more into a wide rectangle, with the short edge towards you.

→

Wholegrain rye and buttermilk loaf

Repeat the rolling process, then use the heel of your hand to seal the seam at the bottom. Use a dough scraper to peel the dough off the bench, and tidy any seams by pinching them together.

Place your dough in the tin, seam side down. Sprinkle the top generously with rye flour, then cover with a damp cloth and leave in a warm place for around 3 hours, or until the dough has risen by about a third. It should have risen about 2.5 cm (1 in) in the tin, and the flour on top will have split into a striking cracked pattern.

Bake your bread
Place a baking tray at the bottom of the oven, and preheat the oven to the maximum temperature. When the oven is hot, boil the kettle and pour around 150–200 ml (5–7 fl oz) of boiling water into the tray.

Place the tin on the middle shelf of the oven and bake for 20 minutes, until the loaf is starting to colour, then reduce the temperature to 200°C (390°F) and bake for a further 20–25 minutes, until the loaf is a dark golden colour, and firm to touch.

Use the tap test to check the bread: turn the loaf out of the tin and tap the bottom of the loaf. If it sounds hollow, it is ready. You can also use a temperature probe to check the inside temperature of the loaf. I have found an internal temperature of 98°C (208°F) to be the one at which we get the best crumb. If the loaf doesn't reach this temperature, the crumb can appear underbaked and gummy.

Turn the loaf out of the tin and place it on a cooling rack. Leave the bread for at least 6 hours before eating. Rye bread needs this time for the crumb to develop and the flavour to mature. It will be even better two days after baking, and will last for up to a week stored in an airtight container at room temperature.

100% whole-wheat sourdough

Makes one loaf

Ingredients

Starter build
50 g (1¾ oz) starter
50 g (1¾ oz) whole-wheat flour
50 g (1¾ oz) water

Dough
80 g (2¾ oz) starter
420 g (15 oz) whole-wheat flour
300 g (10½ oz) water
10 g (¼ oz) salt
whole-wheat flour, for dusting

Bakery notes

Always keep wholegrain flours in the fridge. Proper wholegrain flour will go rancid faster than other flours because it retains the oils with the germ. If you can, use fresh wholegrain from a good farmer or miller; the end result will be worth it.

We give this dough more folds than our basic sourdough. The higher proportion of bran and germ in the flour makes it harder to fold a well structured loaf, and it will take longer to build strength in the dough.

100% wholegrain breads have outstanding flavour and nutrition. This is the style of bread that most people would have eaten before breadmaking was industrialised and wheat became a commodity. For centuries this was the only bread available. It was made with very fresh stone-milled flour and baked in community bakeries or wood-fired ovens.

Starter build
Around 4–6 hours before you plan to mix your dough, combine the starter, flour and water for the starter build, mixing well to combine (see 'How to make and maintain a starter', page 16). You will use 80 g (2¾ oz) of this for the dough; retain the rest for maintaining your starter.

Build the dough
At least 30 minutes before you plan to mix the dough, combine the flour and water in a large mixing bowl. Mix them with your hands until thoroughly combined, then cover with a damp cloth and set aside for the autolyse (see 'Mixing the dough', page 19).

When the starter is ripe and bubbly, mix it with the flour and water, then sprinkle over the salt and finish mixing the dough. Cover with a damp cloth and set aside in a warm place for at least 30 minutes, before your first set of folds.

Complete six sets of folds, resting the dough in between each one for 30 minutes (see 'Turn and fold', page 20). Whole-wheat can take extra folds, as it has proportionately less protein in the flour than baker's wheat flour. It needs some extra work to build a strong dough.

After your last set of folds, cover your dough with a damp cloth and leave to prove at room temperature for 2–3 hours (see 'Bulk prove', page 20).

Shape and final prove
If you have multiplied the recipe, divide the dough into individual loaves before you pre-shape. Pre-shape the dough, then cover with a damp cloth and leave it to rest on the bench for 15–20 minutes (see 'Pre-shaping', page 20).

When the dough has relaxed, shape the dough as desired, then place it seam side up in a lightly floured proving basket (see 'Shaping', page 20). Cover with a damp cloth and set aside for a few hours, or in the fridge overnight, until ready to bake (see 'Final prove', page 22).

Bake your bread
Preheat the oven to the maximum temperature and bake according to your preferred method (see 'The bake', page 23). Once baked, tip the bread out of the pan onto a wire rack to cool.

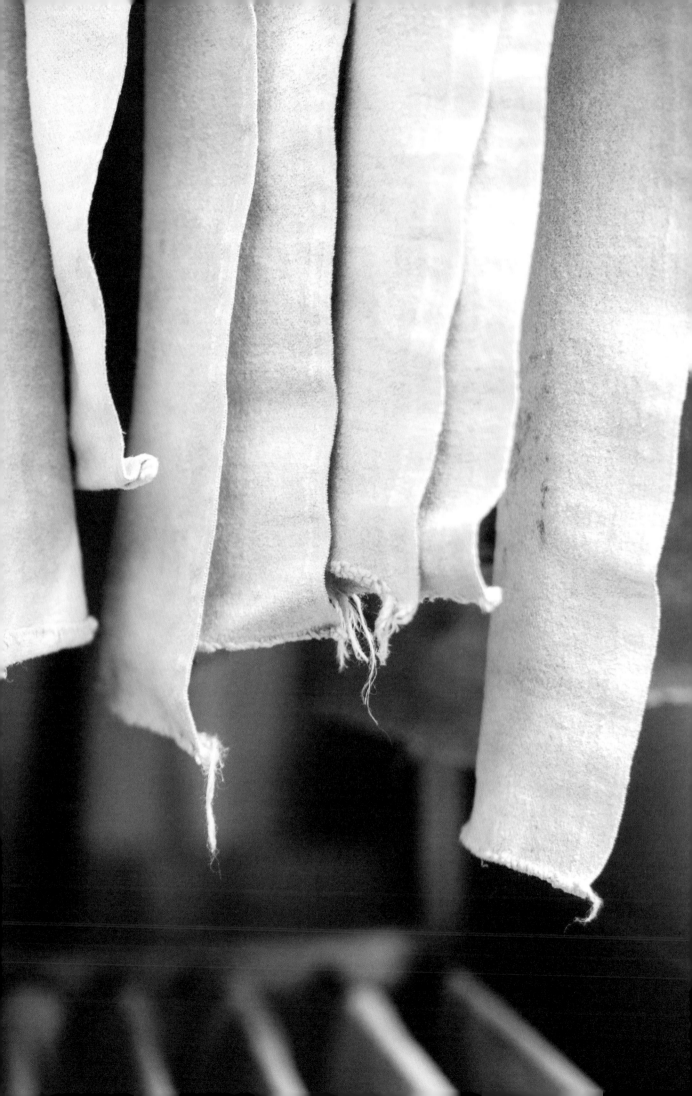

Wattleseed, macadamia and honey loaf

Makes one loaf

Ingredients

Starter build
50 g (1¾ oz) starter
25 g (1 oz) bakers flour
25 g (1 oz) whole-wheat flour
50 g (1¾ oz) water

Dough
100 g (3½ oz) starter
220 g (8 oz) bakers flour
100 g (3½ oz) whole-wheat flour
300 g (10½ oz) water
30 g (1 oz) red gum honey
7 g (¼ oz) salt

15 g (½ oz) wattleseed, ground in
    a mortar and pestle
70 g (2½ oz) macadamia nuts, lightly
    toasted and roughly chopped
semolina, for dusting

Bakery notes
Use a pestle and mortar to grind the wattleseed before using. This will keep the baked loaf from having a gritty texture, and will give a more pronounced wattleseed flavour to complement the macadamias and honey. Most native and rare spices and seeds can be obtained online. If you don't have wattleseed, you could use a combination of mixed spice and cocoa powder.

This bread was inspired by a wattleseed and rye bread made by Ben Shewry at Attica. Native ingredients aren't widely used in modern baking, and I wanted to explore the possibilities. We now use a variety of Australian native ingredients, as the flavour profiles are unique and extremely interesting.

This is one of my favourite breads to eat – the wattleseed gives a dark roasted coffee, chicory-like flavour that combines beautifully with the sweet creamy macadamias and the red gum honey. It's an excellent all-round bread, and pairs particularly well with blue cheese.

Starter build
Around 4–6 hours before you plan to mix your dough, combine the starter, flour and water for the starter build, mixing well to combine (see 'How to make and maintain a starter', page 16). You will use 100 g (3½ oz) of this for the dough; retain the rest for maintaining your starter.

Build the dough
At least 30 minutes before you plan to mix the dough, combine the flours and water in a large mixing bowl. Mix them with your hands until thoroughly combined, then cover with a damp cloth and set aside for the autolyse (see 'Mixing the dough', page 19).

When the starter is ripe and bubbly, mix it with the flour and water mixture, then add the honey and massage the mixture for a minute or so, until fully incorporated. Sprinkle over the salt and finish mixing the dough. Cover with a damp cloth and set aside in a warm place for at least 30 minutes, before your first set of folds.

Add the ground wattleseed and roughly chopped macadamias to the dough as you do the first turn and fold, ensuring they are evenly incorporated. Complete four sets of folds, resting the dough in between each one for 30–45 minutes (see 'Turn and fold', page 20).

After your last set of folds, cover your dough with a damp cloth and leave to prove at room temperature for 2–3 hours (see 'Bulk prove', page 20).

Shape and final prove
If you have multiplied the recipe, divide the dough into individual loaves before you pre-shape. Pre-shape the dough, then cover with a damp cloth and leave it to rest on the bench for 15–20 minutes (see 'Pre-shaping', page 20).

When the dough has relaxed, shape the dough as desired, then place it seam side up in a lightly floured proving basket (see 'Shaping', page 20).

Cover with a damp cloth and set aside for a few hours, or in the fridge overnight, until ready to bake (see 'Final prove', page 23).

Bake your bread
Preheat the oven to the maximum temperature and bake according to your preferred method (see 'The bake', page 22). If using the Dutch oven, bake for 25 minutes with the lid on, then reduce the temperature to 200°C (390°F) and bake for another 4–5 minutes without the lid. The honey in the dough will caramelise the crust quite quickly, so keep an eye on the loaf in the final third of the bake. The wattleseed will give off an amazing aroma as the bread bakes.

Sprouted buckwheat loaf

Makes one loaf

Ingredients

Starter build
50 g (1¾ oz) starter
25 g (1 oz) bakers flour
25 g (1 oz) whole-wheat flour
50 g (1¾ oz) water

Dough
90 g (3 oz) starter
60 g (2 oz) buckwheat groats
300 g (10½ oz) bakers flour
65 g (2¼ oz) whole-wheat flour
280 g (10 oz) water
7 g (¼ oz) salt
20 g (¾ oz) buckwheat flour
20 g (¾ oz) water at 60°C (140°F)
100 g (3½ oz) buckwheat groats,
   crushed

Bakery notes

You can sprout almost anything and throw it into this loaf; we've had success with rye, wheat, quinoa and lentils. They all add their own unique flavour and texture.

The buckwheat, which has no gluten but lots of flavour, is added by making a slurry with hot water and buckwheat flour, and folding that into your developed dough. Low- or no-gluten flours are added later in the mixing process so that they don't impact the development of the dough. We make them into a slurry to maintain hydration and so it's easier to mix through the dough. We also use this technique at the bakery to add purple corn or polenta to our basic sourdough.

Buckwheat groats or kernels are available online, at whole food stores and specialty grocers. Some supermarkets also stock them.

A bit of a misnomer, buckwheat is not related to wheat; it's not even a grass. The seed is high in complex carbohydrates, amino acids, dietary fibre, protein and minerals, and is sometimes referred to as a 'pseudo cereal'. It is not only great nutritionally, but also extremely beneficial to soil health and good crop rotation.

This is a great loaf for getting into the world of sprouted grains. Buckwheat is delicious and very easy to sprout. We add a bit of buckwheat slurry to this loaf, to bring out the earthy flavour of the buckwheat.

Sprout the buckwheat

Rinse the 60 g (2 oz) buckwheat groats three times in cool running water, and put them in a small bowl. Cover with tepid water and leave to soak for 30 minutes.

Cover the base of a tray with a warm, damp cloth. Strain the buckwheat and spread it onto the tray, then cover it with another warm, damp cloth. Leave it to sprout in a warm place – this should take about 24–48 hours.

Once sprouted, the buckwheat is ready to use, but it will also keep in a sealed container in the fridge for up to three days.

Starter build

Around 4–6 hours before you plan to mix your dough, combine the starter, flours and water for the starter build, mixing well to combine (see 'How to make and maintain a starter', page 16). You will use 90 g (3 oz) of this for the dough; retain the rest for maintaining your starter.

Build the dough

At least 30 minutes before you plan to mix the dough, combine the bakers flour, whole-wheat flour and water in a large mixing bowl. Mix them with your hands until thoroughly combined, then cover with a damp cloth and set aside for the autolyse (see 'Mixing the dough', page 19).

When the starter is ripe and bubbly, mix it with the flour and water mixture, then sprinkle over the salt and finish mixing the dough. Cover with a damp cloth and set aside in a warm place for at least 30 minutes, before your first set of folds.

To make the buckwheat slurry, mix the buckwheat flour and 60°C (140°F) water in a small bowl, to form a loose paste. Add the slurry and the sprouted buckwheat to the dough as you do the first turn and fold, ensuring they are evenly incorporated. Complete four sets of folds, resting the dough in between each one for 30–45 minutes (see 'Turn and fold', page 20).

After your last set of folds, cover your dough with a damp cloth and leave to prove at room temperature for 2–3 hours (see 'Bulk prove', page 20).

Sprouted buckwheat loaf

Shape and final prove

If you have multiplied the recipe, divide the dough into individual loaves before you pre-shape. Pre-shape the dough, then cover it with a damp cloth and leave it to rest on the bench for 15–20 minutes (see 'Pre-shaping', page 20).

To crush the buckwheat, wrap it in a tea (dish) towel and roll over the top with a rolling pin. Place the crushed buckwheat groats in a wide bowl. When the dough has relaxed, shape the dough as desired (see 'Shaping', page 20). Spray the top of the loaf with water or roll it over a damp tea towel, then roll it in the crushed groats to cover the loaf.

Place it seam side up in a proving basket. You don't need to flour the banneton for this bread, as the crushed buckwheat will stop it from sticking. Just make sure it is well covered over the surface. Cover with a damp cloth and set aside for a few hours, or in the fridge overnight, until ready to bake (see 'Final prove', page 22).

Bake your bread

Preheat the oven to the maximum temperature and bake according to your preferred method (see 'The bake', page 23). Once baked, tip the bread out of the pan onto a wire rack to cool.

VIENNOISERIE

The term Viennoiserie means 'things of Vienna', and legend has it that the Austrians created a crescent-shaped pastry modelled on the crescent on the Turkish flag following the defeat of Ottoman invaders. This was translated to the French 'croissant' when an Austrian man, August Zang, opened his boulangerie Viennoise in Paris, in the late 1830s.

Croissant pastry is a particular challenge. It takes time and experience to get a feel for the dough, and the variances caused by changes in temperature and humidity. No two days are the same on the croissant bench – that's what makes croissant production so interesting for me. It's one of the reasons I switched from being a chef to a baker. Producing something that is flaky but also soft and buttery is a mix of science and true craft that brings endless discovery.

Our daily range of Viennoiserie includes croissant, pain au chocolat, escargot (like a traditional pain au raisin, but different), fruit and savoury Danishes, morning buns and almond croissant. We also like to experiment by laminating different sugars into the pastry, or creating interesting shapes. Once you get the hang of the pastry, what you can produce is limited only by your imagination.

Croissant pastry

Makes 1.4 kg (3 lb 1 oz) pastry

Ingredients

<u>Ferment (optional)</u>
40 g (1½ oz) bakers flour
25 g (1 oz) water, at 26°C (79°F)
pinch fresh or dry yeast

<u>Dough</u>
50 g (1¾ oz) spelt flour
550 g (1 lb 3 oz) bakers flour
60 g (2 oz/⅓ cup) soft brown sugar
14 g (½ oz) salt
175 g (6 oz) water, at room
    temperature
175 g (6 oz) full-cream (whole) milk,
    at room temperature
18 g (¾ oz) fresh yeast
60 g (2 oz) ferment (optional)
250 g (9 oz) unsalted butter, chilled,
    82% fat and preferably cultured,
    for laminating

Bakery notes
This recipe takes a couple of days. On the first day you will prepare the dough and the butter for lamination, and on the second you will laminate the dough. Lamination is the process of rolling and folding the butter into the dough, to create very fine distinct layers of butter and pastry. This is what creates all those lovely flaky layers when baked.

The ferment in this dough contributes additional flavour, but the recipe will still work without it. You can make a simple ferment as detailed in the recipe, keeping it in the fridge for one to three days before you want to start.

I prefer to use the paddle attachment when I mix croissant dough; others prefer the dough hook. Try both and use whichever you feel more comfortable with.

Our croissant dough is 25% butter, so be sure to use the highest quality you can find. The block of butter used for laminating needs to contain at least 82% fat – a cultured European-style butter is ideal, if you can get it. It will make a world of difference to the flavour of the finished product, as well as to the performance of your dough.

You also need a high-protein bakers flour to get more volume and more pronounced layers. I've added spelt for its nutty flavour, and also because it's more extensible than wheat, which will give you a more elastic dough. If you can't find spelt flour, use bakers flour.

Ferment
Combine the flour, water and yeast in a small bowl and mix well. Leave the ferment at room temperature for 6–8 hours before using. It can be stored in the fridge in an airtight container for up to 3 days.

Prepare the dough
Combine the flours, sugar and salt in the bowl of a stand mixer fitted with a paddle attachment. Stir briefly to combine, then add the water, milk, yeast and ferment (if using). Mix on a low speed for at least 10 minutes, until the dough is smooth and elastic, and coming away from the sides of the bowl.

Turn the dough onto a lightly floured bench and knead it gently for a couple of minutes, then shape it into a rectangular block about 4 cm (1½ in) thick. The dough should be shiny and stretchy, not wet or tacky. Place the dough in a container with a lid, or wrap well in plastic wrap, and refrigerate for 1 hour.

On a lightly floured bench, roll your dough into a rectangle roughly 20 × 40 cm (8 × 16 in), with the long edge towards you.

Fold the left-hand third of the pastry into the middle, and then the other third over that, as if folding a letter. Put the dough back into the container or plastic wrap and refrigerate for at least 3 hours.

→

Prepare the butter

Remove the butter from the fridge and leave at room temperature for 30–60 minutes, until it's malleable but not too soft. Lay it between two sheets of greaseproof paper and roll it out into a rectangle about 13 × 16 cm (5 × 6¼ in), and 1 cm (½ in) thick. Wrap well in plastic wrap and return it to the fridge with your dough for at least 2 hours.

Laminate the pastry

Remove the butter from the fridge and leave at room temperature for 30–60 minutes, until it's malleable but not soft. When you laminate, the temperature of the butter is very important – if it's too cold it will crack and won't fold nicely into the dough; if it's too warm it will leak into the dough, creating a doughy, buttery mess when you bake it. Ideally, it should be between 14 and 18°C (57–64°F), to ensure better lamination and butter fat plasticity. Check it by gently pressing into the surface with your finger; it's ready to use when the surface offers slight resistance.

Remove your dough from the fridge and lay it on a lightly floured bench. Roll it into a rectangle 20 × 30 cm (8 × 12 in), with the long edge towards you.

Lay the butter vertically up the centre of the rectangle so that the short edge of the butter block is towards you (see Step 1, page 80). Fold the sides of the dough over the butter block so that it is completely covered, and the edges of the dough meet in the middle (see Step 2 and 3, page 80). This is called 'locking in' your butter. You want your butter sheet to be a bit shorter than the pastry, so that when you fold over it it is completely enclosed within the pastry (but not sealed).

Gently press down on the pastry to encase the butter and then roll the pastry vertically, with the joined ends running up the middle of the block, until you have a rectangle of even thickness, roughly 45 cm (18 in) high × 20 cm (8 in) wide. It is important that the consistency of the dough and butter is similar, so you maintain distinct layers while laminating. If the butter is too hard and you feel it start to crack, cover the pastry block loosely with plastic wrap and leave it on the bench for 10 minutes to let the butter soften. If the butter appears soft and is starting to seep out the ends, wrap your pastry with the butter locked in, and return to the fridge for 10 minutes before trying again.

Trim the short ends to neaten up the corners, saving any trimmings to use as ferment for your next batch. Fold the top third of the rectangle down into the centre of the pastry sheet (see step 4, page 81) and then cover with the bottom third, as if folding a letter (see step 5, page 81). This is your first single fold (see step 6, page 81). Wrap well in plastic wrap and refrigerate for 20–30 minutes.

Repeat the rolling and folding process twice more, each time beginning with the spine of the 'letter' on the left, so that the block is rotated 90 degrees each time you perform a fold. Rotating the block of pastry ensures that the dough will not become tight, and will produce a more even lamination throughout the block. Cover and refrigerate for 20–30 minutes between each fold.

After the third fold is complete, cover and return to the fridge for at least 1 hour. After an hour, the dough is ready to be rolled out and shaped into your viennoiserie of choice (see recipes to follow).

1.

2.

3.

4.

5.

6.

Croissant

Makes 8–10

Ingredients
1 quantity croissant pastry
 (see page 78)
1 egg
50 g (1¾ oz) full-cream (whole) milk
pinch salt

Bakery notes
*Croissants freeze really well. Refresh
from frozen in a 180°C (360°F) oven
for 5 minutes.*

*We add a pinch of salt to our egg wash
before brushing the pastries. Salt denatures
the proteins in the egg and produces a
runnier texture, which is easier to use.*

Shape your pastries
Roll your rested pastry out into a rectangle roughly 20 × 55 cm (8 × 22 in), and about 8 mm (¼ in) thick, with the long edge towards you.

Trim the edges of your rectangle, then mark notches 8 cm (3¼ in) apart along the bottom edge. Along the top edge, make a notch 4 cm (1½ in) from the left, then continue in 8 cm (3¼ in) increments so that the top and bottom notches are offset.

Working from the left-hand side of your rectangle, place a ruler to join the first top and bottom notch, creating a diagonal line. Use a sharp knife to cut along the diagonal, then swing the bottom of the ruler along to the next notch to cut your first triangle.

Continue cutting in a zigzag pattern, using the notches as your guides, until you have all the triangles cut. The only excess pastry should be at either end. Any scraps can be used as ferment for your next batch of croissant dough (these will keep in the fridge for three days, or in the freezer for a month).

Lay the triangles flat in a container or on a tray, and cover loosely with plastic wrap. Return them to the fridge to rest for 30 minutes.

Line two trays with baking paper. To roll your croissants, take one of the triangles and, holding the base of the triangle towards your body, gently stretch it away from you, elongating it slightly.

Starting from the bottom, roll the croissant into the spiral shape using light, even pressure. Gently press the stretched tip into the bottom of the spiral to seal it, then place it on a tray with the tip underneath the croissant.

Repeat with the remaining triangles, leaving space between each croissant to allow for the eventual rise (you will get 4–5 croissant on a standard baking tray).

It's hard to beat a beautifully flaky, buttery croissant. When you get it right, you will have fine layers that melt over your tongue and taste sublime.

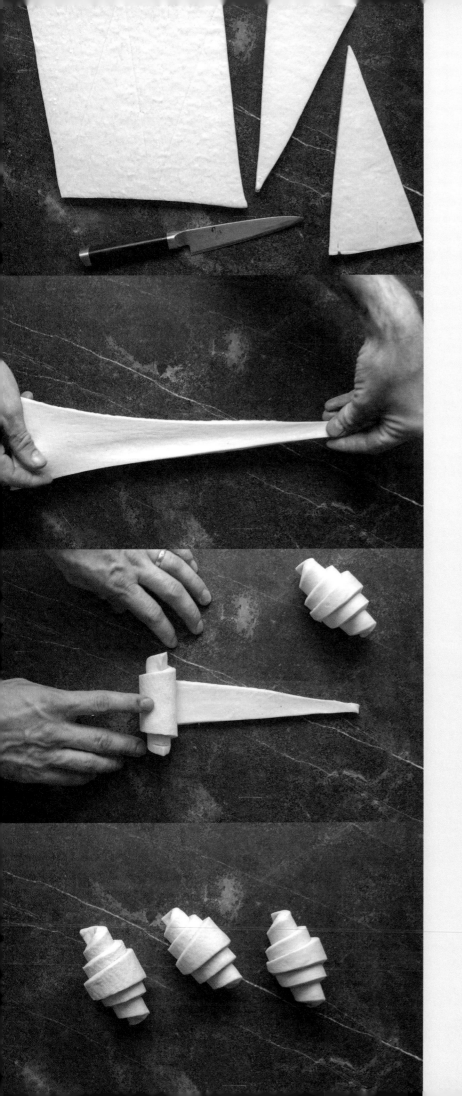

Croissant

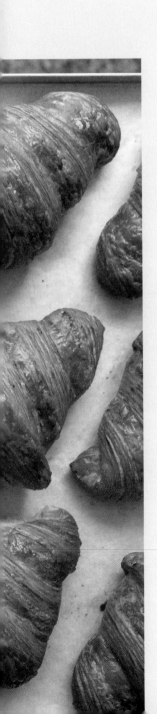

The prove

Lightly cover the trays with plastic wrap and leave them in a warm place (ideally 22–26°C/72–79°F) to rise. At the bakery we have the luxury of a prover/retarder that provides the ideal conditions for proving pastries, but when I'm at home I gauge the weather and adjust my method accordingly. On a cool day, you can use your oven as a proving box by placing a roasting pan filled with hot water at the bottom of the oven and leaving it for about 5 minutes, to create steam. Once the oven is slightly warm, place the trays of croissants (still lightly covered in plastic wrap) in to prove. On a warm day you can just leave them lightly covered on a bench to prove.

Leave the croissants until they have risen by half – the time will vary depending on the temperature and humidity of the day, but this should take around 1–2 hours. You should be able to see the layers in the pastry, and you can test to see if it's ready by lightly pressing into the dough. If your finger leaves a dent in the pastry, it's ready; if the dough springs back it needs some more time proving.

Bake your pastries

Preheat the oven to 190°C (370°F). (If you've used the oven to prove your croissants, make sure you remove them and the tray of water before you turn the oven on!)

Make an egg wash by lightly beating together the egg, milk and salt. Take your first tray of croissants and lightly brush the surface of each with egg wash. Refrigerate the other tray until ready to bake.

Place the tray on the middle shelf of the heated oven, and reduce the temperature to 170°C (340°F). Bake for 10 minutes, then check your croissants and turn the tray, if needed, and bake for a further 4–5 minutes, until they are golden and flaky.

Remove the first tray from the oven, return the temperature to 190°C (370°F) and repeat with the second tray. (You may find you can bake two trays at once if you have a good fan-forced oven.) Cool the croissants slightly on the trays before serving.

Pain au chocolat

This is an indulgence,
with just a little chocolate
punctuating the rich,
buttery pastry. Use good
quality dark chocolate
for a sophisticated
breakfast treat.

Makes 10

Ingredients

1 quantity croissant pastry
  (see page 78)
150 g (5½ oz) dark (semisweet)
  chocolate (at least 58% cocoa
  solids), either in buttons or roughly
  chopped
1 egg
50 g (1¾ oz) full-cream (whole) milk
pinch salt

Bakery notes

*At the bakery, we use little purpose-made
logs of chocolate for pain au chocolat.
You can get them at specialty cookery or
baking shops. You could also use chocolate
buttons, or roughly chopped chocolate.*

Shape your pastries

Roll your rested pastry out into a rectangle roughly 30 × 40 cm (12 × 16 in) and
about 8 mm (¼ in) thick, with the long edge towards you. Trim all the edges to
create a neat rectangle and then, starting from the left-hand side, mark notches
8 cm (3¼ in) apart along the top and bottom edge.

Use a ruler to align the first top and bottom notch and cut a straight vertical
line using a sharp knife. Continue working your way along the notches until
you have 5 long rectangles. Cut each rectangle in half so you have 10 pieces of
pastry roughly 8 × 15 cm (3¼ × 6 in). Lay the rectangles flat in a container or on
a tray, and cover loosely with plastic wrap. Refrigerate for 30 minutes, to rest.

Line two trays with baking paper. Take the rectangles from the fridge and lay
them out on a lightly floured surface with the short edges towards you.

For each piece of pastry, place a horizontal line of chocolate about a quarter
of the way down from the top edge, then gently fold the top of the pastry down
to cover the chocolate.

Place a second line of chocolate below the edge that you've just folded, and
roll the pastry from the top so the chocolate is encased and the seam is on
the bottom. Don't pull it too tight – you don't want a cylinder, you want an
oval-shaped pastry with a flat bottom. Transfer the pastries to a tray lined with
baking paper, leaving space between each one (you will get 4–5 pastries on
a standard baking tray).

The prove

Lightly cover the trays with plastic wrap and leave them in a warm place (ideally
22–26°C/72–79°F) to rise.

Leave the pain au chocolat until they have risen by half – the time will vary
depending on the temperature and humidity of the day, but this should take
around 1–2 hours. On a cool day, you can use your oven as a proving box by
placing a roasting pan filled with boiling water at the bottom of the oven and
leaving it for about 5 minutes, to create steam. Once the oven is slightly warm,
place the trays of pastries (still lightly covered in plastic wrap) in to prove. You
should be able to see the layers in the pastry, and you can test to see if it's ready
by lightly pressing into the dough. If your finger leaves a dent in the pastry,
it's ready; if the dough springs back quickly it needs some more time proving.
Check it again in 10–15 minutes.

Bake your pastries

Preheat the oven to 190°C (370°F). Make an egg wash by lightly beating
together the egg, milk and salt. Take your first tray of pastries and lightly brush
the surface of each with egg wash. Refrigerate the other tray until ready to
bake. Place the tray on the middle shelf of the heated oven, and reduce the
temperature to 170°C (340°F). Bake for 10 minutes, then check your pain au
chocolat and turn the tray, if needed, and bake for a further 4–5 minutes, until
they are golden and flaky.

Remove the first tray from the oven, return the temperature to 190°C (370°F)
and repeat with the second tray. (You may find you can bake two trays at once
if you have a good fan-forced oven.) Cool slightly on the trays before serving.

Seasonal fruit Danish

Makes 12

Ingredients

1 quantity croissant pastry
(see page 78)
½ quantity pastry cream
(see page 262)
seasonal fruit (see Bakery notes)
1 egg
50 g (1¾ oz) full-cream (whole) milk
pinch salt
2 tablespoons apricot or
strawberry jam, for glazing
½ cup nuts, roughly chopped
icing (confectioners') sugar, to finish
(if desired)

Bakery notes

Judge the quantities depending on the fruit you are using. For example, you may need half a large plum per Danish, or several slices of smaller plums. Feel free to change up the finishing touches, too. Hazelnuts pair beautifully with quince, and pistachios with berries. You are limited only by your tastes and imagination.

We make both savoury and fruit Danish at Tivoli Road – the pastry base can be a platform for so many different things! For our fruit Danish, we use berries, figs and stone fruit in summer, and poached rhubarb and poached pears in winter. Some berries hold up better in baking than others – for example, we might bake the Danish with strawberries, and then add fresh blueberries or raspberries after baking.

Shape your pastries

On a lightly floured surface, roll your rested pastry out into a rectangle roughly 20 × 55 cm (8 × 22 in) and about 8 mm (¼ in) thick, with the long edge towards you.

Trim all the edges to create a neat rectangle, then mark notches along the edges of the pastry 9 cm (3½ in) apart. You will use these as a guide for cutting your pastry squares.

Working from left to right, use a ruler to align the first top and bottom notch and cut a straight line vertically with a sharp knife. Continue working your way along the notches until you have 6 long rectangles. Cut each of these in half so you are left with 12 squares of pastry, roughly 9 × 9 cm (3½ in).

Lay the Danish out on two trays lined with baking paper, leaving space between each one to allow for the eventual rise. Loosely cover your trays with plastic wrap and refrigerate for 30 minutes, to rest.

Prepare your fruit

The style of presentation can vary according to your tastes, and depending on the size of the fruit. Use hulled strawberries whole, or cut in half if large. Stone fruit can be pitted and halved, or sliced and fanned out over the pastry. As a general guide, we use 2–3 strawberries or half a stone fruit per Danish.

Spoon roughly 2 teaspoons of pastry cream into the middle of each pastry square, leaving a 2 cm (¾ in) border, and place the fruit on top. Press the fruit gently into the pastry cream to hold it in place.

The prove

Lightly cover the trays with plastic wrap and leave them in a warm place (ideally 22–26°C/72–79°F) to rise. At the bakery we have the luxury of a prover/retarder that provides the ideal conditions for proving pastries, but when I'm at home I gauge the weather and adjust my method accordingly. On a cool day, you can use your oven as a proving box by placing a roasting pan filled with boiling water at the bottom and leaving it for about 5 minutes, to create steam. Once the oven is slightly warm, place the trays of pastries (still lightly covered in plastic wrap) in to prove. On a warm day you can just leave them lightly covered on a bench to prove.

Leave the Danish until they have risen by half – the time will vary depending on the temperature and humidity of the day, but this should take around 1–2 hours. You should be able to see the layers in the pastry, and you can test to see if it's ready by lightly pressing into the dough. If your finger leaves a dent in the pastry, it's ready; if the dough springs back it needs some more time proving.

Bake your pastries

Preheat the oven to 190°C (370°F). (If you've used the oven to prove your Danish, make sure you remove them and the tray of water before you turn the oven on!)

Make an egg wash by lightly beating together the egg, milk and salt. Take your first tray and lightly brush the border of each pastry with egg wash. Refrigerate the other tray until ready to bake. Place the tray on the middle shelf of the heated oven, and reduce the temperature to 170°C (340°F). Bake for 10 minutes, then check your Danish and turn the tray, if needed, and bake for a further 4–5 minutes, until they are golden and flaky.

Remove the first tray from the oven, return the temperature to 190°C (370°F) and repeat with the second tray. (You may find you can bake two trays at once if you have a good fan-forced oven).

While the second tray is baking, warm the jam in a small saucepan over a low heat, and thin with a little water if necessary, to make a glaze. Before serving, brush the fruit with the glaze and leave to cool slightly. Finish each pastry with extra fresh berries, toasted nuts and icing sugar, as desired.

SAINT DAVID DAIRY

Ben and Bianca Evans set up Saint David Dairy in Fitzroy, Melbourne, in 2013, reviving a forgotten history of inner-city dairies supplying their local communities. We use their full range of delicious, undoctored dairy products. Ben told us a bit about their business.

How did you come to be where you are?

I was born in Port Fairy and grew up in Koroit, in south-west Victoria. Being a huge farming area, a lot of the town was involved in some way. My mother was one of ten children on a dairy farm in Toolong, and I ended up finishing school to begin a cadetship in dairy technology at the local Murray Goulburn factory. My sister is a dairy farmer and my uncle is the manager of the local factory in Koroit today, so we are embedded in the industry.

Travelling overseas cheesemaking, and while at college, I saw the small-scale factories and fell in love with them. After working in the huge processing plants, the large scale of people and machinery lost something, whereas in the small factories I still felt like the milk was valued, and could be seen, smelled and tasted.

What prompted you to start a dairy in inner-city Melbourne?

I had planned for years to start a small factory of my own one day, but never thought of having it so inner-city. After returning from an overseas working holiday, I moved to Melbourne and saw the growing interest in food origins, supporting local business, slow food and sourcing direct from the producer. My wife was studying in Fitzroy and I saw the sign in St David Street saying 'Food factory for lease'. We sold everything we owned, quit our jobs, and twelve months later we were hand-bottling milk.

What particular challenges does an inner-city dairy face?

Parking, neighbours, noise and hours of operation are all affected by our location. The space restrictions will certainly keep our growth in check. But it is such a part of the story of our business, and the local support has been awesome.

What's the overriding philosophy driving your business?

We wanted to provide a small, transparent business that was focused on quality rather than quantity. We sourced the milk, processed it, delivered it, and did it all in the local community with them. We didn't want to play with the milk. We don't standardise our full-cream (whole) milks at all; how it comes from the farm is how it goes in the bottle. People who are looking at products such as ours have expectations around the sourcing of the milk and practices, and also regarding paying a fair price to the farmers.

Ethics and sustainability are embedded in our philosophy, and we needed to find a farm that fitted well with us. While we use carbon neutral electricity at the factory, for instance, the farming family that supply our milk have over 2 acres of pasture per cow, which is quite a low stocking rate for Gippsland. It is only 100 km (62 miles) from our door to theirs, reducing the food miles as much as possible. Bobby calves are sold locally to be raised. We pay the farm a far better price than they were receiving before, which adds to their passion for supplying great milk to us. They even stretch the milk in the dairy after each milking as a test to make sure it is perfect!

Is there seasonal variation in dairy production? Does that make it difficult to manage customer expectations, given that people expect everything to be available all the time?

There is certainly seasonal variation in the milk, and our largest stress is ensuring the milk will stretch year round, when various factors during the summer months can affect this. This played into our choice of the farm we source our milk from, being pasture-based, and with split calving over the year to give fresh lactation throughout. Seasonality also affects milk proteins, which affects things like the strength of the yoghurt set, so while we don't use any stabilisers or gums in our yoghurt, we battle through spring to maintain the thickness.

How do you culture butter?

We culture our butter by warming fresh cream, adding our blend of cultures, and leaving it to ferment for 24 hours. We monitor the culture activity and once the cream has soured to the desired levels, it goes back in the fridge to cool and allow the fat to crystallise before churning.

Escargot

This is our take on the French pain au raisin – spiced fruit studded through rolls of croissant pastry. We like to add custard after baking, and finish with a sprinkle of pistachios to create textural contrast.

Makes 12

Ingredients
50 g (1¾ oz) currants
50 g (1¾ oz) raisins
50 g (1¾ oz) sultanas
½ teaspoon ground cinnamon
¼ teaspoon freshly grated nutmeg
¼ teaspoon ground allspice
1 quantity croissant pastry
    (see page 78)
½ quantity vanilla custard
    (see page 262)
1 egg
50 g (1¾ oz) full-cream (whole) milk
pinch salt

2 tablespoons apricot or strawberry
    jam, for glazing
½ cup raw pistachios, finely chopped

Bakery notes
Feel free to adjust the fruits and spices to your taste here. For a more traditional pain au raisin, you can omit the custard when finishing your escargot.

This shape and the filling makes escargot a more forgiving pastry. At the bakery we combine all the scraps and trimmings from the croissant production, give it a fold and roll it out to make our escargot.

Soak the fruit
Place the currants, raisins and sultanas in a small bowl. Cover with warm water and leave to soak at room temperature for 1 hour. Drain well, then combine with the spices and mix thoroughly. Refrigerate until ready to use.

Shape your pastries
On a lightly floured surface, roll your rested croissant pastry out into a rectangle roughly 30 × 40 cm (12 × 16 in) and about 8 mm (¼ in) thick, with the long edge towards you.

Trim all the edges to create a neat rectangle, then use a spatula to spread a thin layer of custard (around ¼ cup) over the surface of the dough, leaving a 2 cm (¾ in) border along the bottom edge. Reserve the rest of the custard for finishing the pastries after baking. Spread the spiced fruit evenly over the custard.

Starting from the top edge of your dough sheet, roll the pastry down firmly and evenly towards you, being careful not to stretch the pastry, as this will make the dough too tight and affect the final shape of your escargots. When you've finished rolling you should have a long cylinder with a spiral of fruit running through the middle and the seam on the bench, underneath the roll of pastry.

Line two trays with baking paper. Use a bread knife to trim one end of the roll of pastry, then cut it into 3 cm (1¼ in)-wide pieces.

Take one piece, holding it with a spiral facing up. Stretch the end of the roll out a little and tuck it in under the base of the pastry (this will stop them unravelling when they bake). Repeat for each escargot, placing them with the tucked-in end underneath the pastry, and spacing them out evenly on the trays to allow for the eventual rise.

The prove
Lightly cover the trays with plastic wrap and leave them in a warm place (ideally 22–26°C/72–79°F) to rise. At the bakery we have the luxury of a prover/retarder that provides the ideal conditions for proving pastries, but when I'm at home I gauge the weather and adjust my method accordingly. On a cool day, you can use your oven as a proving box by placing a roasting pan filled with boiling water at the bottom and leaving it for about 5 minutes, to create steam. Once the oven is slightly warm, place the trays of pastries (still lightly covered in plastic wrap) in to prove. On a warm day you can just leave them lightly covered on a bench to prove.

Leave the escargot until they have risen by half – the time will vary depending on the temperature and humidity of the day, but this should take around 1–2 hours. You should be able to see the layers in the pastry, and you can test to see if it's ready by lightly pressing into the dough. If your finger leaves a dent in the pastry, it's ready; if the dough springs back it needs some more time proving.

Bake your pastries

Preheat the oven to 190°C (370°F). (If you've used the oven to prove your escargot, make sure you remove them and the tray of water before you turn the oven on!)

Make an egg wash by lightly beating together the egg, milk and salt. Take your first tray and lightly brush the border of each pastry with egg wash. Refrigerate the other tray until ready to bake.

Place the tray on the middle shelf of the heated oven, and reduce the temperature to 170°C (340°F). Bake for 10 minutes, then check your escargot and turn the tray, if needed, and bake for a further 4–5 minutes, until they are golden and flaky.

Remove the first tray from the oven, return the temperature to 190°C (370°F) and repeat with the second tray. (You may find you can bake two trays at once if you have a good fan-forced oven).

While the second tray is baking, gently warm the jam in a small saucepan over a low heat, and thin with a little water if necessary, to make a glaze. Once baked, transfer the escargot to a wire rack and allow them to cool for a few minutes before brushing with the warmed glaze.

Once cooled, pipe or spoon a little vanilla custard into any gaps, as desired, then sprinkle with pistachios and serve.

Morning buns

Makes 12

Ingredients

Morning bun sugar
zest of 1 orange
2 teaspoons ground cinnamon
¼ cup light brown sugar
¼ cup caster (superfine) sugar

Morning buns
50 g (1¾ oz) butter, for greasing
½ cup caster (superfine) sugar, for
    lining trays and finishing the buns
1 quantity croissant pastry
    (see page 78)
½ quantity vanilla custard
    (see page 262)

Bakery notes
A good tip is to leave the buns in the muffin tray for a minute or two after baking to allow the caramelised sugar to properly coat the pastry, then carefully tip them onto a wire rack so the sugar can cool and harden, giving you a nice caramel crust on top. If you leave them too long, the caramel will set and the pastries will get stuck. If this happens, return the pan to the oven or a hot surface to heat just enough to melt the sugar again.

Morning buns look amazing, and always attract attention. The gentle notes of cinnamon and orange sugar rolled into the pastry infuse each mouthful. The vanilla custard fills the centre and provides creamy contrast to the flakiness of the pastry.

To make the morning bun sugar, place all the ingredients in a small bowl, and mix well.

Prepare a 12-hole muffin tray to bake the pastries in. Soften the butter and brush the sides and base of each muffin well. Sprinkle over the caster sugar to coat, shaking off any excess sugar. Set aside the remaining caster sugar in a bowl, to dust the buns once baked. Place 1 teaspoon of morning bun sugar in each well, spreading it out to cover the base.

Shape your pastries
Roll your rested croissant pastry out into a rectangle roughly 20 × 60 cm (8 × 24 in) and about 8 mm (¼ in) thick, with the long edge towards you.

Trim all the edges to create a neat rectangle, then use a spatula to spread a thin layer of custard over the surface of the dough, leaving a 1 cm (½ in) border along the bottom edge. Reserve the rest of the custard for finishing the pastries after baking.

Sprinkle the remaining morning bun sugar over the pastry sheet, ensuring that the surface is covered in a thin, even layer of sugar.

Starting from the top edge of your dough sheet, roll the pastry firmly and evenly towards you, being careful not to stretch the pastry, as this will make the dough too tight and affect the final shape of your buns. When you've finished rolling you should have a long cylinder with a spiral of sugar running through the middle and the seam on the bench, underneath.

Use a bread knife to trim the ends of the roll, and slice the rest into 12 even pieces (approx. 4 cm/1½ in wide). Sit each piece in a well of your prepared muffin tin, with the spiral visible from the top.

The prove
Lightly cover the trays with plastic wrap and leave them in a warm place (ideally 22–26°C/72–79°F) to rise. At the bakery we have the luxury of a prover/retarder that provides the ideal conditions for proving pastries, but when I'm at home I gauge the weather and adjust my method accordingly. On a cool day, you can use your oven as a proving box by placing a roasting pan filled with boiling water at the bottom and leaving it for about 5 minutes, to create steam. Once the oven is slightly warm, place the tray of morning buns (still lightly covered in plastic wrap) in to prove. On a warm day you can just leave them lightly covered on a bench to prove.

Bake your pastries

Preheat the oven to 190°C (370°F) and place a clean, rimmed tray on the bottom shelf, to catch any drips.

Place your tray of buns on the middle shelf of the oven, then reduce the oven temperature to 170°C (340°F) and bake for 20 minutes.

Check on the buns to see that they're not colouring too quickly, then turn the tray and bake for a further 10–15 minutes, until golden and flaky. Tip the buns out onto a wire cooling rack, being careful to avoid the caramelised sugar on the base, which will be extremely hot. Carefully position the buns so that they're sitting caramel-side-up and leave them to cool.

Once cool, dust the buns with the remaining caster sugar, to coat. Pipe or spoon a small amount of vanilla custard into the centre of each bun to finish.

Almond croissant

Makes 10

Ingredients

Frangipane
230 g (8 oz) butter, softened
285 g (10 oz) caster (superfine) sugar
45 g (1½ oz) plain (all-purpose) flour
285 g (10 oz) ground almonds
5 eggs
1 teaspoon vanilla or 1 vanilla bean
zest of ½ a lemon

Sugar syrup
100 g (3½ oz) caster (superfine) sugar
zest of ½ a lemon
½ cinnamon stick
1 star anise
1 bay leaf

Assembly
500 g (1 lb 2 oz) flaked almonds
10 one-day old croissants
icing (confectioners') sugar,
   for dusting

Bakery notes
*If you're making the frangipane ahead
of time it will keep in the fridge for up to
a week. You'll just need to bring it out of the
fridge a couple of hours before you need it,
so it's soft enough to use.*

This is essentially a delicious way of using up leftover croissants. Another very popular way is to slice the croissant in half, place sliced cheese and ham in the middle, and bake for a couple of minutes in a hot oven. Either way, croissants take so much effort to make, it would be criminal to waste them!

Frangipane
In a stand mixer fitted with the paddle attachment, cream together the butter and caster sugar until fluffy and pale.

Mix the flour and ground almonds in a bowl. In a separate bowl, lightly whisk the eggs, vanilla and lemon zest.

Gradually add the egg mixture to the butter and sugar with the paddle still going, ensuring that each addition is fully incorporated before adding the next one.

Once all the eggs mix is in, add the dry ingredients and mix with the paddle until just combined. Put the mixture into a piping (icing) bag, ready to use.

Sugar syrup
Combine the caster (superfine) sugar, lemon zest, cinnamon, star anise and bay leaf in a small saucepan with 200 ml (7 fl oz) of water. Bring the syrup to a simmer over a medium heat, stirring constantly until the sugar has dissolved. Cool completely, and then strain the spices out, reserving the syrup in a bowl.

Assembly
Put the flaked almonds in a large mixing bowl.

Slice each croissant in half horizontally, leaving the two pieces just attached at one edge, and open them up. Brush the insides with sugar syrup.

Spread a layer of frangipane about 1 cm (½ in) thick over the bottom half of each croissant. Replace the top half, then pipe a line of frangipane roughly 1 cm (½ in) thick over the length of the croissant.

Press the top of each croissant into the almond flakes so they stick to the frangipane. Arrange the croissants on a baking tray and refrigerate them for half an hour so the frangipane can firm up.

Bake your pastries
Preheat the oven to 160°C (320°F). Remove the tray from the fridge and put it straight into the oven.

Bake for 10 minutes, then reduce the heat to 150°C (300°F) and bake for a further 15–20 minutes, until they are a nice golden brown. If you find they are colouring too quickly, reduce the temperature a bit. It's important to cook out the frangipane without burning the croissant.

Leave to cool, then dust with icing sugar to serve.

SAVOURY

To complement our breads
and sweet baking, we make
a range of savoury pies, sausage
rolls, sandwiches and salads
to satisfy the lunch crowds.
Everything we sell needs
to be delicious, so we have
taken classical techniques
and recipes, and used them
in our savoury section to
make the tastiest sandwiches
or pies we can. It's a creative
outlet for this former chef,
but everyone in the kitchen
contributes to these recipes.

The pies and sausage rolls are a great
item to make up in a large batch and
freeze, to be baked when required when
time is short to cook a meal. The salads
are designed to be sustaining as a
meal on their own, but also work really
well with simple roasted meats or
fish. Our sandwiches were created to
showcase our breads and complement
the flavours. They are a big hit all year
round and are actually our biggest selling
items at the bakery.

Khorasan, cheddar and chive scones

Makes 8 scones

Ingredients

200 g (7 oz/1⅓ cups) wholegrain
   khorosan flour
300 g (10½ oz/2 cups) plain
   (all-purpose) flour
2 teaspoons baking powder
½ teaspoon bicarbonate of soda
   (baking soda)
2 teaspoons salt
220 g (8 oz) unsalted butter
240 g + 50 g (8½ oz + 1¾ oz) cheddar
   cheese, grated
1 bunch chives, snipped
2 eggs
225 g (8 oz) sour cream
60 ml (2 fl oz/¼ cup) thick cream

Bakery notes

It's important to start with chilled butter so that it doesn't melt through the dough. You want to retain little lumps of butter to produce a beautiful flaky crumb.

Khorasan is an ancient grain, also known as kamut, and is available in health food stores. If you can't find it you can use any wholegrain flour, or substitute with plain flour.

We first made this savoury scone as an alternative to a sweet scone for our farmers' market stall. Over time, they sold out more and more quickly, and then customers started asking for them in the bakery. They've since become a firm favourite of our bakery repertoire.

Cheddar and chive is such a classic combination. Using really good cheddar will give these scones a delicious umami bite. We add whole-wheat flour for more depth of flavour – it also improves the soft, flaky texture of the scone. These are great to eat fresh from the oven for a mid-morning snack, just as they are or with some good-quality butter.

Cut the butter into 1 cm (½ in) dice, then put it in the freezer to get it really cold while you weigh up the rest of your ingredients.

Combine the flours, baking powder, bicarbonate of soda and salt in a large mixing bowl, then whisk to combine, removing any large lumps. Tip the dry ingredients out onto a clean bench top and scatter over the cubed butter. Use a rolling pin to break the butter into the flour, gathering the flour in as you roll until you have a crumbly textured mixture with pea-sized lumps of butter still visible. Having small chunks of butter helps the scones rise, so be careful not to overmix it at this stage. Return the mixture to the bowl, add the grated cheese and chives, and toss to combine.

In a separate bowl, lightly whisk together the eggs and sour cream, then make a well in the dry ingredients and pour the egg mixture into the middle. Use a spoon to gently 'cut' the flour into the wet mix until you have an even crumble texture.

Tip the mixture onto a lightly floured bench and use your fingertips to finish working it lightly into a firm dough. You want to bring it together into a dough, handling it as little as possible so you don't melt the butter pieces or overwork the gluten in the flour.

Roll the dough into a slab roughly 20 × 20 cm (8 × 8 in), and 4 cm (1½ in) high. Trim the edges and cut the dough into 8 rectangles 5 × 10 cm (2 × 4 in) and place them, evenly spaced, on a tray lined with baking paper. The trimmings can be rolled back together and combined into another scone. Cover loosely with plastic wrap and refrigerate for a couple of hours to set the butter back into the dough.

When you're ready to bake, preheat the oven to 200°C (390°F). Gently warm the cream if necessary, to bring it to a slightly runny consistency. Brush the scones with the cream and sprinkle a little bit of extra grated cheese on each one. Reduce the oven temperature to 180°C (360°F) and bake for 15–17 minutes. Turn the tray and bake for another couple of minutes, until golden.

Sandwiches

These sandwiches really are a meal, satisfying enough to get you through to dinner without that mid-afternoon slump.

Our chicken sandwiches are extremely popular. People appreciate that they taste like real roasted chicken, and that there is integrity in the ingredients we use. It's such a nice, simple and humble lunch. The chicken is roasted whole and then we chop the skin and juices through the meat so you get all the best bits and so much flavour. Use super fresh bread, and keep everything else simple so the chicken is the hero. You could roast your chicken in advance, or use leftovers from the night before (reduce quantities of other ingredients accordingly).

We make a variety of pickles and ferments at the bakery, which we love to incorporate into our sandwiches. They just make everything more lively and interesting, and can be a great way to create variety in texture. The pickles, chutneys and relishes in the Larder chapter are often used to make simple, tasty lunch options. For example:

- *Ham, cheddar and piccalilli (see page 272)*

- *Pastrami, gruyère, sauerkraut (see page 269) and bread and butter pickles (see page 268)*

- *Cheddar and red onion chutney (see page 271) with apple, celery and walnuts*

- *Bacon and egg with tomato chilli jam (see page 270).*

The open sandwich-style dishes are great brunch and lunch options, and have been designed for quick assembly, once all the elements are prepared.

Roasted chicken with horseradish mayonnaise, butter lettuce and pickles

Makes 6 sandwiches

Ingredients

Roasted chicken
1 whole chicken, roughly 1.6 kg (3½ lb)
1 lemon
½ bulb garlic, sliced horizontally so
   the cut sides of garlic are visible
a few sprigs of thyme
30 ml (1 fl oz) olive oil
salt and freshly ground black pepper,
   to taste

Horseradish mayonnaise
100 g (3½ oz) mayonnaise
   (see page 269)
1 tablespoon freshly grated
   horseradish
¼ bunch parsley, picked and
   roughly chopped
¼ bunch tarragon, picked and roughly
   chopped
¼ bunch dill, picked
1 large shallot, peeled and thinly sliced
salt and freshly ground black pepper,
   to taste

Assembly
12 slices sourdough bread
1 butter lettuce, washed, leaves
   separated
½ cup bread and butter pickles,
   drained of brine (see page 268)

This is such a simple and delicious sandwich, with the kick of heat from the horseradish perfectly complementing the roasted chicken. If you're using left-over roast chicken, combine the ingredients for the horseradish mayonnaise separately, then use enough to just coat the chicken. Any left-over mayonnaise can be kept in the fridge for up to one week and used on other sandwiches. This mayonnaise is also great with rare roast beef and watercress.

To roast your chicken, preheat the oven to 210°C (410°F). Open up the cavity of the chicken and spread the legs to allow the heat to circulate while cooking. Place the lemon, garlic and thyme inside the chicken, and season the skin with salt and pepper. Rub the olive oil into the skin all over, then place the chicken onto a roasting tray, breast side up.

Roast for 30 minutes, then reduce the heat to 160°C (320°F) and cook for a further 40–50 minutes. Test the chicken by inserting a knife into the thickest part of the thigh – the juices will run clear when it's cooked. Rest the chicken at room temperature for an hour.

Take the skin off the chicken and roughly chop it. Pick the meat off the carcass, shredding it into roughly bite-sized pieces as you go.

Put all the meat into a large mixing bowl, and add the chopped skin. Remove the lemon from inside the chicken and squeeze the juice over the meat. Skim the top layer of fat from the roasting tray, then pour the juices over the chicken. Add the mayonnaise, horseradish, herbs and shallot to the chicken and season to taste with salt and pepper. Mix through with your hands until well combined.

To assemble your sandwiches, lay out your slices of bread and place a generous handful of chicken mix onto half of each sandwich. Top the chicken with 6–8 slices of pickle and three leaves of lettuce per sandwich. Top with the other slice of bread and eat!

Roasted chicken with pickled carrots and garlic mayonnaise

The pickled carrots in this recipe provide a lovely crunch that gives way to a burst of vibrant pickly flavours, and the mellow roasted garlic complements them perfectly. This sandwich is a firm favourite with customers and staff alike.

You will need to start a few hours ahead to roast the chicken and garlic. Roasting the garlic takes around 2 hours. You can prepare it the day before, if you like. At home I like to roast big batches of garlic when it's in season, then I squeeze the flesh out of the cloves and freeze it in ice cube trays.

The pickled carrots are ready to use once the liquor has cooled down, but will continue to develop flavour if stored in the pickling liquor in the fridge. If you want to make the pickle in a large batch ahead of time, ensure you sterilise your jars – the pickle will last indefinitely this way. If you are doing a quick pickle it's best to use slim carrots, and slice them before pickling.

Makes 6 sandwiches

Ingredients

Roasted chicken
1 whole chicken, roughly 1.6 kg (3½ lb)
1 lemon
½ bulb garlic, sliced in half horizontally
3 sprigs of thyme
30 ml (1 fl oz) olive oil
salt and freshly ground black pepper, to taste

Garlic mayonnaise
100 g (3½ oz) mayonnaise (see page 269)
1 bulb garlic, whole

Pickled carrots
20 baby carrots
700 g (1 lb 9 oz) white-wine vinegar
80 g (2¾ oz/⅓ cup) caster (superfine) sugar
½ teaspoon black peppercorns
½ teaspoon caraway seeds
½ teaspoon dill seeds

Assembly
12 slices sourdough bread
4 large handfuls of rocket (arugula), washed and dried
salt and freshly ground black pepper, to taste

To roast your chicken, preheat the oven to 210°C (410°F). Open up the cavity of the chicken and spread the legs to allow the heat to circulate while cooking.

Place the lemon, garlic and thyme inside the chicken, and season the skin with salt and pepper. Rub the olive oil into the skin all over, then place the chicken onto a roasting tray, breast side up. Roast for 30 minutes, then reduce the heat to 160°C (320°F) and cook for a further 40–50 minutes. Test the chicken by inserting a knife into the thickest part of the thigh – the juices will run clear when it's cooked. Rest the chicken at room temperature for an hour.

Meanwhile, wrap the whole garlic bulb in foil and place in a small baking tray with 1 cm (½ in) of water in the bottom of the tray. Place this in the oven with the chicken when you turn the temperature down to 160°C (320°F), and roast for 2 hours, until soft. Once cool enough to handle, cut the bulb in half width-ways and squeeze out the flesh of the garlic into a small container.

To prepare your pickle, scrub the carrots under running water with a brush to remove any dirt, then slice them in half horizontally and place them in a heatproof container.

Put the white-wine vinegar, sugar, peppercorns, caraway and dill seeds in a saucepan with 300 ml (10 fl oz) water and bring it to a simmer, stirring to dissolve the sugar. As soon as the sugar has dissolved, pour the pickling liquor over the carrots and leave to cool.

Once the chicken is rested, remove the skin and roughly chop it. Pick the meat off the carcass, shredding it into roughly bite-sized pieces as you go.

Put all the meat into a large mixing bowl, and add the chopped skin. Remove the lemon from inside the chicken and squeeze the juice over the meat. Skim the top layer of fat from the roasting tray, then pour the juices over the chicken. Add the mayonnaise and mix through with your hands until well combined, then mix through the roasted garlic, to taste, and season with salt and pepper.

To assemble your sandwiches, lay out your slices of bread and place a generous handful of chicken mix onto half of each sandwich. Lay drained slices of pickled carrot over the chicken, then add some rocket leaves. Top with the other slice of bread and eat!

Chargrilled zucchini and pepita pesto with feta, tomato and pickled red onion

Makes 6 sandwiches

Ingredients

Pepita pesto
100 g (3½ oz) pepitas (pumpkin
    seeds)
40 g (1½ oz) sunflower seeds
20 g (¾ oz) poppy seeds
25 g (1 oz) parmesan, finely grated
1 clove garlic, peeled and finely
    chopped
40 g (1½ oz) pitted kalamata olives
½ lemon, juiced
65 ml (2¼ fl oz) olive oil
salt and freshly ground black pepper,
    to taste

Pickled onions
1 red onion, peeled and finely sliced
100 ml (3½ fl oz) red-wine vinegar
45 g (1½ oz) caster (superfine) sugar
1 clove garlic
10 g (¼ oz) table salt
½ teaspoon black peppercorns

Chargrilled zucchini
6 medium zucchini (courgettes)
40 ml (1¼ fl oz) olive oil
salt and freshly ground black pepper,
    to taste

Assembly
12 slices sourdough or olive bread
3 tomatoes, sliced
240 g (8½ oz) feta
1 oak leaf lettuce, leaves washed
    and separated

This sandwich has been a sneaky hit and is certainly not 'just another vegetarian sandwich'. The combination of so many different seeds in the pesto provides beautiful richness, and the pickle lightens it all up, creating perfect balance.

This pesto is so tasty and versatile, you'll want to put it on everything! Feel free to make a larger batch – it will last up to a week in the fridge. If storing larger batches, cover the surface with a thin layer of oil to prevent discolouration.

We love making pickles at the bakery, and the pickled onions in this sandwich make everything taste better. They are great to have on hand in the fridge, and work well in salads or even grilled cheese on toast.

To make the pesto, blitz the pepitas, sunflower seeds, poppy seeds, parmesan, garlic, olives and lemon juice in a food processor. Blitz until the seeds break down, but stop before it becomes a paste. Reduce the speed to low and slowly pour in the oil until the mixture becomes a thick, spreadable paste.

To prepare the onion for pickling, blanch it in boiling water for 1 minute, then drain well and transfer to a heatproof container.

Combine the vinegar, sugar, garlic, salt and peppercorns in a pan over a high heat. Bring to a boil, stirring to dissolve the sugar, then pour it over the onion while still hot, and leave to cool. This is a quick pickle that will be ready to use once cool, but it will also keep well in the fridge for up to a week.

To chargrill the zucchini, preheat a large griddle pan over a high heat. Cut the zucchini in half lengthways, then cut each half into two pieces so you have two shorter pieces, each with a flat side and a round side. Toss the zucchini in a bowl with the oil, and season to taste with salt and pepper.

Place the zucchini cut side down on to the hot griddle pan for 2 minutes, then turn over and cook on the rounded side for 1 minute. You want them to be lightly marked and just cooked.

To assemble your sandwiches, lay out your slices of bread and spread a generous layer of pepita pesto onto one half of each sandwich. Arrange the zucchini, tomato and pickled onion over the pesto. Crumble the feta over it, then finish with a few leaves of lettuce. Top with the other slice of bread and eat!

Smoky baba ghanoush with grilled broccolini, sesame and chilli

Makes 6 sandwiches

Ingredients

Baba ghanoush
2 medium sized eggplant (aubergine)
1 clove garlic, peeled and finely
  chopped
2 tablespoons tahini
1 tablespoon olive oil
½ tablespoon lemon juice
1 teaspoon cumin seeds, lightly
  toasted
¼ bunch parsley, washed and roughly
  chopped
¼ bunch mint, washed and roughly
  chopped
salt and freshly ground black pepper,
  to taste

Assembly
1 bunch broccolini, trimmed
40 ml (1¼ fl oz) olive oil
1 tablespoon sesame seeds
1 long red chilli, finely sliced
3 spring onions, finely sliced
¼ bunch coriander (cilantro), washed,
  picked and torn
2 handfuls spinach, washed and dried
12 slices sourdough bread
salt and freshly ground black pepper,
  to taste

This fragrant sandwich is full of bold flavours – smoky eggplant, umami sesame, and a little hit of chilli. It's great on a sourdough baguette, or slices of multigrain.

We prepare the eggplants over an open flame on the gas hob. This produces a beautiful smoky flavour. You can also roast them in a hot oven for 40–45 minutes, until soft.

To make the baba ghanoush, place the eggplants on a gas hob over a low flame and turn them every 10 minutes or so for 40–45 minutes, until the skin is blackened and they are soft to touch. Set aside to cool for half an hour. When cool enough to handle, cut them in half vertically and scrape the flesh out with a spoon into a colander. Try not to get any of the blackened skin mixed through, as it will make the baba ghanoush taste bitter.

Sprinkle some salt over the eggplant, then leave it over the sink for an hour to drain any juices.

Place the eggplant in a mixing bowl and add the garlic, tahini, oil and lemon juice. Mix it through until you get a thick, chunky paste, then add the cumin, parsley and mint. Stir to combine and season to taste.

Preheat a griddle pan or barbecue chargrill until very hot. Cut the broccolini in half horizontally to separate the tops from the stalks, then toss the pieces in olive oil and season lightly with salt and pepper.

Chargrill the stalks first, turning occasionally as you cook, to colour. This will take a few minutes; you want them to be slightly undercooked so they still have some crunch. Set the stalks aside and do the same with the tops (they will be a bit quicker).

Combine the sesame seeds, chilli, spring onion and coriander in a mixing bowl, and toss the cooked broccolini through to coat.

Lay out your slices of bread and spread a generous amount of baba ghanoush over the bottom half of each sandwich. Divide the broccolini over the top and finish with a small handful of spinach. Top with the other slice of bread and eat!

Roasted pork with Tuscan slaw and crackling

Makes 6 sandwiches

Ingredients

Roasted pork
800 g (1 lb 12 oz) pork belly, skin on
 and well scored
sea salt

Tuscan slaw
300 g (10½ oz) white cabbage, finely
 shredded
½ a large fennel, finely shaved on a
 mandolin
60 g (2 oz) sultanas, soaked in warm
 water for half an hour, then drained
60 g (2 oz) walnuts, lightly toasted
 and roughly chopped
30 g (1 oz) capers
2 spring onions, finely sliced
2 handfuls parsley, washed and
 roughly chopped
juice and zest of ½ lemon
60 ml (2 fl oz/¼ cup) olive oil
30 g (1 oz) parmesan, finely grated
salt and freshly ground black pepper,
 to taste

Assembly
12 slices multigrain sourdough
100 g (3½ oz) mustard mayonnaise
 (see page 269)

Bakery notes
We prepare the skin of the pork by scalding it with boiling water, then drying it out. To do this, place well-scored pork, skin side-up on a rack over the sink, then pour a kettle full of boiling water over the pork to scald the skin. Pat the rind dry with paper towel and refrigerate, uncovered, for at least 2 hours.

In preparation for the weekend, we get in lovely pork loins from Western Plains Pork that we roast whole. For smaller numbers at home we use the belly, always with the skin on. If your household is anything like the bakery, it might be worth making double the crackling, just to make sure there's some left for the sandwiches! The smell and sight of the crackling on the just-roasted pork is more temptation than most can bear.

The zingy slaw cuts through the richness of the pork, and would also make a delicious side dish for any roasted meats.

Preheat the oven to 210°C (410°F). Rub the skin of the pork with a generous amount of salt, making sure you get it right into the scores. Place the pork in a roasting tray, skin side up, and roast for 20 minutes.

Reduce the heat to 150°C (300°F) and continue cooking for a further 1½–2 hours, until tender. You should meet no resistance when you press it with a fork. Rest the pork at room temperature for an hour. Once rested, remove the crackling and break it into bite-sized pieces. Slice the belly, removing any bones, and season with salt to taste.

For the Tuscan slaw, combine the cabbage, fennel, sultanas, walnuts, capers, spring onions and parsley together in a large mixing bowl. Add the lemon zest and juice, and the olive oil. Toss to coat the salad with the dressing, then toss through the parmesan. Season to taste with salt and pepper.

To assemble your sandwiches, lay out your slices of bread and spread a thin layer of mustard mayonnaise onto each slice. Place a generous handful of Tuscan slaw onto half of each sandwich. Lay several slices of pork belly on top of the slaw, then add a few pieces of crackling to each sandwich. Top with the other slice of bread and eat!

Lovage-cured salmon on rye with remoulade

Serves 4

Ingredients

Lovage-cured salmon
65 g (2¼ oz) lovage leaves, picked
65 g (2¼ oz) flaked sea salt
55 g (2 oz/¼ cup) caster (superfine) sugar
zest and juice of 1 lemon
4 black peppercorns
2 juniper berries, crushed
½ side salmon, pin boned and skin on

Remoulade
240 g (8½ oz) kohlrabi
100 g (3½ oz) crème fraîche
100 g (3½ oz) mayonnaise (page 269)
1 teaspoon caraway seeds, toasted and roughly chopped
4 teaspoons capers
a few sprigs each of tarragon, dill and chives, roughly chopped
zest and juice of ½ a lemon

Assembly
8 slices 100% rye sourdough
1 punnet mustard leaf, washed and dried
extra virgin olive oil, for drizzling
freshly cracked black pepper, to taste

Bakery notes
You need to start this recipe two days ahead to cure the salmon. You can also use ocean trout, if you prefer. If you have any left-over cured fish, it's great in salads or sandwiches.

If you prefer a lighter rye bread, this is also lovely on multigrain. And if you can't get mustard leaves, any small, lightly bitter leaves would be great to finish this dish.

Lovage is a herb that you find growing in hedgerows in England. It's lovely and refreshing, with notes of celery seed and parsley. In Cornwall they make an alcoholic lovage cordial, which is drunk mixed with brandy. It is the perfect tonic for a cold Cornish evening. We always have a bottle in the cupboard to drink during the winter months. Good garden shops will sell lovage plants, or you could try a good greengrocer or farmers' market. If you can't find fresh lovage, you could use a combination of dill, tarragon and parsley.

To cure the salmon, put the lovage into a blender with 10 g (¼ oz) of the salt. Blend until the lovage is broken up and the salt mixed through. Transfer the lovage to a bowl with the remaining salt, sugar, lemon juice and zest, peppercorns and juniper berries, and mix to combine.

Pour half of the cure mixture into a non-reactive tray or plastic container that is large enough to contain the fish, and spread it over the base. Place the fish on top, skin side down, and gently rub the remaining cure mix over the salmon, packing it on top. Cover with a lid or plastic wrap and refrigerate for 24 hours.

The next day, gently turn the fish over. Rub any curing mix that has fallen off back into the flesh. You will find that some liquid has been drawn out of the fish – this is nothing to worry about; it just becomes part of the cure. Cover or wrap again, then refrigerate for another 24 hours.

The next day, remove the salmon from the fridge and gently rinse it under cold running water, just to remove the curing mix. Pat it dry with kitchen towel, and it's ready for slicing. Use a long sharp knife to cut slices horizontally across the surface of the fish.

Prepare the remoulade on the day you are serving. Peel the kohlrabi and cut it into matchsticks. Combine the crème fraîche and mayonnaise in a small mixing bowl and stir together. Add the caraway seeds, capers, tarragon, dill, chives, lemon zest and juice, and kohlrabi, and mix with your hands until everything is evenly coated. Season to taste with salt and pepper.

To assemble, lay out the slices of bread on the bench. Divide the remoulade evenly over the slices, and spread it out to cover. Place a small handful of mustard leaves on top the remoulade, then lay thin slices of salmon over the top. Finish with a drizzle of olive oil and some freshly cracked black pepper to taste.

Heirloom tomatoes on sourdough with stracciatella and lemon verbena

Serves 6

Ingredients

Verbena oil
50 ml (1¾ fl oz) olive oil
60 ml (2 fl oz/¼ cup) vegetable oil
8 g (¼ oz/small handful) fresh verbena leaves
zest of ½ a lemon, in strips

6 large heirloom tomatoes, sliced into 6–8 wedges each
12 cherry tomatoes, halved
small handful fresh verbena leaves, roughly torn
½ bunch chives, finely chopped
a few sprigs lemon thyme, leaves picked
1 teaspoon nigella seeds
2 teaspoons white balsamic vinegar
salt and freshly cracked black pepper, to taste
6 thick slices sourdough
450 g (1 lb) stracciatella

Bakery notes

You will need to start this recipe the day before to infuse the verbena oil. You'll end up with more oil than you need – store it in a sealed jar in the fridge and it will retain the vibrant verbena flavour for up to two weeks. Use it up on salads, or even drizzled over steamed vegies to serve with roasted chicken.

We use a combination of black Russian, oxheart and whatever other tomatoes are in season. You may need to adjust quantities depending on how large your tomatoes are.

Stracciatella is a fresh stretched-curd Italian cheese. You could substitute with mozzarella or burrata, both of which would provide a firmer texture.

Lemon verbena is a fragrant herb native to South America. It's used widely in both savoury and sweet dishes, and makes a delicious infusion to drink as a tea. It's not all that common at the greengrocer, but you should be able to pick up a small plant at any good nursery. The verbena plant is hardy and easy to grow, and makes a great addition to your herb selection. If you can't find verbena leaves for this recipe, you could substitute another fragrant soft herb, such as basil or lemon thyme.

This dish is another of those classic combinations – bread, tomatoes and fresh cheese, lifted by the addition of some aromatic verbena oil.

To make the verbena oil, warm all the ingredients in a small saucepan over a low heat to around 65°C (150°F). Turn off the heat and pour the oil into an airtight container – a small jar is ideal. Refrigerate overnight to infuse, then strain the oil through a fine sieve. Discard the zest and verbena leaves and return the oil to the jar until you are ready to use it.

The next day, put the tomatoes in a mixing bowl along with the herbs, nigella seeds, vinegar and 4 tablespoons of the verbena oil. Gently toss everything together with your hands, ensuring the tomatoes and herbs are well-coated with the dressing. Season to taste with salt and pepper, then set aside for a few minutes to allow the flavours to come together.

When you're ready to eat, toast the sourdough slices and place them on plates to serve. Spread each slice generously with stracciatella and top with the tomato mixture. The juices from the bottom of the bowl make a delicious dressing, so be sure to spoon this over the top to finish.

Grilled asparagus on sourdough with Comté and pickles

Serves 6

Ingredients

Pickled shallots
2 banana shallots, peeled and
  finely sliced
250 ml (8½ fl oz/1 cup) white-wine
  vinegar
100 g (3½ oz) sugar

Béchamel
50 g (1¾ oz) butter
50 g (1¾ oz/⅓ cup) plain (all-purpose)
  flour
500 g full-cream (whole) milk
1 tablespoon dijon mustard
½ nutmeg, grated
salt and freshly cracked black pepper,
  to taste

Assembly
2–3 bunches of asparagus (we use
  around 5 spears per serve,
  depending on thickness)
20 ml + 100 ml (¾ fl oz + 3½ fl oz)
  olive oil
6 thick slices of sourdough

60 g (2 oz) Comté, grated
50 g (1¾ oz) sunflower seeds
2 sprigs oregano, leaves picked
2 sprigs bronze fennel, fronds picked
½ lemon, for juice
salt and freshly cracked black pepper,
  to taste

Bakery notes
The pickled shallots are zingy and fresh the day they're made. The pickle will continue to develop flavour, and certainly won't go off if you keep it for a few days, but I like to eat it fresh. Keep the left-over pickling liquor to use again – just strain it into a clean jar and store it in the fridge, ready to use for your next batch.

I love Comté, but there are lots of other cheeses that would work here. Any gruyère, cheddar, blue or a hard goat's milk cheese would also be delicious.

We use bronze fennel at the bakery, but if this is unavailable, green fennel or any other small leaves would be just as lovely.

I'm always excited to see asparagus at the market. Along with broad beans, asparagus is one of the first signs of spring after the cold of winter. Here we combine asparagus with one of my all-time favourite cheeses, Comté.

A rich béchamel and quick pickle bring it all together, making this dish a pleasure to eat. It's perfect for a light lunch or supper.

To pickle the shallots, put them in a heatproof bowl. Put the vinegar and sugar in a small saucepan and bring to a simmer over a high heat, stirring to dissolve the sugar. Pour the liquor over the shallots and set aside to cool. They're ready once the liquor is completely cool.

Next, make the béchamel. Melt the butter in a medium saucepan over a medium heat, then add the flour and stir over the heat for a couple of minutes until it forms a thick, sandy coloured paste. Gradually whisk in the milk until the mixture thickens and comes to the boil. Remove from the heat, add the mustard and nutmeg, and season to taste with salt and pepper. Set aside in the fridge to cool.

Preheat your grill (broiler) to a medium–high heat, and preheat a griddle pan over a high heat – you want it hot and smoking. Toss the asparagus well in 20 ml (¾ fl oz) of the olive oil, and season lightly with salt and pepper. Spread the asparagus over the griddle pan for a minute, then gently move them around to spread the heat for another minute. You want them lightly coloured but still a bit undercooked, as you are going to apply more heat under the grill once you've assembled your open sandwiches.

While the griddle pan is still hot, brush your bread slices with the remaining olive oil and place them on the pan. Toast for 1–2 minutes on each side until the slices are warm and lightly charred.

Drain the shallots well. To assemble your open sandwiches, lay the toasted slices of bread on two trays lined with baking paper. Spread each slice with a generous amount of béchamel and top with the grilled asparagus spears. Sprinkle the grated Comté over the top, and grill for 4–5 minutes until the cheese is melted and just starting to colour. Finish with slices of pickled shallot, a sprinkling of sunflower seeds, the herbs and a few drops of lemon juice. Season to taste and eat immediately.

MOUNT ZERO

Mount Zero is a family business that grows olives, grains and pulses in the Wimmera in western Victoria. General manager Richard Seymour's parents started the business. He took some time to tell us about what they do there.

How did you come to be where you are?

My parents Jane and Neil bought an abandoned 50-year-old olive grove in the Grampians in the mid-90s – just when I was finishing high school. They worked harder than they ever had to bring the grove back into production and take the produce to market. I joined Mount Zero full time in 2004 with the aim of bringing our farm and the produce from our region directly to restaurant tables and retail shelves.

You don't just make olives – can you tell us a bit about your range?

Following successive years of drought in the early days, we realised that we could not sustain ourselves on just the produce of the Mount Zero olive block. We began working with neighbouring farms to bring locally grown lentils and grains to markets in Australia (they had previously been commodity exported). We have slowly grown that range from two key lentil varieties to more than twelve premium lentil and grain varieties. In 2009 we began working with the Barengi Gadjin Land Council to harvest natural salt from Pink Lake in Dimboola (80 km/50 miles west of Mount Zero).

How do you work around the seasons with all the products you make?

While olives are harvested between April and June each year, there is a lot more to what we do than just harvesting and pressing. Immediately following harvest, in June, we spend at least three months pruning the olive grove. Every three months we spray the whole farm with a biodynamic preparation called 500, which inoculates the soil with living microbes to aid soil and tree health. We harvest salt from Pink Lake in early April, before the lake fills with winter rains and after most of the summer heat has gone from the lake – it can be baking out there.

What's the overriding philosophy driving your farming practices?

Our biodynamic farming practices influence the philosophies of our business. As a sustainable farm, we are keen to make sure that our business follows good basic principles of sustainability, local supply and custom, as well as quality. Sustainability for us represents not only the farming methods, but also the financial viability. The business also needs to be socially sustainable, hence our work with local communities and farmers to bring our produce to our local market.

What are the benefits of cold-pressing olive oil?

To be classified extra virgin, olive oil must be cold pressed and pressed only once. The careful handling of the fruit from the tree to the press to the bottle provides incredible flavour and unrivalled health benefits. No other edible oil has the depth and diversity of flavour that extra virgin olive oil has. The balance of fruit and the bitterness and pepperiness of olive oil is celebrated in the cuisines of Europe, the Middle East and Northern Africa. Flavour is reflective of the variety of the fruit and the region that it is grown in. Extra virgin olive oil is high in antioxidants, great for heart health, helps to lower cholesterol and prevent the onset of diabetes – the list goes on.

How does biodynamic farming differ from conventional farming?
The key focus of biodynamic farming is the health of the soil, the belief being that healthy soils
will provide healthy plants and crops that are more resistant to disease and pest infestation.
So rather than treat the symptoms, we are preventing the cause. Key to biodynamic soil
health is increasing soil humus through cropping and composting, and then promoting the
microorganisms in the soil to aid the breakdown of the soil humus, which then feeds the plants
or crops in as natural a way as possible.

What are the advantages to brining olives naturally?
Naturally brining olives is a process whereby the olives are simply picked and placed in brine
(salt and water) to naturally ferment out many of the extremely bitter compounds. This process
can take between four and twelve months, but the result is a fruit that is still full of flavour and
retains the antioxidant and health properties that olive oil is famous for. The quick way of curing
olives is to treat them in a strong alkaline solution (most often caustic based) before brining.
While this method is quick and often better preserves the colour of the olive, the flavour is
almost always entirely stripped from the fruit, along with many of the health properties.

MOUNT ZERO OLIVES
5383 8280
Hours: 10am - 5pm
OPEN

Pies and sausage rolls

In Australia, a bakery is often judged on its meat pie, so I knew that I had to have good pies available when we opened Tivoli Road.

For such a seemingly simple thing, there are several elements that can make all the difference. We are careful to source great ingredients to start with, and put a lot of care and attention into the technique and seasoning when preparing the filling. Using a good quality stock (preferably homemade) will also make a big difference to the flavour. It has to be delicious, and stand on its own (any of these fillings are also great served over rice, pasta or polenta, or with a thick slice of sourdough toast). We also use two different types of pastry – puff pastry for a flaky, golden lid, and savoury shortcrust for the base, to hold it all together.

We make our pies and sausage rolls in large batches each week, and bake what we need from frozen each day. The pastry comes up beautifully – you can tell they're done when you have a flaky golden crust. Always eat your pies on the day they're baked to avoid soggy pastry.

You might find it helpful to prepare the filling the day before, so you're not chained to the stove all day. These fillings all freeze really well if you want to make large batches for later use.

We use 11-cm (4-¼ in) diameter individual pie tins when making our pies, but the simplest way to prepare these recipes for a crowd is in a large pie dish, topped with puff pastry. In this case, lightly grease the dish before filling it, and seal the pastry onto the edges. Brush with egg wash and pierce the top so the steam can escape during cooking.

Pork, caramelised apple and fennel sausage roll

Makes 8 large sausage rolls

Ingredients
2 teaspoons fennel seeds + extra to
  sprinkle
1 tablespoon vegetable oil
3 medium brown onions, peeled
  and diced
4 cloves garlic, peeled and finely
  chopped
8 sprigs sage, picked and finely
  chopped
3 sprigs rosemary, leaves picked
  and finely chopped
5 sprigs thyme, leaves picked and
  finely chopped
20 g (¾ oz) unsalted butter
2 granny smith apples, peeled and cut
  into ½ cm (⅛ in) dice
1 tablespoon caster (superfine) sugar
1 tablespoon sherry vinegar
1.2 kg (2 lb 10 oz) pork mince
65 g (2¼ oz) breadcrumbs
12 g (½ oz) table salt
1 quantity puff pastry (see page 252)
1 egg, lightly beaten

Bakery notes
If we ever have the end of a loaf of bread leftover, instead of throwing it away, I dry it to make crumbs, then freeze them. That way, I always have them handy for recipes like this.

After baking so many sausage rolls at Bourke Street Bakery and seeing them become a cult item, I knew we had to develop our own delicious version to please the crowds. These are often the first lunch item to sell out.

These sausage rolls are great for picnics, and they will be a smash hit at your next children's party. If you like, you could pipe the sausage mix a bit thinner and make smaller slices for party-sized sausage rolls.

If using store-bought puff pastry, you may need to adjust the size and produce a different number, depending on the size and shape your pastry is rolled to.

Toast the fennel seeds in a large, dry frying pan over a low heat for 1–2 minutes, until fragrant. Crush lightly in a mortar and pestle and set aside.

Using the same pan, heat the vegetable oil over a low heat. Sweat off the onions and garlic for 8–10 minutes until lightly caramelised, to give a bit of sweetness. Add the toasted fennel seeds, sage, rosemary and thyme and set aside to cool.

Wipe out the pan then melt the butter in it over a medium–high heat. Add the apples and toss gently in the butter for 2 minutes, then add the sugar. Continue to cook, stirring constantly, until the sugar is lightly caramelised, then add the vinegar to deglaze the pan. Set aside.

Combine the mince, breadcrumbs, salt and apples in a large mixing bowl. Add the onion and garlic mixture and mix it through with your hands for 3–5 minutes, until all the elements are evenly distributed through the mince.

On a lightly floured work surface, roll out the puff pastry into a sheet roughly 30 × 50 cm (12 × 20 in), and 5 mm (¼ in) thick. Cut it into four pieces 15 × 25 cm (6 × 10 in), with the long edges towards you.

Divide the sausage mix evenly between the four sheets, making a line of filling from left to right a third of the way up each sheet. (At the bakery we use a large piping [icing] bag for this.)

Lightly brush the beaten egg along the top edge of each piece, then roll the pastry up from the bottom of each roll, away from you, folding it over the sausage mix. Seal the roll on the egg-washed edge so the seam sits underneath the meat.

Egg wash the top and sides, then sprinkle with fennel seeds and lightly pierce along the top with a fork. Cut each roll in half, then lay your sausage rolls on a tray lined with baking paper and rest them in the fridge for half an hour.

Preheat the oven to 180°C (360°F). Bake the sausage rolls from cold for 10 minutes, then reduce the heat to 160°C (320°F) and bake for a further 30 minutes until golden. Allow the sausage rolls to rest for 10 minutes before eating.

Beef cheek, stout and treacle pie

Makes 8 individual pies or 1 family pie

Ingredients

Filling
100 ml (3½ fl oz) vegetable oil
800 g (1 lb 12 oz) beef cheeks
300 ml (10 fl oz) stout
30 ml (1 fl oz) black treacle
  (use molasses if unavailable)
1 litre (34 fl oz/4 cups) beef stock
20 g (¾ oz) unsalted butter
2 medium brown onions, peeled
  and diced
2 garlic cloves, peeled, finely chopped
1 large carrot, peeled and diced
10 button mushrooms, sliced
½ bunch thyme, leaves picked and
  roughly chopped
3 teaspoons cornflour (cornstarch)
salt and freshly ground black pepper,
  to taste

Assembly
1 quantity savoury shortcrust pastry
  (see page 255)
½ quantity puff pastry (see page 252)
1 egg, lightly beaten
1 tablespoon poppy seeds

This is certainly our most popular pie – it rarely comes off the menu. Beef cheeks have a good amount of marbling and a high proportion of surface area, so you get lots of caramelisation when you're browning the meat, and they retain their moisture and shape in the braising process. You could use any slow-cooking cut of beef, such as chuck steak, gravy beef or brisket. This recipe works just as well for a large family pie (see page 133) as it does for smaller, individual pies.

Roll out the savoury shortcrust pastry into a sheet roughly 4 mm (⅛ in) thick. Wrap the sheet in plastic wrap and place it in the fridge. Roll the puff pastry into a sheet roughly 3 mm (¼ in) thick, wrap it in plastic wrap and place it in the fridge. Let the pastry rest after rolling it out – this will stop it shrinking once cut.

To make the filling, heat 40 ml (1¼ fl oz) of the vegetable oil in a large frying pan until hot. Season the beef cheeks with salt and pepper, and cook them over a medium heat until they are brown and caramelised on all sides.

Transfer the beef cheeks to a large pan with the stout, treacle and beef stock. Bring it to a simmer and then reduce to a low heat – you barely want to see a ripple while it's simmering. Braise on the stove, uncovered, for 1½–2 hours, until the beef just begins to come apart with gentle pressure. Remove the cheeks from the stock and set aside to cool. Increase the heat and simmer the stock until reduced by half.

While the beef is cooking, you can prepare your vegetables. Place a large saucepan over medium heat and add the remaining 60 ml (2 fl oz/¼ cup) of oil, and the butter. Gently fry the onions and garlic until soft and translucent, then add the carrots and cook for another 5 minutes, stirring occasionally to avoid sticking. Add the mushrooms and cook for another 5 minutes, stirring occasionally, then stir in the thyme and remove from heat.

Once cool enough to handle, chop the beef cheeks into roughly 2 cm (¾ in) square chunks. Put the beef and the cooked vegetables into a large pan together with the reduced stock and bring to the boil. In a small bowl, mix the cornflour with a little water and stir until you have a loose paste or slurry, adding more water if needed. Stir the cornflour slurry into the pie mixture until it begins to thicken. Turn off the heat and leave it to cool slightly, then season to taste with salt and pepper and leave to cool.

Before you assemble the pies, preheat the oven to 180°C (360°F) and lightly grease your pie dishes. Lay the savoury shortcrust pastry on a lightly floured bench, and cut out 8 discs of pastry for the bases, 2 cm (¾ in) wider in diameter than the base of your pie dishes.

Line each pie dish with a round of shortcrust pastry and press it well into the corners of the base with your thumb. Trim off any excess and lightly brush the edges with the beaten egg. Lay out your sheet of puff pastry and cut 8 discs slightly larger than the diameter of the top of your pie dishes. Fill each pie generously with the filling and top each with a puff pastry lid. Press the edges of the pastry base and lid together to seal.

Brush the top of each pie with egg wash, pierce it a couple of times with a sharp knife or a fork, and sprinkle with the poppy seeds. Bake at 180°C (360°F) for 10 minutes, then reduce the heat to 160°C (320°F) and bake for a further 30–40 minutes, until the pies are nice and golden. Allow them to rest for 10 minutes before eating.

Chicken curry pie

**Makes 8 individual pies or
1 family pie**

Ingredients
1 quantity savoury shortcrust pastry
   (see page 255)
½ quantity puff pastry (see page 252)

Marinade for the chicken
2 cloves garlic, peeled and crushed
2 thumbs ginger, peeled and finely
   chopped (approx. 10 cm/4 in)
2 teaspoons ground turmeric
juice of ½ lemon
80 ml (2½ fl oz/⅓ cup) vegetable oil

1 kg (2 lb 3 oz) skinless chicken
   thighs, diced

Curry paste
1 bunch coriander (cilantro), washed
   and roughly chopped (including
   the stalks)
½ bunch mint, washed, picked and
   roughly chopped

1 medium brown onion, peeled
   and roughly chopped
2 green chillies, roughly chopped
1 thumb ginger, peeled and roughly
   chopped (approx. 5 cm/2 in)
4 cloves garlic, peeled and
   roughly chopped
1 teaspoon black pepper,
   freshly ground
1 teaspoon ground cinnamon
2 teaspoons cumin seeds
1 teaspoon coriander seeds
1 clove
1 tablespoon caster (superfine) sugar
juice of 1 lemon

Filling
2 teaspoons cornflour (cornstarch)
100 g (3½ oz) plain yoghurt
salt and freshly ground black pepper,
   to taste

Assembly
1 egg, lightly beaten
1 tablespoon nigella seeds

Roll out the savoury shortcrust pastry into a sheet roughly 4 mm(⅛ in) thick.
Wrap the sheet in plastic wrap and place it in the fridge. Roll out the puff pastry
into a sheet roughly 3 mm (⅛ in) thick, wrap it in plastic wrap and place it in the
fridge. Let the pastry rest after rolling it out – this will stop it shrinking once cut.

To make the chicken marinade, combine the garlic, ginger, turmeric, lemon
juice and oil in a large bowl and mix to form a thin paste. Add the chicken and
massage the marinade into it. Cover and leave overnight in the fridge.

For the curry paste, blitz the coriander, mint, onion, chillies, ginger and garlic
in a blender or food processor to form a paste. (You may need to add a little
water.) Toast the whole spices separately in a dry frying pan over a medium heat
for 1 minute, until fragrant, moving the pan constantly to avoid burning them.
Grind the toasted spices, then mix them into the paste with the black pepper
and cinnamon. Add the sugar and lemon juice, and stir to combine, then
refrigerate in an airtight container until ready to use.

Put the marinated chicken and the curry paste in a large, heavy based pan,
and mix to combine. Cook it over a medium–low heat and bring to a simmer
for roughly 40 minutes, stirring occasionally, until the sauce thickens slightly.

Mix the cornflour with a little water and stir until you have a loose paste, adding
more water if needed. Add the cornflour to the chicken and stir until the
sauce thickens a little more, then add the yoghurt and season to taste with salt
and pepper. Cool to room temperature or refrigerate overnight.

Before you assemble the pies, preheat the oven to 180°C (360°F) and lightly
grease your pie dishes. Lay the savoury shortcrust pastry on a lightly floured
bench, and cut out 8 discs of pastry for the bases, 2 cm (¾ in) wider in diameter
than the base of your pie dishes. Line each pie dish with a round of shortcrust
pastry and press it well into the corners of the base with your thumb. Trim off
any excess and lightly brush the edges with the beaten egg.

Lay out your sheet of puff pastry and cut 8 discs slightly larger than the diameter
of the top of your pie dishes. Fill each pie generously and top each with a puff
pastry lid. Press the edges of the pastry base and lid together to seal. (To make
one family-sized pie, see page 133.)

Brush the top of each pie with egg wash, pierce it a couple of times with a sharp
knife or a fork, and sprinkle with the nigella seeds. Bake at 180°C (360°F)
for 10 minutes and then reduce the heat to 160°C (320°F), before baking for
a further 30–40 minutes, until the pies are nice and golden. Allow them to rest
for 10 minutes before eating.

Our chef Charlie made this chicken curry to eat with rice at home, and decided it would be great in a pie. The curry is beautifully fragrant and mildly spiced.

Start this recipe one day ahead to marinate the chicken. The curry paste can be made ahead of time, if you like. It will keep in the fridge for up to three days, and it also freezes well.

Lamb and pearl barley pie

**Makes 8 individual pies or
1 family pie**

Ingredients
1 quantity savoury shortcrust pastry
  (see page 255)
½ quantity puff pastry (see page 252)

Filling
5 lamb shanks
salt and freshly ground black pepper
25 ml (¾ fl oz) vegetable oil
25 g (1 oz) unsalted butter
2 large carrots, peeled and diced
2 large onions, peeled and diced
2 cloves garlic, peeled and finely
  chopped
½ bunch thyme, leaves picked and
  roughly chopped
1 bay leaf

25 g (1 oz) tomato paste
25 g (1 oz) plain (all-purpose) flour
660 ml (22½ fl oz) red wine
400 g (14 oz) tinned whole tomatoes
65 g (2¼ oz) pearl barley

Assembly
1 egg, lightly beaten
1 tablespoon cumin seeds

This pie makes a nourishing mid-winter dinner. The pearl barley gives the lamb and vegetable braise a beautiful texture, and makes a hearty meal out of a simple pie. Because the lamb is cooked on the bone you get lovely marrow richness through the filling.

Roll out the savoury shortcrust pastry into a sheet roughly 4 mm (⅛ in) thick. Wrap the sheet in plastic wrap and place it in the fridge. Roll the puff pastry into a sheet roughly 3 mm (⅛ in) thick, wrap it in plastic wrap and place it in the fridge. Let the pastry rest after rolling it out – this will stop it shrinking once cut.

To prepare the filling, preheat the oven to 170°C (340°F). Season the lamb with salt and pepper.

Place a large, heavy based casserole dish on a medium heat and add the vegetable oil. Brown off the lamb in batches, and set aside. Melt the butter in the same pan over a medium heat, then add the carrots and onions. Cook these for around 5 minutes, stirring occasionally to avoid sticking, until they start to colour.

Add the garlic, thyme and bay leaf, and continue to cook for another 5 minutes, stirring occasionally. Turn the heat down and add the tomato paste and flour, and mix well. Cook for a few more minutes, stirring occasionally, then add the red wine and tomatoes. Bring the pan to a simmer and skim off any scum.

Remove from the heat, add the pearl barley and lamb, cover with a lid and braise in the oven for 2½ hours. The filling is ready when the meat is falling off the bone, and you should have a nice, thick gravy. Reduce the liquid further on the stove if necessary. Cool slightly, and when cool enough to handle, remove the bones and break up the meat, making sure all the ingredients are well mixed. Leave to cool to room temperature or refrigerate overnight.

Before you assemble the pies, preheat the oven to 180°C (360°F) and lightly grease your pie dishes. Lay the savoury shortcrust pastry on a lightly floured bench, and cut out 8 discs of pastry for the bases, 2 cm (¾ in) wider in diameter than the base of your pie dishes.

Line each pie dish with a round of shortcrust pastry and press it well into the corners of the base with your thumb. Trim off any excess and lightly brush the edges with the beaten egg. Lay out your sheet of puff pastry and cut 8 discs slightly larger than the diameter of the top of your pie dishes. Fill each pie generously with the filling and top each pie with a puff pastry lid. Press the edges of the pastry base and lid together to seal. (To make one family-sized pie, see page 133.)

Brush the top of each pie with egg wash, then pierce it a couple of times with a sharp knife or a fork, and sprinkle with the cumin seeds. Bake at 180°C (360°F) for 10 minutes and then reduce the heat to 160°C (320°F), before baking for a further 30–40 minutes, until the pies are nice and golden. Allow them to rest for 10 minutes before eating.

Chicken, lemon and sweet potato pie

**Makes 8 individual pies or
1 family pie**

Ingredients
1 quantity savoury shortcrust pastry
  (see page 255)
½ quantity puff pastry (see page 252)

Filling
1 small sweet potato (roughly 200 g/
  7 oz), peeled
30 ml + 20 ml (1 fl oz + ¾ fl oz)
  vegetable oil
2 medium brown onions, peeled
  and roughly diced
2 cloves garlic, peeled and finely
  chopped

1 kg (2 lb 3 oz) chicken thighs, skin
  off, diced
100 ml (3½ fl oz) white wine
400 g (14 oz) tinned whole tomatoes
3 teaspoons cornflour (cornstarch)
20 g (¾ oz) preserved lemon, rind
  only, finely chopped
100 g (3½ oz) peas (frozen are fine)
¼ bunch coriander (cilantro), washed,
  leaves picked
¼ bunch parsley, washed, leaves
  picked
salt and freshly ground black pepper,
  to taste

Assembly
1 egg, lightly beaten
1 tablespoon sesame seeds

We always have an abundance of lemons at the bakery, so we preserve boxes of them when they're in season and use them throughout the year in salads, sandwiches and pies. The salty piquancy brings out wonderful flavours in a variety of savoury dishes.

Roll out the savoury shortcrust pastry into a sheet roughly 4 mm (⅛ in) thick. Wrap the sheet in plastic wrap and place it in the fridge. Roll the puff pastry into a sheet roughly 3 mm (⅛ in) thick, wrap it in plastic wrap and place it in the fridge. Let the pastry rest after rolling it out – this will stop it shrinking once cut.

To make the filling, preheat the oven to 180°C (360°F). Chop the sweet potato into 2 cm (¾ in) dice, and toss it in a roasting tray with 30 ml (1 fl oz) of the oil. Roast for 20 minutes, until softened and just starting to brown.

Sweat off the onions and garlic with the remaining oil in a medium sized pan over a low heat for 10 minutes, stirring occasionally, until soft and translucent. Add the chicken and turn up the heat to brown lightly.

Add the wine and tomatoes and bring to the boil, then reduce to a low heat and simmer for around 30–40 minutes, until the chicken is tender and the sauce is slightly reduced.

Mix the cornflour with a little water and stir until you have a loose paste or slurry, adding more water if needed. Add the cornflour slurry to the chicken and stir until the sauce thickens a little more. Add the sweet potato, preserved lemon and peas, and mix thoroughly. Leave to cool before mixing through the herbs, then season to taste with salt and pepper.

Before you assemble the pies, preheat the oven to 180°C (360°F) and lightly grease your pie dishes. Lay the savoury shortcrust pastry on a lightly floured bench, and cut out 8 discs of pastry for the bases, 2 cm (¾ in) wider in diameter than the base of your pie dishes.

Line each pie dish with a round of shortcrust pastry and press it well into the corners of the base with your thumb. Trim off any excess and lightly brush the edges with the beaten egg. Lay out your sheet of puff pastry and cut 8 discs slightly larger than the diameter of the top of your pie dishes. Fill each pie generously with the filling and top each pie with a puff pastry lid. Press the edges of the pastry base and lid together to seal. (To make one family-sized pie, see page 133.)

Brush the top of each pie with egg wash, pierce it a couple of times with a sharp knife or a fork, and sprinkle with the sesame seeds. Bake at 180°C (360°F) for 10 minutes and then reduce the heat to 160°C (320°F) before baking for a further 30–40 minutes, until the pies are nice and golden. Allow them to rest for 10 minutes before eating.

Potato, mushroom and taleggio pie

**Makes 8 individual pies or
1 family pie**

Ingredients
1 quantity savoury shortcrust pastry
   (see page 255)
½ quantity puff pastry (see page 252)

Filling
500 g (1 lb 2 oz) kipfler potatoes,
   washed
4 sprigs rosemary
50 ml (1¾ fl oz) vegetable oil
75 g (2¾ oz) unsalted butter
1 brown onion, peeled and diced
2 cloves garlic, peeled and finely
   chopped

200 g (7 oz) button mushrooms,
   quartered
40 g (1½ oz) plain (all-purpose) flour
400 ml (13½ fl oz/1⅔ cups) full-cream
   (whole) milk
200 g (7 oz) taleggio, chopped into
   small pieces
2 sprigs tarragon, picked and roughly
   chopped
salt and freshly ground black pepper,
   to taste
12 cornichons, cut in half lengthways

Assembly
1 egg, lightly beaten

Roll out the savoury shortcrust pastry into a sheet roughly 4 mm (⅛ in) thick.
Wrap the sheet in plastic wrap and place it in the fridge. Roll the puff pastry
into a sheet roughly 3 mm (⅛ in) thick, wrap it in plastic wrap and place it in the
fridge. Let the pastry rest after rolling it out – this will stop it shrinking once cut.

To make the filling, put the potatoes in a large saucepan, cover with water
and season with salt. Bring to the boil, then reduce the heat and simmer for
20 minutes. The potatoes will fall off a sharp knife when done. Strain the
potatoes and refresh them briefly under cold water. Quarter them lengthways,
then cut into 2 cm (¾ in) slices and place in a large mixing bowl.

Strip the leaves from three sprigs of rosemary and finely chop. Heat 20 ml
(¾ fl oz) of the oil and 20 g (¾ oz) of the butter in a large saucepan, then add
the onion and garlic and sweat them off until soft and translucent. Remove
from the heat, stir through the rosemary and add the mixture to the potato.

Heat a large frying pan over a high heat, then add the remaining oil and
15 g (½ oz) of the butter. Fry the mushrooms for 5 minutes, until softened
and starting to colour, then add to the potato and onions.

Melt the remaining 40 g (1½ oz) of butter in a saucepan over a medium heat.
Add the flour and stir over the heat until it forms a thick, sandy coloured paste.
Gradually whisk in the milk, then continue to stir until the mixture is thick and
comes to the boil. Remove from the heat, add the taleggio and continue
whisking until smooth.

Pour the cheese sauce over the potatoes, onions and mushrooms. Add the
tarragon and gently turn the mixture until everything is well coated in the sauce.
Season to taste with salt and pepper. Set aside to cool completely.

Before you assemble the pies, preheat the oven to 180°C (360°F) and lightly
grease your pie dishes. Lay the savoury shortcrust pastry on a lightly floured
bench, and cut out 8 discs of pastry for the bases, 2 cm (¾ in) wider in diameter
than the base of your pie dishes.

Line each pie dish with a round of shortcrust pastry and press it in well with
your thumb. Trim off any excess and lightly brush the edges with the beaten
egg. Lay out your puff pastry and cut 8 discs slightly larger than the top of your
pie dishes. Fill each pie generously with the filling and place three slices of
cornichon on top. Top each pie with a puff pastry lid and press the edges of the
base and lid together to seal. (To make one family-sized pie, see page 133.)

Brush the top of each pie with egg wash, then pierce it a couple of times with
a sharp knife. Strip the leaves from the remaining sprig of rosemary and sprinkle
them over the top. Bake at 180°C (360°F) for 10 minutes and then reduce the
heat to 160°C (320°F), before baking for a further 30–40 minutes, until
the pies are nice and golden. Allow them to rest for 10 minutes before eating.

This might seem like an
unusual filling for a pie, but
it has a great conversion
rate with the sceptics.
The filling was inspired by
a pizza that used similar
flavours. We don't do pizza
nights (yet!), so we made
a pie instead. We make a
cheesy béchamel to hold
the potato and rosemary,
making it an excellent
winter pie that's creamy
and hearty, with a nice zing
from the cornichons.

If you can't get taleggio you
could use almost any hard,
washed rind or blue cheese
with a good strong flavour.

Salads

Every day we make one large salad to serve for
lunch. We use a combination of vegetables, grains,
seeds, protein and lots of herbs, so they provide
a sustaining meal on their own. The trick is making
sure there's enough variety in the salad to ensure
that every mouthful combines all the elements in
varying proportions, so the palate doesn't get
bored halfway through.

Any of these salads would also work beautifully as
a side dish to simply roasted meats and fish; as a
dish to bring along to your next barbecue; or served
alongside one of our pies.

Yellow bean and farro with fennel, pecorino and radicchio

Serves 8 as a substantial lunch; 12 or more as part of a larger meal

Ingredients
250 g (9 oz) farro
1 kg (2 lb 3 oz) yellow beans, tops trimmed
40 ml + 75 ml (1¼ fl oz + 2½ fl oz) extra virgin olive oil
½ radicchio, washed and roughly chopped into 1 cm (½ in) slices
1 large fennel, thinly shaved on a mandolin
½ red onion, thinly shaved on a mandolin
2 handfuls baby spinach, washed
75 g (2¾ oz) sunflower seeds
½ bunch oregano, washed, leaves picked
½ bunch parsley, washed, leaves picked and roughly chopped
juice and zest of 1 lemon
salt and freshly ground black pepper, to taste
75 g (2¾ oz) pecorino, shaved
½ teaspoon dried chilli flakes

The term 'farro' refers to spelt, emmer and einkorn grains, all types of wheat that cannot be threshed. Ours is a beautiful biodynamically grown grain produced by our friends at Mount Zero in the Wimmera, in the west of Victoria. This dish keeps the contrasting elements simple, really highlighting the nutty beauty of the grain.

Put the farro in a large saucepan and cover with 1.5 litres (51 fl oz/6 cups) cold water. Bring to the boil and then reduce to a simmer for 30 minutes, until tender. Strain and set aside to cool.

Preheat a large griddle pan or barbecue chargrill until very hot. Toss the beans in 40 ml (1¼ fl oz) oil until they're well coated, and season lightly with salt and pepper.

Lay the beans in an even layer on the griddle pan and cook for 3 minutes, turning occasionally so that all sides of the beans are nicely chargrilled and they still have some crunch. Remove them from the griddle and spread them out on a tray to cool.

Combine the beans, farro, radicchio, fennel, onion, spinach, sunflower seeds, herbs, lemon juice and zest and remaining olive oil in a large mixing bowl and toss, making sure the dressing coats everything well. Season to taste with salt and pepper.

Gently toss most of the pecorino through the salad and transfer it to a serving dish, or divide it between bowls if serving separately. Sprinkle the salad with the chilli flakes and the remaining pecorino before serving.

Broccolini and pearl barley with zucchini, and tahini yoghurt dressing

Serves 8 as a substantial lunch; 12 or more as part of a larger meal

Ingredients

Salad
250 g (9 oz) pearl barley
75 g (2¾ oz) currants
3 bunches broccolini, trimmed
40 ml (1¼ fl oz) extra virgin olive oil
salt and freshly ground black pepper, to taste
3 small zucchini (courgettes), thinly sliced on a mandolin
½ red onion, peeled and thinly sliced
1 long red chilli, seeds in, thickly sliced
1 handful spinach, washed
1 handful wild rocket, washed
½ bunch mint, leaves picked and roughly torn
½ bunch parsley, washed, leaves picked and roughly chopped
75 g (2¾ oz) sesame seeds, toasted

Dressing
200 g (7 oz) Greek yoghurt
1½ teaspoons honey
1 tablespoon tahini
1 tablespoon extra virgin olive oil
juice and zest of ½ a lemon
1 tablespoon red-wine vinegar
salt and freshly ground black pepper, to taste

Lots of people throw away the stem of the broccolini but I like to include it. It provides a lovely variation in texture and avoids waste, which we hate. In this salad we chargrill the stems and the tops. Another nice way of using up broccoli (or cauliflower) stems is to shave them into your salad raw, for freshness and to add texture.

Put the pearl barley in a large saucepan and cover with 1.5 litres (51 fl oz/6 cups) cold water. Bring to the boil and then reduce to a simmer for 30 minutes, until tender. Strain and set aside to cool.

Place the currants in a small bowl and just cover with warm water. Leave them to soak for half an hour.

Meanwhile, make the dressing by whisking all the ingredients together in a bowl. Set aside until ready to assemble.

Preheat a griddle pan or barbecue chargrill until very hot. Cut the broccolini in half horizontally to separate the tops from the stalks. Toss them in olive oil and season lightly with salt and pepper. Chargrill the stalks first, turning occasionally as you cook, to colour. This will take a few minutes; you want them to be slightly undercooked so they still have some crunch. Set the stalks aside and do the same with the tops (they will be a bit quicker).

Drain the currants well. Toss the pearl barley, broccolini, zucchini, onion, chilli, spinach, rocket, mint, parsley, sesame seeds and drained currants in a large mixing bowl to combine. Pour over the dressing and gently toss to coat.

Roasted pumpkin and chickpea with barberries, feta and dukkah

With every change of season we have something to look forward to. Autumn brings the vibrant butternut pumpkin, which we use for our savoury Danishes, sandwiches and this warm and earthy salad. Barberries are small dried berries that have a sharp and slightly acidic flavour. They help to give balance, and accent the more mellow flavours in this dish. Barberries are available from most health food stores – if you can't find them, you could use currants.

For quick assembly on the day, make the dukkah ahead of time. I like to at least double the recipe, so I always have some to hand for use in everything from salads, to avocado on toast, to pumpkin soup. It will retain good flavour for up to a month stored in an airtight container in your spice cupboard. You could also cook the chickpeas the day before, or substitute a 400 g (14 oz) tin of chickpeas.

Serves 8 as a substantial lunch; 12 or more as part of a larger meal

Ingredients

Dukkah
1 teaspoon fennel seeds
1½ teaspoons cumin seeds
1 tablespoon coriander seeds
½ teaspoon nigella seeds
40 g (1½ oz) macadamia nuts, lightly toasted and roughly chopped
1 tablespoon pepitas (pumpkin seeds), lightly toasted
1½ teaspoons pink peppercorns
½ teaspoon smoky paprika
¼ teaspoon sea salt

Roasted pumpkin
1 butternut pumpkin (squash) (roughly 1–1.2 kg/2 lb 3 oz– 2 lb 10 oz)
150 ml (5 fl oz) extra virgin olive oil
1 teaspoon cumin seeds
¼ teaspoon ground cinnamon
¼ teaspoon smoky paprika
½ teaspoon coriander seeds, gently crushed in a pestle and mortar
salt and freshly ground black pepper, to taste

Assembly
250 g (9 oz) dried chickpeas, soaked overnight in water
100 g (3½ oz) barberries
½ red onion, peeled and thinly sliced
1 handful spinach, washed and dried
1 handful wild rocket, washed and dried
¼ bunch coriander (cilantro), washed and stems attached
¼ bunch mint, washed, leaves picked and roughly torn
¼ bunch parsley, washed, leaves picked and roughly torn
40 g (1½ oz) sesame seeds, toasted
40 g (1½ oz) pepitas (pumpkin seeds), toasted
40 g (1½ oz) sunflower seeds, toasted
juice and zest of 1 lemon
75 ml (2½ fl oz) extra virgin olive oil
salt and freshly ground black pepper, to taste
150 g (5½ oz) feta

To make the dukkah, gently toast the fennel, cumin, coriander and nigella seeds seperately in a dry frying pan over a low heat for around 1 minute, until fragrant. Move the pan around continuously to avoid burning the spices. Set aside to cool slightly, and then gently break them up with a mortar and pestle – you just want to release the fragrance, not grind the spices to a powder. Combine the spices in a small bowl with the remaining dukkah ingredients and stir to combine well. Set aside.

Place the chickpeas in a saucepan and cover with 1.5 litres (51 fl oz/6 cups) cold water. Bring to the boil and then reduce to a simmer for 45–50 minutes, until tender. Strain and set aside to cool.

Place the barberries in a small bowl and just cover with warm water. Leave them to soak while you roast the pumpkin.

Meanwhile, preheat the oven to 200°C (390°F). Peel and roughly chop the pumpkin into large bite-sized chunks. Toss them together with 150 ml (5 fl oz) of the oil and the spices, and season to taste with salt and pepper.

Spread the pumpkin out on a roasting tray and cook it in the oven for 10 minutes. Take the pan out of the oven and gently agitate it to stop the pumpkin sticking and to make sure it's roasting evenly. Return to the oven

→

for another 10–15 minutes, until the pumpkin is tender and just starting to caramelise. Set aside to cool.

Drain the barberries well. To assemble your salad, place the pumpkin, chickpeas, onion, spinach, rocket, herbs, toasted seeds and lemon zest in a large mixing bowl. Pour the lemon juice and oil over the salad, then toss with your hands to mix and coat everything well. Season to taste with salt and pepper.

Transfer to a serving bowl (or individual bowls if using) and top with crumbled feta and a sprinkling of dukkah.

Green wheat, borlotti and green bean with goat's cheese, walnuts and mint

**Serves 8 as a substantial lunch;
12 or more as part of a larger meal**

Ingredients
100 g (3½ oz) cracked freekeh
1 kg (2 lb 3 oz) green beans, topped
1 kg (2 lb 3 oz) borlotti beans, podded
½ bunch mint, roughly chopped
handful parsley, roughly chopped
2 handfuls baby spinach, washed
3 spring onions, finely sliced
200 g (7 oz) shelled walnuts, lightly
   toasted and roughly chopped
juice and zest of 1 lemon
75 ml (2½ fl oz) olive oil
2 teaspoons apple-cider vinegar
salt and freshly ground black pepper,
   to taste
200 g (7 oz) goat's cheese

Borlotti beans have a short season, so it's special when you get to use them fresh. If they're out of season, you can substitute with dried beans. Cannellini beans are a good alternative, as they maintain their texture better when dried. Use 250 g (9 oz) dried beans.

Green wheat, or freekeh, is wheat that has been harvested before it's fully dried on the plant, and then roasted. Freekeh refers to the harvesting and drying process, and not the grain, so while it is most commonly wheat, it can be made with any grain. Because the grains are harvested when they're still green, they retain a lot of their nutritional value and are high in fibre, vitamins and minerals.

I like to use a fairly fresh, soft goat's cheese for this salad, and just break it over the dish before serving.

Put the freekeh in a large saucepan and cover with 1.5 litres (51 fl oz/6 cups) cold water. Bring to the boil and then reduce to a simmer for 30 minutes, until tender. Strain and set aside to cool.

Bring a large pan of salted water to the boil. Blanch the green beans for 2–3 minutes until tender, then remove with a slotted spoon and refresh them in ice cold water.

Add the podded borlotti beans to the boiling water and reduce to a simmer, then cook for 45 minutes. Drain and refresh them in ice cold water.

Combine the freekeh, beans, herbs, spinach, spring onions, walnuts and lemon zest in a large mixing bowl. Pour over the oil, vinegar and lemon juice, and toss with your hands to mix and coat everything in the dressing. Season to taste with salt and pepper. Transfer to a serving bowl (or individual bowls if using), crumble the goat's cheese over the top, then serve.

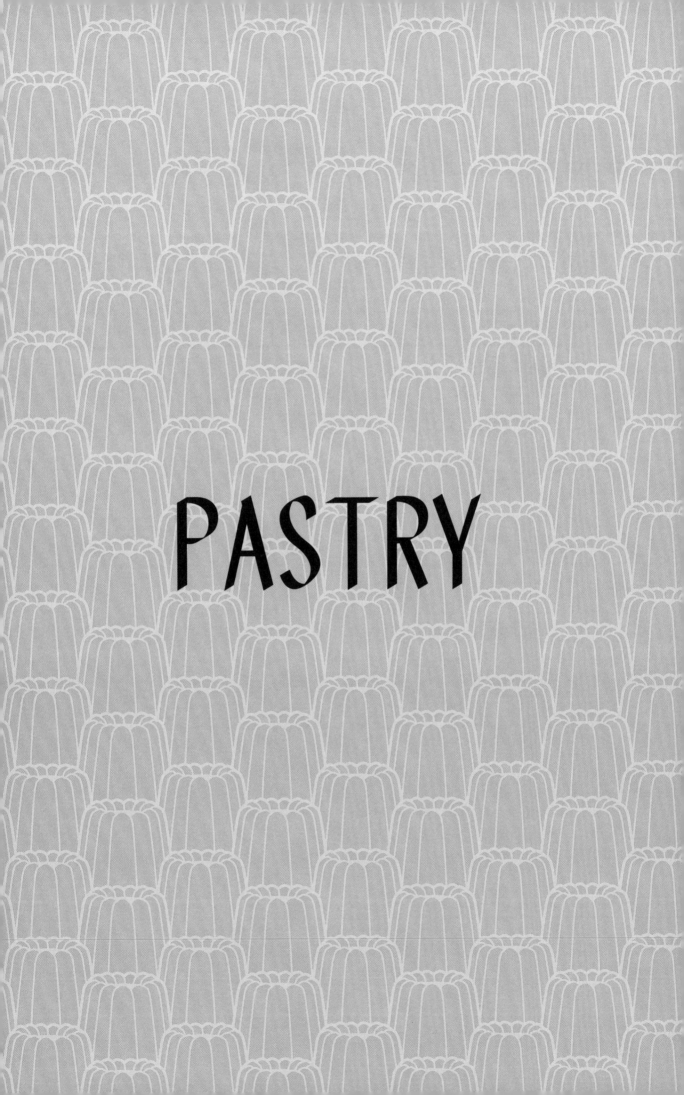

PASTRY

We make a large range of sweet pastry items at the bakery. Some of the recipes are drawn from my background as a chef working on the pastry section in busy kitchens in London, and a lot we happily credit to our head chef Charlie Duffy. Charlie is also English and comes from a background working in Michelin kitchens.

We follow the seasons when selecting produce and use what we have available to us. Seasonal fruits inspire us when creating new items, or are adapted to suit existing recipes. Our range has expanded over the years to include simple treats like cookies, teacakes and brownies to reinvented classics like palmiers and éclairs. We like to explore unusual flavour combinations, using herbs more traditionally used in savoury cooking, or Australia native ingredients.

Here we have included some easy recipes as well as some more technically challenging recipes so there should be something for everyone.

Wholegrain spelt and blood plum galettes

Makes 6

Ingredients

Pastry

225 g (8 oz) unsalted butter
250 g (9 oz) wholegrain spelt flour
100 g (3½ oz) plain (all-purpose) flour
¾ teaspoon table salt
120 g (4½ oz) crème fraîche
2 teaspoons water, chilled

Assembly

6 blood plums
90 g (3 oz) caster (superfine) sugar
½ vanilla pod, seeds scraped, or
   ½ teaspoon vanilla bean paste
½ teaspoon ground cinnamon
1 egg, lightly beaten
100 g (3½ oz) raw (demerara) sugar

Bakery notes

This is quite a rough, sticky dough, so don't worry if it tears while you're rolling it out. If the pastry sticks to the bench, use a dough scraper to lift it off, scrape it back together and patch it where needed. I like to use cultured butter in the pastry, to give a more complex flavour, but this is not essential.

This recipe is right at the heart of who we are and what we do: good ingredients used in season, treated with respect, and showcased simply using good technique. This galette lives or dies on the quality of the fruit you choose, so smell and taste before selecting. Underripe fruit will be hard and sour, and overripe fruit will turn mushy during baking. If blood plums are out of season, try something different – rhubarb, cherries and other stone fruits will all work just as well.

These galettes are perfect for afternoon tea (preferably eaten outside, under a tree), or serve them with crème fraîche for a rustic dessert.

Pastry

Cut the butter into 1 cm (½ in) dice and chill it in the freezer while you prepare the rest of your ingredients. Sift together the flours and salt onto a clean bench, then scatter the cubed butter over the flours. Use a rolling pin to roll the butter into the flour, gathering the flour in as you go. Keep rolling until the mixture has a crumbly texture, with pea-sized lumps of butter still visible.

Transfer the mixture to a large mixing bowl and make a well in the middle. In a separate bowl, lightly whisk the crème fraîche and water together, then pour them into the well. Use a spoon to gently 'cut' the flour into the wet mix until you have an even crumble texture. Using your fingertips, gently push it together into a rough dough. It should have a thick, smooth and slightly sticky texture. Place the dough on a lightly floured bench and roll it out into a rectangle roughly 2 cm (¾ in) thick, with the long edge towards you (exact dimensions are not important here). Fold one-third of the pastry into the middle, then the other third over the top of that, as if folding a letter. Rotate the pastry 90 degrees and roll it out again, into a rectangle roughly 2 cm (¾ in) thick. Repeat the letter fold. Don't worry about making these folds perfectly neat – this is just to finish bringing the dough together and work the flour a bit. Roll the pastry out once more into a rectangle 2 cm (¾ in) thick, then wrap it in plastic wrap and rest it in the fridge for 1 hour.

Remove the pastry from the fridge and roll it out between two sheets of baking paper, into a sheet 4 mm (⅛ in) thick. Return it to the fridge for another 30 minutes.

Lay the pastry out on a lightly floured bench and cut out six 16 cm (6¼ in) discs. Any scraps can be pushed back together, rolled again and cut into discs. Lay the discs on a tray lined with baking paper and refrigerate them while you prepare the fruit.

Wholegrain spelt and blood plum galettes

Assembly

Slice the plums in half and de-stone them. Leave six of the halves intact, and slice the other six into five slim wedges each. Combine the plum halves and wedges in a medium sized bowl. In a separate bowl, mix the caster sugar, vanilla and cinnamon to create a lightly spiced sugar mix. Add the sugar mix to the plums and toss gently with a spoon so the sugar evenly coats the fruit.

Remove the tray of pastry discs from the fridge. Using five of the slim wedges of plum per galette, make a circle 2 cm (¾ in) in from the edge of the pastry, with the thin side of the wedges facing the outer rim of the circle. Fold the 2 cm (¾ in) margin of pastry in towards the centre, over the plum wedges, and crimp the edges together to seal the pastry in place with the plums underneath. This will leave a gap in the centre. Place one intact half of plum here, cut side up. Repeat for the remaining galettes and chill in the fridge for half an hour. While the galettes are chilling, preheat the oven to 175°C (350°F).

Remove the galettes from the fridge. Brush the exposed pastry with the lightly beaten egg and sprinkle with raw sugar. Ensure the galettes are spaced evenly on the tray, with 4 cm (1½ in) between, to get an even bake.

Bake for 15 minutes and then check the plums. If they are starting to colour too quickly, loosely place a small sheet of foil over each galette. Reduce the temperature to 165°C (330°F) and bake for another 10–15 minutes, until the pastry is golden brown. Set aside to cool for 10–15 minutes before serving. They are delicious when still slightly warm, but also good at room temperature.

Baked custard tart

Makes one 23 cm (9 in) tart (serves 8)

Ingredients
½ quantity sweet pastry, chilled
  (see page 255)

Egg custard
585 g (1 lb 5 oz) double (heavy) cream
75 g (2¾ oz) full-cream (whole) milk
½ vanilla pod, seeds scraped, or
  ½ teaspoon vanilla bean paste
180 g (6½ oz) egg yolk (approx.
  9 yolks)
65 g (2¼ oz) caster (superfine) sugar
½ nutmeg, for grating

Bakery notes
If there are any cracks in the pastry after blind baking, brush a little egg yolk over them before filling the tart to seal them up. For slightly larger holes or tears, use a little excess pastry to fill the gap, and return to the oven for a few minutes.

Place the tart case on the oven rack and then pour the custard in, to avoid any spillage. Removing the upper shelves before preheating the oven can make this easier.

You can also use this recipe to make small, individual tarts. You'll just need to reduce the bake time to account for the lower volume of custard.

This tart combines simple, quality ingredients to create something sublime. The flavours are classically English, and the freshly grated nutmeg gives the rich, silky custard an aromatic lift.

On a lightly floured bench, roll the pastry out into a large disc, 5 mm (¼ in) thick. Lightly grease a 23 cm (9 in) round tart tin with butter, then gently lay the pastry over it. Using your thumb, press the pastry firmly into the base, then trim the excess off with a knife. Place the tart shell in the fridge to rest for 1 hour. While the shell is resting, preheat the oven to 160°C (320°F).

To blind bake the tart shell, line the rested pastry case with baking paper and fill with dried beans, rice or baking weights. Bake for 20 minutes, then remove the paper and beans and return the tart shell to the oven for a further 10 minutes, or until lightly golden. Set the shell aside to cool in the tin, and reduce the oven to 110°C (230°F).

To make the filling, gently heat the cream, milk and vanilla in a medium saucepan over a low heat, stirring, until combined and just warm.

Meanwhile, in a large mixing bowl gently whisk the eggs and sugar together until combined. Slowly pour the warmed cream and milk mixture over the eggs and sugar, whisking to emulsify. Strain the mixture through a fine sieve into a measuring jug.

Line a tray with baking paper and place the tart shell on top. Place the tray in the oven on the lowest shelf, then gently pour in the custard. Bake for around 50 minutes. The centre of the custard should have a slight wobble, like a jelly, but no colour on top. The residual heat will finish setting the custard.

Place the tart on a wire rack to cool, then remove the tart from the tin and transfer onto a serving dish. Grate the nutmeg over the top before serving.

Strawberry and chamomile tarts

Makes 10 small tarts

Ingredients
1 quantity sable pastry (see page 254)
1 egg, lightly beaten
1 tablespoon raw (demerara) sugar

Strawberry glaze
250 g (9 oz) strawberries
10 ml (¼ fl oz) water
15 g (½ oz) sugar
3 g (⅛ oz) pectin

Chamomile cream
220 g (8 oz) full-cream (whole) milk
10 g (¼ oz) dried chamomile flowers
1 gold gelatine leaf
4 egg yolks
40 g (1½ oz) sugar
15 g (½ oz) cornflour (cornstarch)
15 g (½ oz) cocoa butter
45 g (1½ oz) crème fraîche
75 g (2¾ oz) butter, softened, in
   1 cm (½ in) dice

Assembly
2 punnets strawberries

Bakery notes
For the strawberry glaze, the pectin and sugar are measured as a percentage of the juice you get out of your strawberries. This will vary depending on the quality and water content of the berries. The pectin should be 2% and the sugar 10% of the eventual weight of the juice.

You can keep any left-over strawberry pulp and freeze it to use in a later batch of jam or smoothies, or spoon it over your breakfast.

You will need metal pastry rings that will cut through hard pastry. We use 8 cm (3¼ in) rings, though you can use any size you like.

When making the chamomile cream, I use a stick blender to achieve a smooth velvety texture with no aeration. You can whisk the ingredients in one by one at the end, but you will need to strain the cream afterwards to achieve the desired texture.

On a lightly floured bench, roll the pastry out into a large disc, 7 mm (¼ in) thick, then freeze it for 1 hour so that it sets hard.

Preheat the oven to 160°C (320°F). Remove the pastry from the freezer and use the pastry rings to cut out discs. Leave the rings on the discs and place them on a tray lined with baking paper, leaving space between them so they bake through evenly. Brush some egg over the top of each disc, then sprinkle with raw sugar.

Bake the discs for 15–17 minutes, until golden. As soon as they're out of the oven, remove the rings so they don't stick (use a tea towel so you don't burn your hands). Set the discs aside to cool.

For the strawberry glaze, hull the strawberries and cut them in half. Place the berries in a metal mixing bowl that fits over a saucepan like a double boiler, and cover the bowl tightly with plastic wrap. Half fill the saucepan with water, ensuring that the water won't touch the bowl, then place it on the stove on a low heat.

Without removing the plastic wrap, sit the bowl of strawberries over the pan and leave to cook for 2 hours, until the berries produce a clear red juice (check the water in the saucepan occasionally to ensure it doesn't boil dry). Strain the juice through a sieve and discard any remaining strawberries (or set aside for a later use).

Weigh 150 g (5½ oz) of the juice into a small saucepan. Mix the sugar and pectin together, then sprinkle the mixture into the juice, whisking until it dissolves. Place the saucepan over a medium heat and bring the mixture to a simmer for 3–5 minutes to activate the pectin. The glaze should be shiny and have

The subtle flavour of the chamomile really adds balance and depth of flavour to this tart. You could also use elderflower, lemon myrtle or lemon verbena for an equally delicious result.

Strawberry and chamomile tarts

a thicker consistency. Pour it into a container and refrigerate until you're ready to assemble the tarts.

To make the chamomile cream, first make an infusion by combining the milk and chamomile in a saucepan and bringing to a simmer over a medium heat. Set aside for 15 minutes, then strain the infusion through a fine sieve. Use a spoon to squeeze as much of the milk as possible out of the chamomile, then weigh 180 g (6½ oz) of the infused milk into a small saucepan and set aside. Discard the rest of the infused milk.

Soak the gelatine leaf in water, and set aside for 5 minutes, to soften. Whisk the egg yolks and sugar together in a medium sized bowl, then add the cornflour and whisk again until combined.

Return the infused milk to the heat and bring to a simmer, then pour it over the egg mixture and whisk to combine. Return the mixture to the saucepan over a medium heat, whisking constantly, until the mixture becomes thick and just starts to bubble. Remove it from the heat immediately and pour into a tall measuring jug.

While the mixture is still hot, add the cocoa butter and use a stick blender to emulsify. Squeeze the water out of the gelatine leaf, then add to the mixture and blend again. Add the crème fraîche and blend again. Add the butter, one piece at a time, blending to emulsify after each addition.

Pour the mixture into a clean bowl, cover the surface with plastic wrap to avoid a skin forming, and leave to cool in the fridge for 1½–2 hours, until set.

Hull the remaining two punnets of strawberries and slice them 2 mm (⅒ in) thick, horizontally. Place them in a large mixing bowl along with 2 tablespoons of the glaze, and gently turn the strawberries until they are coated (add more glaze if needed).

To assemble your tarts, lay out your pastry discs on the bench and put the chamomile cream into a piping (icing) bag. Pipe a thick layer of chamomile cream onto the centre of each disc, leaving a 1 cm (½ in) rim at the edges. Fan the strawberries over the top of the cream, layering them until the pastry base is completely covered and you have a small strawberry mound. Transfer the tarts to serving plates and serve.

Raspberry and goat's milk tarts with lemon myrtle cream

Makes 10

Ingredients
1 quantity sable pastry (see page 254)
1 egg, lightly beaten
1 tablespoon raw (demerara) sugar

Lemon myrtle cream
75 g (2¾ oz) lemon juice
5 lemon myrtle leaves
1 gold gelatine leaf
2 eggs
35 g (1¼ oz) caster (superfine) sugar
110 g (4 oz) butter, diced and softened

Goat's milk cream
1 gold gelatine leaf
4 egg yolks
40 g (1½ oz) caster (superfine) sugar
15 g cornflour (cornstarch)
180 g (6½ oz) goat's milk
15 g cocoa butter
80 g (2¾ oz) goat's curd
70 g (2½ oz) butter, diced and softened

Assembly
4 punnets raspberries

Bakery notes
You will need metal pastry rings that will cut through hard pastry. We use 8 cm (3¼ in) rings, though you can use any size you like.

When making the goat's milk cream, I use a stick blender to achieve a smooth velvety texture with no aeration. You can whisk the ingredients in one by one at the end, but you will need to strain the cream afterwards to achieve the desired texture.

There are quite a few elements here. It's a good idea to get the creams and the pastry bases done ahead of time – then you can just assemble the tarts when you're ready to eat them.

Lemon myrtle is a native Australian flowering plant that grows in subtropical southern Queensland. It has the highest 'citral' purity of any plant, and a very clean, sweet citrus flavour, which pairs beautifully with the goat's milk and fresh berries in this tart.

You can buy lemon myrtle fresh at some farmers' markets when in season, and dried leaves are available online. If you can't get hold of lemon myrtle, you could substitute with lemon verbena or lemon zest.

On a lightly floured bench, roll the pastry out into a large disc, 7 mm (¼ in) thick, then freeze it for 1 hour so that it sets hard.

Preheat the oven to 160°C (320°F). Remove the pastry from the freezer and use the tart rings to cut out discs. Leave the rings on the discs and place them on a tray, leaving space between them so they bake through evenly. Brush some egg over the top of each disc, then sprinkle with raw sugar.

Bake the discs for 15–17 minutes, until golden. As soon as they're out of the oven, remove the rings so they don't stick (use a tea towel so you don't burn your hands). Set the discs aside to cool.

To make the lemon myrtle cream, bring the lemon juice and lemon myrtle leaves to a simmer over a medium heat. Remove from the heat and leave to infuse for 30 minutes.

Soak the gelatine leaf in water, and set aside for 5 minutes, to soften. Strain the infused lemon juice through a fine sieve, then set aside. In a metal mixing bowl that fits over a saucepan like a double boiler, whisk the eggs and sugar together until slightly pale, then add the infused lemon juice. Half-fill the saucepan with water, ensuring that the water won't touch the bowl, then place it on the stove on a low heat.

Sit the bowl over the saucepan and heat the mixture, whisking until it thickens and reaches 80°C (180°F) on a sugar thermometer. Strain again through a fine sieve into a medium sized bowl.

Squeeze out the water from the gelatine and add it to the mixture. Add the butter one piece at a time, using a stick blender continuously to emulsify. Cool in the fridge for 2 hours or until you are ready to assemble your tarts.

To make the goat's milk cream, soak the gelatine leaf in water, and set aside for 5 minutes, to soften. In a medium sized bowl, whisk the egg yolks and sugar until combined, then add the cornflour and whisk again to combine.

Bring the goat's milk to a simmer in a saucepan over medium heat, then pour it over the egg mixture and whisk to combine. Return the mix to the saucepan and whisk constantly over a medium heat until the mixture becomes thick and just starts to bubble. Remove it from the heat immediately and pour into a tall measuring jug.

While the mixture is still hot, add the cocoa butter and use a stick blender to emulsify. Squeeze out the water from the gelatine, then add it to the mixture and blend again. Add the goat's curd and blend again. Add the butter, one piece at a time, blending to emulsify after each addition. Pour the mixture into a clean bowl, then cover the surface with plastic wrap to avoid a skin forming and refrigerate for 1½–2 hours, until set.

To assemble the tarts, put both the creams into piping (icing) bags, and lay out your sable pastry bases on the bench. Pipe a small disc of goat's milk cream onto the centre of each disc, leaving a 1 cm (½ in) rim at the edges. Arrange the raspberries around the edge, securing them on the edge of the cream, and pile a few in the centre. Finish your tarts by piping a few dots of lemon myrtle cream irregularly among the raspberries.

Canelé

Canelé are a traditional Bordelaise pastry that went out of fashion during times of ration but have regained popularity in the past 30–40 years. They are deceptively tricky – it's the little things that really make the difference here.

The copper moulds used to make canelé are key, because they conduct heat so well. This is what creates the crisp exterior. Using beeswax to line the moulds is equally important, as it creates a seal and adds a gentle flavour. We use wax from Raw Honey, which really improves the end result.

We use Stroh rum, which is a spiced 80% proof rum made in Austria. Because it's so strong you only need a little, which means the batter has a higher proportion of fat-carrying liquid such as milk. Fat equals flavour, so this rum makes a marked difference.

Makes 10

Ingredients
450 g (1 lb) full-cream (whole) milk
80 g (2¾ oz) plain (all-purpose) flour
¼ teaspoon table salt
200 g (oz) icing (confectioners') sugar
80 g (2¾ oz) eggs (approx. 2 small eggs)
30 g (1 oz) egg yolk (approx. 2 small yolks)
½ vanilla bean, seeds scraped
40 g (1½ oz) butter
12 g (⅓ oz) rum
100 g (3½ oz) beeswax, grated

Bakery notes
Make the batter two days ahead, then leave it to mature for two days (or up to seven). We have noted all the ingredients by weight, because you need absolute precision to achieve the correct balance. Don't rush any of the steps, and if your first batch isn't perfect, keep practising – your patience and precision will be rewarded by a truly superior canelé.

If you can't get beeswax you can use clarified butter (or ghee) instead. You will miss the waxy perfume, and the result will have a slightly different finish.

If you're buying new copper moulds, you'll need to season them before your first batch of canelé. To do this, preheat the oven to 180°C (360°F). Grate some beeswax into a small saucepan and melt it over a very low heat. Place the moulds in the oven for 2 minutes, then remove them from the oven and pour beeswax into one until ¾ full. Using a pair of tongs, swirl the wax around to fully coat the inside of the mould, then pour the wax into the next mould, and so on, working quickly so the wax doesn't set. Place each wax-coated mould upside down over a wire rack with kitchen paper underneath to catch any excess. Turn the moulds upright on a tray and return to the oven for 10 minutes, then leave to cool. Repeat these steps four more times to complete the seasoning process.

In a medium saucepan, heat the milk to 85°C (185°F) over a medium heat. Pour into a small bowl and cover it with plastic wrap. Pierce the plastic wrap a few times so the steam can escape, then leave it in the fridge overnight. Scalding the milk denatures the proteins, which improves the crumb of your canelé.

The next day, sift the flour, salt and icing sugar together into a medium sized bowl, then set aside. Combine the eggs, egg yolks and vanilla in a narrow measuring jug, and use a stick blender to bring them together without incorporating any air. (You can use a whisk instead of a stick blender, but you will need to strain the mixture through a sieve to achieve the desired consistency.)

Weigh 400 g (14 oz) of the chilled scalded milk into a saucepan. Add the butter and bring it back to 85°C (185°F) over medium heat, stirring occasionally. Pour the milk over the flour mixture, stirring gently with a whisk. It's important not to overwork the flour at this stage. Slowly add the egg mixture, whisking gently as you go. Finally, add the rum and gently incorporate it, then strain the finished batter through a fine sieve and leave it in the fridge for two days to mature.

On the day of baking, line the moulds with beeswax following the method you used to first season them (see Bakery notes, above), but only follow the process once, rather than five times. Once all your moulds are lined and cool, place them in the freezer for half an hour. This will help to create a better crust when you pour the batter in.

Preheat the oven to 190°C (370°F), and remove the batter from the fridge. It will have separated a little – mix it very gently with a spoon, just to re-combine. Put the batter into a measuring jug and pour 75 g (2¾ oz) of batter into each canelé mould. (You can either weigh each individual mould as you fill it, or put all the moulds on a baking tray and then set the tray on your kitchen scales.)

Bake for 20 minutes, and then turn the tray 180 degrees, reduce the oven temperature to 175°C (350°F) and bake for another 20 minutes. Turn the tray again and bake for another 10 minutes, or until you have a lovely dark caramel colour on top. Remove the tray from the oven and immediately use a pair of tongs to flip each canelé out of its mould and onto a wire rack to cool. Cool for 1 hour before eating.

Coconut blossom palmiers

Makes 8

Ingredients
1 quantity puff pastry (see page 252)

Coconut sugar mix
125 g (4½ oz) coconut blossom sugar
100 g (3½ oz) soft brown sugar
150 g (5½ oz) raw (demerara) sugar
½ teaspoon ground cinnamon
¼ teaspoon table salt

Bakery notes

Before laminating the sugar into the pastry, apply a very fine film of water over the pastry so the sugar doesn't slide off when you fold or roll the pastry. A spray bottle is ideal for this – you get just enough water to bind the sugar without drenching the pastry. A pastry brush, dipped in water and lightly applied, will also work.

I prefer to bake these on a very sturdy tray that will hold its shape in the heat of the oven. If the base is firm, you will get more even caramelisation and a crispy texture.

Coconut blossom sugar is extracted from the sap inside the flower buds of the coconut palm. It is commonly used throughout South-East Asia as a natural sweetener in baked goods as well as in savoury dishes such as curries and soups. We use it for its lovely butterscotch and molasses flavours, which give added depth and a slight bitterness to this flaky, buttery pastry. Coconut blossom sugar is widely available at Asian grocers and health food stores.

Put all the ingredients for the sugar mix in a medium sized mixing bowl, and toss to combine.

Roll out the puff pastry into a rectangle roughly 12 cm × 24 cm (4¾ in × 9½ in), and 1 cm (½ in) thick, with the long edge towards you. Lightly spray some cold water over the surface of the pastry to ensure the sugar sticks; be careful not to use too much. Sprinkle the pastry with a thin layer of the sugar mixture, ensuring the surface is evenly covered.

Starting from the right-hand side of the rectangle, fold one third of the pastry into the middle, then the other third over the top of that, as if folding a letter. Wrap your pastry in plastic wrap and refrigerate for 1 hour. Roll it out again into a rectangle 12 cm × 24 cm (4¾ in × 9½ in), and 1 cm (½ in) thick, then repeat the folding process. Wrap and rest in the fridge for another hour.

Roll the pastry out into a rectangle roughly 20 cm × 48 cm (8 in × 19 in), and 7 mm (¼ in) thick. Position it on the bench so the short edge is towards you. Lightly spray some cold water over the pastry, then generously sprinkle with the sugar mix, ensuring that the entire surface is covered evenly.

Make notches in the pastry 23.5 cm (9¼ in) and 24.5 cm (9¾ in) from the bottom edge. Fold the top and bottom edges in to meet these notches. You will be left with a 1 cm (½ in) gap in the middle.

Spray the newly exposed surfaces of dough with water, then generously cover with the sugar mix. Fold the top half down over the bottom, using the 1 cm (½ in) gap as a hinge.

Spray the newly exposed surfaces of dough with water, and generously cover the surface with the sugar mix. Carefully flip the dough over and repeat so that both sides of the pastry block are covered with sugar. You should have roughly 50 g (1¾ oz) of sugar mix left after this.

Cut 2.5 cm (1 in) slices through the cross-section of the pastry so that each slice is held together by the hinged edge. Keeping the sliced block together, gently transfer it onto a tray lined with baking paper. Wrap the tray in plastic wrap and freeze it for at least 6 hours, or overnight. The palmiers will last in the freezer for up to two weeks.

To bake your palmiers, preheat the oven to 175°C (350°F) and line two trays with baking paper. Remove the palmiers from the freezer, separate each slice from the block, and lay them out on the bench cut-side up.

Sprinkle the remaining sugar mix over the top and then turn them upside down onto the lined trays, leaving a 5 cm (2 in) gap between each one. Bake in the oven for 25–30 minutes, until they are a deep golden colour and the pastry has expanded considerably.

Remove from the oven and leave to cool on the trays for 10 minutes. Once the caramel has set, turn the palmiers over and break off any excess bits of sugar, then place on a wire rack to cool completely before serving.

Chocolate and wattleseed éclairs

Éclairs can be truly awful or truly sublime, and the difference is often in the precision and patience of the cook. Measuring so precisely may sound like a lot of work, but the proof will be in the pudding.

This is our English chef Charlie's Aussie twist on a classic French pastry. The wattleseed provides a bitter chicory flavour to counter the sweetness of the chocolate ganache.

Makes 12

Ingredients

1 quantity choux pastry (see page 254), chilled

Éclair crunch

50 g (1¾ oz) butter, softened
100 g (3½ oz) caster (superfine) sugar
20 g (¾ oz) cocoa powder, sifted
20 g (¾ oz) ground almonds
20 g (¾ oz) plain (all-purpose) flour, sifted
40 g (1½ oz) orange juice

Biscuit

75 g (2¾ oz) butter, softened
90 g (3 oz) soft brown sugar
20 g (¾ oz) cocoa powder
75 g (2¾ oz) plain (all-purpose) flour

Wattleseed ganache

150 g + 150 g (5½ oz + 5½ oz) 35% fat cream
15 g (½ oz) ground wattleseed
1 gold gelatine leaf
90 g (3 oz) 60% dark chocolate, roughly chopped
15 g (½ oz) soft brown sugar
15 g (½ oz) glucose syrup

Chocolate glaze

8 gold gelatine leaves
270 g (9½ oz) 35% fat cream
55 g (2 oz) caster (superfine) sugar
65 g (2¼ oz) cocoa powder, sifted
25 g (1 oz) dark chocolate, at least 60%, roughly chopped

Bakery notes

You need to use strong flour with a high protein content for the choux pastry, so that it holds the structure when baking, resulting in a crisp shell and a hollow centre. A good trick when piping out the choux pastry is to draw an outline on the paper first. Just make sure that the template is on the underside of the paper, so you don't get ink on your pastry.

There are a lot of components in this recipe, so it's a good idea to make the crunch and the biscuit the day before. The assembled éclairs are best eaten on the day they are baked and filled.

You may need to look around a bit to find wattleseed. Suppliers such as Herbie's Spices or the Essential Ingredient stock it, and it is also available online at bushtuckershop.com.au or bushfoodshop.com.au.

Éclair crunch

In a stand mixer fitted with the paddle attachment, cream together the butter and sugar for a couple of minutes, until slightly pale. Slowly incorporate the cocoa powder, ground almonds and plain flour, and mix until just combined. With the paddle still mixing slowly, gradually add the orange juice and mix until just combined. Place the mix in a small bowl and refrigerate, covered, for 1 hour.

Preheat the oven to 175°C (350°F) and line a tray with baking paper. Drop teaspoon-sized dots of the mix onto the paper, leaving a 3 cm (1¼ in) gap between them to allow for spread.

Bake for 8–10 minutes. The mix will bubble up slightly like a brandy snap, and then settle. Leave the crunch until it has set hard and cooled completely, then crush in a mortar and pestle until you have coarse pebbles. The crunch will store in an airtight container for up to five days.

Chocolate and wattleseed éclairs

→

Biscuit

In a stand mixer fitted with the paddle attachment, lightly cream the butter and sugar until it forms a paste. Gently mix in the cocoa powder and flour until the mixture forms a soft dough. Divide the dough in two and press each piece into a disc roughly 1 cm (½ in) thick. The shape is not important, as it can be re-rolled and used again. Wrap each disc in plastic wrap and refrigerate for 30 minutes.

Place one piece of dough between two sheets of baking paper and roll it out into a sheet 2 mm (1⁄10 in) thick. Leaving the baking paper in place, put the dough on a flat tray and freeze for about an hour, until frozen solid. Repeat for the other piece of dough.

Once the dough is frozen, loosen the baking paper by peeling it off the top and placing it loosely back over the dough. Flip the dough sheet over and remove the other piece of paper. Using a sharp knife and a ruler, cut the pastry into rectangles 12.5 cm × 3 cm (5 in × 1¼ in), being careful to avoid cutting through the baking paper underneath. Cover it again with the paper and return to the freezer until you are ready to bake your éclairs. Any excess dough can be re-rolled and used again. Alternatively, it will keep in the freezer for up to two weeks.

Wattleseed ganache

Put 150 g (5½ oz) of the cream in a small saucepan along with the wattleseed and bring to a simmer over a low heat, stirring to combine. Remove from the heat and cover with a lid, then leave to infuse for half an hour.

Meanwhile, soak the gelatine in cold water for 10 minutes. Place the chocolate into a medium sized bowl.

Strain the wattleseed-infused cream through a fine sieve and re-weigh it to 150 g (5½ oz). Return it to the pan and add the brown sugar and glucose syrup. Bring this to a simmer, then remove it from the heat.

Squeeze the water off the gelatine and add it to the cream and sugar mixture, stirring to dissolve it thoroughly. Pour this mixture over the chocolate and stir until thoroughly combined.

Add the remaining 150 g (5½ oz) of cream and mix well. Cover the bowl with plastic wrap and refrigerate for at least 2 hours, until well chilled. Remove from the fridge and whisk until aerated and thick, then place in a piping (icing) bag fitted with a fine-tipped nozzle and refrigerate until you are ready to assemble your éclairs.

Éclairs

Preheat the oven to 180°C (360°F). Take your choux pastry out of the fridge and put it in a piping (icing) bag fitted with a French star nozzle. On a tray lined with baking paper, pipe fingers of choux pastry 12.5 cm (5 in) long and 2 cm (¾ in) wide, leaving 5 cm (2 in) between each one.

Take the portioned biscuits from the freezer and sit one on top of each choux pastry finger.

Bake for 20 minutes, then reduce the heat to 160°C (5½ oz) and continue baking for a further 20 minutes, until golden. The éclairs should feel light and hollow when done, with a light crust. Transfer to a wire rack and leave to cool completely.

Chocolate glaze

Soak the gelatine in cold water for 5 minutes. Heat the cream and sugar in a medium saucepan over a low heat and bring to a simmer.

Remove the pan from the heat and whisk in the cocoa powder. Squeeze off the water from the gelatine and mix it into the cream until dissolved. Add the chocolate and whisk to emulsify.

Strain the mixture through a fine sieve into a tall container, then blend using a stick blender for 2–3 minutes. This will give the glaze a nice gloss.

Assembly

At this point you want the glaze to be around 35°C (95°F) and the consistency of thick honey, so if you made it ahead of time, gently warm it over a very low heat and then allow it to cool slightly.

Using a skewer, make two small holes in the base of each éclair, just in from each end and about 5 cm (2 in) apart. Take the piping (icing) bag filled with the wattleseed cream and gently insert the tip into one of the holes. Fill the éclair until it feels heavy. You should be able to pipe from one end and fill until the cream comes out the other hole, but if it appears blocked or still feels light, place the tip of the nozzle in the second hole and try filling the éclair from the other end. Repeat for the remaining éclairs.

Dip the top of each éclair into the chocolate glaze, shaking gently to allow any excess to drip off, then place upright on a tray.

Sprinkle each éclair with the éclair crunch to finish.

Banana, fig and walnut loaf cake

Makes 1 large loaf

Ingredients

155 g (5½ oz) plain (all-purpose) flour
2 tablespoons cornflour (cornstarch)
1 teaspoon cinnamon
2 teaspoons baking powder
1 teaspoon bicarbonate of soda (baking soda)
½ teaspoon table salt
250 g (9 oz) (approx. 3–4) very ripe bananas, peeled
juice of ½ lemon
2 eggs, at room temperature
½ vanilla pod, seeds scraped
85 g (3 oz) butter, soft
170 g (6 oz) caster (superfine) sugar
115 g (4 oz) walnut halves
225 g (8 oz) dried figs, stems removed and quartered
1 banana (less ripe)
1–2 tablespoons raw (demerara) sugar, for topping

Bakery notes

It's best to use very ripe bananas in the mix for this cake. The browner the banana, the more flavour it will lend to the finished product. You can often find heavily discounted bananas in just the right state of disrepair at your grocer.

This is a great treat that's always nice to have in the pantry. It's a bit like banana bread, but much more special, with the figs and nuts bringing contrasting textures. You could use different dried fruits if you like – we've made this with dates and hazelnuts with excellent results.

Preheat the oven to 160°C (320°F). Grease a 9 × 22 × 10 cm (3½ × 8¾ × 4 in) loaf tin and line it with baking paper.

Sift together the flours, cinnamon, baking powder, bicarbonate of soda and salt. In a separate bowl, mash the very ripe bananas with the lemon juice until soft, then stir in the eggs and vanilla.

In a stand mixer fitted with the paddle attachment, cream the butter and sugar until pale and fluffy. Gradually add the egg and banana mixture, beating well between each addition until fully incorporated. Add the dry ingredients and mix gently until combined, then add the walnuts and figs and mix together.

Peel the other banana and cut two thin slices lengthways. Pour the mixture into your prepared tin, then place the banana slices over the top. (It is important the slices are thin, otherwise they will sink into the batter as the cake bakes.) Sprinkle with raw sugar, as desired, then bake for 50–60 minutes, until the top is golden brown and a skewer inserted into the middle comes out clean. Leave in the tin for a few minutes before transferring to a wire rack to cool.

Chocolate, orange and almond cake

Makes 1 large loaf

Ingredients

Almond topping
50 g (1¾ oz) butter, diced
130 g (4½ oz) soft brown sugar
zest of 1 orange
40 g (1½ oz) honey
150 g (5½ oz) flaked almonds

Cake
170 g (6 oz) plain (all-purpose) flour
50 g (1¾ oz) cocoa powder
1¼ teaspoons bicarbonate of soda
    (baking soda)
¼ teaspoon salt
225 g (8 oz) butter, soft
340 g (12 oz) caster (superfine) sugar
3 eggs, at room temperature
½ vanilla pod, seeds scraped (or
    ½ teaspoon vanilla paste)
160 g (5½ oz) buttermilk

Bakery notes
If the almond topping sticks a bit in the tin or falls off when you invert the cake, you can fix it if you act quickly, before the caramel sets. Use a spoon or spatula to stick it back onto the cake, being careful not to touch the caramel directly, to avoid burning your fingers.

It's best to use a serrated knife to slice this cake, as the top sets quite firm. Gently saw through the almond topping to avoid squashing the cake. It will keep well for a few days in an airtight container.

This decadent moist chocolate cake always gets a good response – the rich brown colour and caramelised almond crust on top draws people in. And once they've tried it, they always come back for more.

Preheat the oven to 160°C (320°F). Grease a 9 × 22 × 10 cm (3½ × 8¾ × 4 in) loaf tin and line it with baking paper.

To prepare the almond topping, melt the butter, sugar, orange zest and honey in a small saucepan over a low heat, stirring constantly until the sugar has dissolved and the mixture is thick and syrupy. Pour the syrup into your prepared tin, then sprinkle the flaked almonds evenly over the top. Set aside to cool.

In a medium bowl, sift together the flour, cocoa, bicarbonate of soda and salt, then set aside. In a stand mixer fitted with the paddle attachment, cream together the butter and sugar until pale and fluffy.

In a separate bowl, whisk together the eggs and vanilla. With the mixer still running on a slow speed, gradually add the egg to the butter mixture a little at a time, ensuring each addition is fully incorporated before adding the next.

Alternate between adding a third of the dry ingredients and a third of the buttermilk to the batter, mixing well between each addition, until all the ingredients have been added and the batter has just come together. Scrape down the sides of the bowl to ensure that the batter is completely mixed.

Pour the batter into the tin over the almonds and caramel, and bake for 60–70 minutes, until the top is firm to touch and a skewer inserted into the middle comes out clean.

Leave to cool for a few minutes, then set a wire rack over a tray lined with paper. Invert the still warm cake onto the wire rack then gently lift off the tin, being careful to avoid the caramel, which will still be extremely hot. Leave to cool completely before serving, to allow the almond caramel top to set.

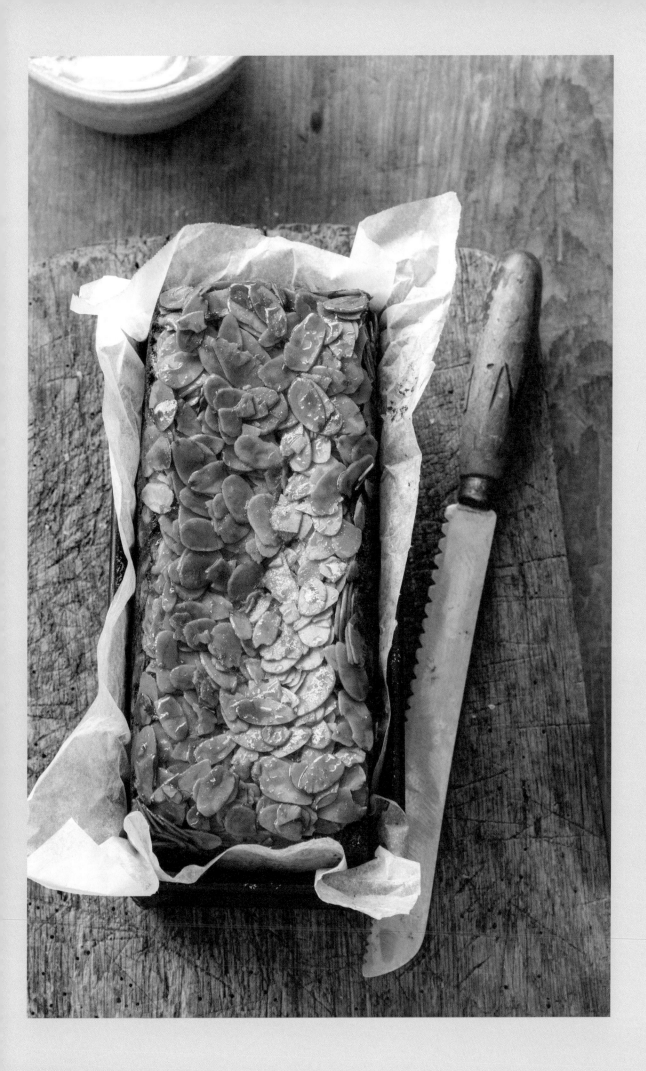

Pistachio cake

Makes 1 large loaf

Ingredients
310 g (11 oz) butter, soft
280 g (10 oz) caster (superfine) sugar
5 whole eggs, at room temperature
zest of 1 lemon
½ vanilla bean, seeds scraped
85 g (3 oz) plain (all-purpose) flour
1¼ teaspoons baking powder
¼ teaspoon salt
125 g (4½ oz) ground almonds
125 g (4½ oz) ground pistachios

Bakery notes
You could cool this cake either in the tin or on a wire rack. As a general baking rule, if you like a softer crust, cool the cakes in the tins. If you prefer more contrast between the crust and the centre, remove from the tin and cool on a wire rack.

To get a nice even finish on your cakes, use a wet hand to spread the batter evenly into the tin before baking.

If ground pistachios are difficult to come by, just grind your own from unsalted raw, shelled pistachios. The pistachio meal will keep well for a few days in an airtight container.

For a lovely variation, try baking berries into the cake. Fill your tin two-thirds of the way, spread a layer of berries over (100–150 g [3½–5½ oz], frozen is fine), then top with the remaining batter and bake according to the recipe.

Our loaf cakes are a permanent feature in our pastry cabinet and we rotate them regularly. This elegant cake is moist and delicious. The rich green of the pistachios contrasts beautifully when served with berries and cream, and the lemon zest lifts their sweetness.

Preheat the oven to 160°C (320°F). Grease a 9 × 22 × 10 cm (3½ × 8¾ × 4 in) loaf tin and line it with baking paper.

In a stand mixer fitted with the paddle attachment, cream the butter and sugar until pale and fluffy.

Crack the eggs into a separate bowl, then add the lemon zest and vanilla. Gradually add the egg mixture to the creamed butter and sugar, mixing well between each addition until fully incorporated. Scrape down the sides of the bowl if necessary to ensure the ingredients are thoroughly mixed.

Sift the flour, baking powder and salt into a large mixing bowl, add the ground almonds and pistachios, and whisk to combine. Fold the dry mixture into the wet ingredients, then gently mix with the paddle until the mixture just comes together.

Pour the mixture into the tin and bake for 50–60 minutes, until a skewer inserted into the middle comes out clean.

Ginger cake

Makes 1 large loaf

Ingredients

180 g (6½ oz) butter, diced

290 g (10 oz) golden syrup (use honey or maple syrup if unavailable)

160 g (5½ oz) soft brown sugar

230 g (8 oz) plain (all-purpose) flour

1½ teaspoons baking powder

1 teaspoon bicarbonate of soda (baking soda)

2½ tablespoons ground ginger

½ teaspoon mixed spice

½ nutmeg, finely grated

1 teaspoon ground cinnamon

200 ml (7 fl oz) full-cream (whole) milk

3 eggs, at room temperature

Bakery notes

This is a simple recipe that requires bringing all the elements together without overworking the flour. It should have a tight, but still light, crumb. Over-whisking it will make it a bit gummy.

Luxuriously dark and sticky, this quick and simple loaf is extremely popular, especially through the winter months – definitely one to snuggle up with on a dreary afternoon. If you're feeling decadent, toast a slice under the grill (broiler) and enjoy it with some salted butter or a dollop of clotted cream.

Preheat the oven to 160°C (320°F). Grease a 9 × 22 × 10 cm (3½ × 8¾ × 4 in) loaf tin and line it with baking paper.

In a small pan, melt the butter, golden syrup and brown sugar over a low heat, stirring until the sugar has dissolved and the mixture is nice and syrupy. Pour the syrup into a bowl and set aside to cool slightly.

Sift together the flour, baking powder, bicarbonate of soda and spices in a large mixing bowl. In a separate bowl, mix together the milk and eggs.

Whisk the egg mixture into the cooled syrup, then pour this onto the dry ingredients, whisking as you go, until everything is just combined. The mixture should have the consistency of pancake batter, so don't worry if it seems runny.

Pour the batter into your prepared tin and bake for 50 minutes, until a skewer inserted into the middle comes out clean.

Wholegrain spelt and carrot cake

Makes one 22 cm (8¾ in) round cake

Ingredients

Cake
5 eggs, at room temperature
300 g (10½ oz) honey
200 ml (7 fl oz) light olive oil
250 g (9 oz) wholegrain spelt flour
1 teaspoon salt
2 teaspoons baking powder
1 teaspoon bicarbonate of soda (baking soda)
2 teaspoons ground cinnamon
350 g (12½ oz) carrot, grated
160 g (5½ oz) walnuts, roughly chopped

Cream-cheese icing (frosting)
60 g (2 oz) icing (confectioners') sugar, sifted
60 g (2 oz) butter, diced and soft
1 vanilla pod, seeds scraped (or 1 teaspoon vanilla paste)
375 g (13 oz) cream cheese, roughly chopped, room temperature
120 g (4½ oz) thick cream

walnuts, to decorate (optional)

Bakery notes
If you can't find wholegrain spelt flour, any wholegrain flour will work beautifully. Plain flour will also work well, although you will need to adjust the ratios in the recipe slightly. Use 300 g (10½ oz) plain flour, 4 eggs and 185 ml (6 fl oz) light olive oil instead of the quantities listed.

We are increasingly using wholegrain flours in our baking, for better flavour and nutrition. I absolutely love carrot cakes and was keen to try a wholegrain version. The chopped walnuts add texture, and the honey aromas will drive you crazy with impatience while the cake is baking!

This cake is great for occasions when you need to work ahead, as it is even better the day after baking. It will keep well for a few days in an airtight container.

Preheat the oven to 180°C (360°F). Grease the tin and line it with baking paper.

In a stand mixer fitted with the whisk attachment, whisk the eggs and honey for about 10 minutes, until light and fluffy. Keep whisking and add the oil slowly, as though making a mayonnaise, until emulsified. The batter will thin slightly, so don't panic if it doesn't continue to thicken.

Combine the flour, salt, baking powder, bicarbonate of soda and cinnamon together in a large mixing bowl. Add to the egg mixture in three batches, folding gently between each addition until incorporated. Add the grated carrot and chopped walnuts in three batches, folding gently between each addition until incorporated. Use a spatula to scrape around the sides and bottom of the bowl to ensure they are evenly distributed through the mix, and don't sink to the bottom.

Pour the batter into the prepared tin and reduce the oven temperature to 160°C (320°F). Bake for about 40 minutes, until the top is golden brown and a skewer inserted into the middle comes out clean. Leave the cake in the tin for a few minutes before transferring to a wire rack to cool.

To make the cream-cheese icing, cream together the icing sugar, butter and vanilla in a stand mixer fitted with the paddle attachment, until pale and smooth. Add the cream cheese a little at a time, continuing to mix at medium speed until smooth and creamy. Add the cream and mix until thoroughly combined and you have a spreadable consistency. Be careful not to over mix it, otherwise it will split.

When the cake has cooled, cut it in half horizontally and place the bottom half onto a serving plate. Fill the cake by spreading it with half the cream-cheese icing, and then replace the top. Cover the top with the rest of the icing and decorate with walnuts, if desired.

Pear, almond and brown butter bundt cakes

Makes 12

Ingredients
210 g (7½ oz) brown rice flour
80 g (2¾ oz) ground almonds
35 g (1¼ oz) tapioca flour
2½ teaspoons baking powder
½ teaspoon table salt
1 teaspoon ground cinnamon
350 g (12½ oz) butter
3 eggs
140 g (5 oz) soft brown sugar
150 g (5½ oz) maple syrup
½ vanilla pod, seeds scraped
3 large beurre bosc pears

Cinnamon sugar
150 g (5½ oz) caster (superfine) sugar
½ teaspoon ground cinnamon

½ quantity vanilla custard
    (see page 262)

Bakery notes
We make this cake in silicone mini bundt moulds, but it would also work well in small pudding bowls or muffin tins. You may need to adjust the cooking time, and use the custard as an icing (frosting) instead of a filling.

If you're working in advance, the mixture will last for a couple of days in the fridge. Once baked, the cake will be fine for two days stored in an airtight container at room temperature, but make sure you dust and fill them the day you want to eat them.

This recipe was created in response to requests for a gluten free option to be included in our pastry cabinet. We didn't want to create something gluten free for the sake of it, and this delicate, moist cake definitely stands on its own. The custard filling provides a creamy texture and carries the flavours across your palate. We use a combination of gluten free flours. Brown rice flour provides flavour and structure, ground almonds provide richness, and tapioca flour gives the cakes a light, fluffy texture.

Preheat the oven to 170°C (340°F), and grease 12 cake moulds (or muffin tins).

Sift together the rice flour, ground almonds, tapioca flour, baking powder, salt and cinnamon into a large bowl and set aside.

Melt the butter in a saucepan over medium heat, and leave it until it starts to brown – you will know it's ready when it stops spitting and bubbling, and has a wonderful, nutty aroma. Strain it through a fine sieve to remove any milk solids, then leave to cool slightly. Weigh out 235 g (8½ oz) for use and discard the rest (or keep for another purpose).

In a separate bowl, whisk the eggs, brown sugar, maple syrup and vanilla until combined. Whisk in the browned butter, then fold this mixture into the dry ingredients to form a thick, runny batter.

Peel, core and grate the pears, and place them in a sieve over the sink. Gently squeeze out a small amount of liquid – you don't want the pear completely dry, but you need to remove enough moisture to ensure that the cake isn't wet when baked. Fold the grated pear through the batter.

Divide the batter between your prepared moulds, filling each one to the top. Bake for 15–17 minutes, until the cake springs back when you touch it lightly. Leave to cool in the moulds for 10 minutes, and then turn them out onto a wire rack to cool completely.

Combine the sugar and cinnamon, and put the vanilla custard into a piping (icing) bag. Roll the cakes in the cinnamon sugar to coat completely, and brush off any excess. Fill the centre of each bundt cake with custard, and serve.

Doughnuts

Makes 10

Ingredients
190 g (6½ oz) bakers flour
25 g (1 oz) caster (superfine) sugar
2 g salt
zest of 1 lemon
8 g fresh yeast
40 g water
10 g lemon oil
2 medium eggs, at room temperature
45 g (1½ oz) butter, diced and soft
1 litre (34 fl oz/4 cups) vegetable oil,
    such as rice bran oil or cotton seed
    oil, for deep frying

Cinnamon sugar
125 g (4½ oz) caster (superfine) sugar
½ teaspoon ground cinnamon

Bakery notes

You need to use strong flour for this dough, with a high protein content, so it can hold the structure when frying. If lemon oil is not available, feel free to use a good extra virgin olive oil.

Make the dough the day before you fry the doughnuts. This allows the yeasty flavour to develop, and achieves a strong dough that is easier to handle.

If you can't get fresh yeast, you can substitute with dried yeast, but just remember that fresh yeast is heavier than dried yeast. One teaspoon of fresh yeast is equal to 1 teaspoon of dried yeast, but 10 g (¼ oz) of fresh yeast is equivalent to 5 g (¼ oz) dried yeast.

Mix the flour, sugar, salt and lemon zest in a medium-sized bowl, and set aside. Combine the yeast, half the water, oil and eggs in the bowl of an electric mixer fitted with the dough hook. Add the flour mixture and mix on medium speed for 10 minutes, adding more water as needed to make a smooth dough.

Add the softened butter slowly while continuing to mix. Mix for 5 minutes, until the butter is fully incorporated. The dough should come away from the bowl and form a ball that is smooth, shiny and slightly sticky. Use the windowpane test to check the dough – take a small ball of dough and gently stretch it between your hands. You should be able to stretch it very thin without it breaking. If you find that it breaks easily, continue mixing for a few more minutes to work the gluten in the flour, then test it again. Leave the dough to rest in the bowl, covered with a damp tea towel, for 1 hour.

After an hour, knock back the dough and fold it by lifting one side up and over the other. Do this five or six times to develop strength in the dough. Transfer the dough to a lightly oiled container, then cover with a damp tea towel and refrigerate overnight to develop a complex, yeasty flavour.

Line two trays with baking paper, and spray the paper lightly with oil. Turn the dough out onto a lightly floured bench and cut it into ten equal pieces. With each piece, gently flatten the dough and bring the edges together in the middle to form a rough ball, then turn it over so the seam is at the bottom. Cup your hand over the dough and use firm pressure to roll it on the bench until it forms a nice tight round ball with a smooth, even surface. Cover the doughnuts again with the damp tea towel, and leave them to rest for 15–20 minutes.

Take each doughnut and knock it flat, then fold the edges into the middle and turn it over so the seam is at the bottom. Using firm pressure, roll it in your hand on the bench again. Putting pressure on the doughnut strengthens the dough so it will rise well. Place the doughnuts on the lined trays, evenly spaced to allow for the eventual rise. Lightly cover with plastic wrap and leave to rise for 2–3 hours, or until risen by half. Test the doughnut by gently pressing the surface. If this leaves a dent, they're ready to fry, but if the dough springs back it still needs more time.

Heat the oil for deep frying to 180°C (360°F) in a large, heavy based saucepan or deep fryer. The temperature is important. If it's too hot, the doughnuts will burn and be raw inside, but if it's not hot enough the doughnuts will stew in the oil and become soggy and greasy. Fry the doughnuts a few at a time, being careful not to overcrowd the pan, for about a minute on each side, until golden. Use a slotted spoon to turn them and remove them from the oil, onto a plate lined with paper towel. Set them aside to cool, then dust them in cinnamon sugar and cut a slit in the side, ready for filling.

Growing up, my Gran would take me to the amusement arcade, where I would watch the doughnuts coming out of the fryer into the cinnamon sugar, and eat them warm. I have always preferred filled doughnuts, however – they are a great way to play with new flavours and textures.

This is the most talked about item at our bakery, and the recipe I get asked for the most. Our doughnuts definitely got us through the early days as Melbourne entered something of a doughnut renaissance.

→

You can be as straight-laced or adventurous as you like with your doughnut fillings. Most people can't go past classic vanilla custard (see page 262) or raspberry jam (see page 278). You can also use the custard as a base to carry other flavours, as detailed here.

Other popular versions at the bakery include crème brûlée (filled with custard and covered with brûléed sugar) and lamington doughnuts (see page 204). You could also use the fillings below and add a different garnish, such as honeycomb or freeze-dried berries, to create interesting textures.

The easiest way to fill the doughnuts is to place the filling in a piping (icing) bag. Slit a hole into each doughnut and insert the tip of the piping bag into it. Fill the doughnuts generously, with a good dollop of filling visible on top. To keep things tidy, it's a good idea to place the doughnuts into patty pans – this stops the doughnuts rolling around and gives people something to hold their doughnut in while they eat.

Fillings

SALTED CARAMEL

Ingredients
395 g (14 oz) tin condensed milk
40 g (1½ oz) vanilla custard (see page 262)
1½ teaspoons sea salt, or to taste

Place the still sealed tin of condensed milk in a large saucepan and cover well with water. Bring it to the boil, then reduce to a simmer for 3 hours, carefully flipping the tin over halfway through cooking. Top up with more water as required, ensuring that the tin is always fully submerged. You will end up with a thick, oozing, sweet reduction.

Leave to cool completely in the fridge, then open the tin and scoop the reduction into a medium sized bowl. Add the custard and season to taste with sea salt. Be careful not to overmix it once you've added the custard, otherwise it will become quite runny and is difficult to rescue.

LEMON CURD

Ingredients
95 g (3¼ oz) caster (superfine) sugar
4 egg yolks
15 g (½ oz) cornflour (cornstarch)
90 g (3 oz) lemon juice
95 g (3¾ oz) butter, soft and diced

In a large metal mixing bowl, whisk together the sugar and egg yolks, then whisk in the cornflour, followed by the lemon juice. Place the bowl over a saucepan half-filled with water (make sure the bowl doesn't touch the water). Place the saucepan over a low heat for about 25 minutes, stirring regularly until the mixture reaches 80°C (180°F) on a sugar thermometer, and becomes very thick. You don't want the mixture to boil, just to stay warm so it thickens and all the ingredients are cooked.

Once you have a thick consistency, take the curd off the heat. Gradually add the cubes of softened butter and whisk to emulsify. Cool in the fridge for 2–3 hours before using.

CHOCOLATE CUSTARD

Ingredients
55 g (2 oz) dark chocolate, roughly chopped
½ quantity vanilla custard (see page 262)

Place the chocolate in a metal mixing bowl. Place the bowl over a pan half-filled with water over medium heat (ensuring the bowl doesn't touch the water), and stir the chocolate until it is completely melted, then fold it into the custard (preferably when still warm). Set aside in the fridge until ready to use.

Rapadura and brazil nut cookies

Makes 12 cookies

Ingredients
165 g (6 oz) butter, soft and diced
200 g (7 oz) rapadura sugar
2 egg yolks
1 vanilla bean, seeds scraped, or
   1 teaspoon vanilla bean paste
215 g (7½ oz) plain (all-purpose) flour
½ teaspoon table salt
½ teaspoon bicarbonate of soda
   (baking soda)
150 g (5½ oz) dark chocolate, at
   least 60% cocoa solids, roughly
   chopped
100 g (3½ oz) brazil nuts, roughly
   chopped
sea salt, for sprinkling

Bakery notes
These cookies are baked from frozen at the bakery to produce that lovely crackly crust and soft centre. Baking from frozen allows the dough to hold its shape longer, spreading less at the start of baking. This creates greater contrast between the crunchy outside and the soft inside. Unfrozen cookie dough will spread more quickly, so you'll get a flatter, crunchier cookie. Baking from frozen also means you can keep a stash in the freezer and break them out as needed.

Rapadura is unrefined whole cane sugar, widely used in Central and South America. The juice is collected from the crushed sugar cane, and set into blocks of deep, golden brown sugar. Being such a pure product, it provides a wonderfully complex, rich caramel flavour. If you can't get hold of rapadura sugar, you can substitute soft brown sugar.

In a stand mixer fitted with the paddle attachment, gently cream the butter and sugar together until it forms a paste. In a separate bowl, lightly whisk the yolks and vanilla, and then gradually add to the sugar and butter mixture, beating well after each addition until fully incorporated.

Sift together the flour, salt and bicarbonate of soda and add to the butter mixture, gently beating until the mixture is just combined.

Add the chocolate and brazil nuts and gently mix until they are evenly distributed through the dough. With wet hands, portion the dough into 12 even balls, then transfer them to a container and freeze for at least 2 hours, or overnight.

The day you want to bake them, preheat the oven to 175°C (350°F). Place the cookies onto a tray lined with baking paper, leaving plenty of space between each, as they will spread quite a lot during baking. Bake for 15–17 minutes, turning the tray if necessary, until golden. Sprinkle each cookie with sea salt and then transfer to a wire rack to cool.

Chocolate buckwheat cookies

Makes 12 cookies

Ingredients
35 g (1¼ oz) unsalted butter, diced
270 g (9½ oz) dark chocolate, at
    least 70%, roughly chopped
55 g (2 oz) buckwheat flour
½ teaspoon baking powder
¼ teaspoon salt
2 large eggs
190 g (6½ oz) soft brown sugar
½ vanilla pod, seeds scraped, or
    ½ teaspoon vanilla paste
sea salt, for sprinkling

Bakery notes
This recipe is all about keeping the air in the mixture so you get that crunchy shell and soft centre. Make sure you use good quality chocolate, at least 70% cocoa solids. I use buckwheat flour, but you could use other flours that are low in gluten and won't develop strength in mixing – rye or spelt would both work well.

If not baking straight away, the cookies can be stored in the freezer already prepped. Just pop them in the oven when needed and bake from frozen for 10 minutes. Once baked, these cookies will last 2–3 days in a sealed container at room temperature, although the crunchy shell will soften a little over time.

An absolute favourite of mine, these cookies were inspired by Elisabeth Prueitt's chocolate rye cookies at Tartine Bakery in San Francisco. After trying those cookies I knew we had to make our own version. I love the combination of chocolate and buckwheat – it's earthy, nutty, bittersweet and slightly salty. Yum!

Bring a half-full saucepan of water to a simmer, then place a metal mixing bowl over it, ensuring that the bowl doesn't touch the water. Put the butter and chocolate into the bowl and melt, mixing occasionally with a spatula to bring them together. (Be careful not to overheat the chocolate.) Turn off the heat and leave the mixture until ready to use. If the mixture starts to set, gently heat it through over the pan until it is melted again.

In a separate bowl, sift together the buckwheat flour, baking powder and salt.

In a stand mixer fitted with the whisk, whisk the eggs, brown sugar and vanilla for about 10 minutes on medium speed until pale, light and airy. Use a spatula to gently fold in the chocolate mixture, in three batches. Be careful to fold very gently so you incorporate the chocolate without losing the aeration in the egg mix. Mix until just combined, making sure you scrape the bottom of the bowl.

Sprinkle half the dry ingredients over the surface of the egg and chocolate mix, and gently fold them through. (Sprinkling the dry ingredients means you don't lose too much of the air.) Repeat with the remaining dry ingredients and mix until just combined, ensuring that you scrape the bottom of the bowl to incorporate everything fully. Pour the cookie dough into a clean container, then cover and refrigerate for 6 hours, or overnight.

Preheat the oven to 180°C (360°F) and line two trays with baking paper. With wet hands, portion the dough into 12 even balls and space them evenly onto the trays. The cookies will spread quite a lot during baking, so make sure you leave plenty of space around each one. Sprinkle the top of each cookie with a pinch of flaky sea salt, then bake for 8–10 minutes, until they look shiny and the top starts to crack. Transfer the cookies to a wire rack to cool before eating.

Monte Carlos

Being British, I had never heard of a Monte Carlo until I was introduced to this genius sweet treat by Ashlea Allen, a wonderful pastry chef who worked with us for several years when we first opened. We created these small cookie sandwiches, which are perfect mid-afternoon with a cup of tea.

This version is a nice way to showcase this delicious Davidson plum jam. Davidson plums are a tropical bushfood unique to the rainforest regions of northern Australia. A sour fruit with a deep burgundy flesh and distinct tart flavour, they are becoming widely available throughout Australia and are definitely worth seeking out. If you find them hard to come by, substitute with other red plums, but reduce the quantity of sugar by half. You could also make a tart berry jam using the recipe on page 278.

Makes 12

Ingredients

Davidson plum jam
250 g (9 oz) Davidson plums
250 g (9 oz) caster (superfine) sugar

Shortbread biscuits
525 g (1 lb 3 oz) plain (all-purpose) flour
1¼ teaspoons baking powder
370 g (13 oz) butter, soft
240 g (8½ oz) soft brown sugar
½ vanilla pod, seeds scraped
2 whole eggs

Buttercream
100 g (3½ oz) icing (confectioners') sugar, sifted
125 g (4½ oz) butter, soft
½ vanilla pod, seeds scraped

Bakery notes

To check if your jam is ready, perform the set test. Put a plate in the freezer before you start to make the jam. Take the plate out when you think the jam is about ready, place a couple of drops of jam on the plate and put it in the fridge for a minute. Draw a line through the jam to check the consistency. Return to the heat if it is looser than you would like.

Any dough left over after cutting the biscuits can be rolled together and frozen for use at another time.

You can spoon the jam and buttercream onto the shortbread biscuits, rather than piping them, but you won't get quite as clean a finish as if you were to pipe them.

Davidson plum jam
Pit the plums (each contains two stones) then finely chop the flesh. Heat the plums and sugar in a saucepan over medium heat, and slowly bring to the boil, stirring constantly to dissolve the sugar. Once the sugar has dissolved, turn the heat up to high and boil rapidly for 5–7 minutes until the setting point is reached (see Bakery notes, above). You want a fairly thick jam, so the consistency should be syrupy. Pour into a sterilised jar (see page 279) and cool completely.

Shortbread biscuits
Sift together the flour and baking powder. In a stand mixer fitted with the paddle attachment, cream the butter until pale. Add the brown sugar and vanilla then cream for another 2 minutes, until the mixture is pale. Add the eggs one at a time, mixing between each addition. Gradually add the flour and baking powder and beat until the mixture just comes together. The dough should be soft and slightly sticky. Divide the dough into two and press each batch into a rectangle 2–3 cm (¾–1¼ in) thick. Wrap in plastic wrap and refrigerate for 30 minutes.

Place each piece of dough between two pieces of baking paper and roll into a sheet 1 cm (½ in) thick, then return to the fridge for around 1½ hours, to set firm.

Preheat the oven to 170°C (340°F) and line two trays with baking paper. Use a 6 cm (2½ in) round cookie cutter to cut out 24 discs and place them on the trays, leaving at least 3 cm (1¼ in) between each. Bake for 10–12 minutes, turning the tray halfway through for an even bake, until lightly golden brown. Transfer to a wire rack and set aside to cool completely.

Buttercream
Place all the ingredients in the bowl of a stand mixer fitted with the paddle attachment and cream until very pale and fluffy.

Assembly
Lay out 12 of your cookies, bottom-side up. Fill one piping (icing) bag with the jam and another with the buttercream. If the buttercream feels soft and difficult to handle, refrigerate for 10 minutes to firm it up a little.

Pipe a thin layer of jam (around 1 tablespoon worth) onto each biscuit, leaving a 5 mm (¼ in) border around the edge. Pipe a thick layer of buttercream directly on top of the jam. Sandwich together with a second biscuit (from the remaining 12) bottom-side down, and gently press down until the jam and cream have spread to the edges. Leave them for at least an hour so the buttercream can set.

Dust with icing sugar to serve, if desired. These biscuits are best eaten the next day, so the flavours can mingle and the biscuits can soften slightly.

Chocolate, rye and walnut brownies

Makes one rectangular 33 × 23 cm (13 × 9 in) tray, (around 24 pieces, depending on how big you like them)

Ingredients
500 g (1 lb 2 oz) dark chocolate, at
    least 70% cocoa solids
210 g (7½ oz) unsalted butter
30 ml (1 fl oz) espresso coffee, or
    1 tablespoon strong instant coffee
150 g (5½ oz) wholegrain rye flour
15 g (½ oz) cocoa powder
½ teaspoon sea salt
6 eggs, at room temperature
450 g (1 lb) soft brown sugar
1 vanilla pod, seeds scraped, or
    1 teaspoon vanilla paste
250 g (9 oz) walnuts, lightly toasted
    and roughly chopped

Bakery notes
To achieve the desired gooey centre and crispy top, it's important to maintain as much air in the mixture as possible. Make sure to fold and mix very gently, and as little as possible, until the ingredients are just incorporated. When whisking the eggs, use a medium speed instead of a high speed. It will take longer but the aeration will be more stable because the bubbles will be smaller and less likely to collapse.

Don't overheat the chocolate or it will crystallise, burn and become bitter. Heat it until it is just melted and don't take it any further.

I am a massive chocoholic, and brownies are about as chocolatey as it gets. I love the contrast between the nice crust and classic soft fudgy centre of a great brownie, with walnuts adding another textural element. We use good quality Valrhona chocolate, and the earthiness of the rye flour complements it perfectly, as well as giving the brownie a beautiful soft, light texture.

Preheat the oven to 180°C (360°F). Grease a 33 × 23 cm (13 × 9 in) baking tray, and line with baking paper.

Half fill a saucepan with water and bring to a simmer, then place a metal mixing bowl over the pan, ensuring that the bowl doesn't touch the water. Melt the chocolate, butter and coffee in the bowl, mixing occasionally with a spatula to combine thoroughly. (Be careful not to overheat the chocolate.) Turn off the heat and leave until ready to use. If the chocolate mix starts to set, gently heat it over the pan until it is just melted again.

In a separate bowl, sift together the rye flour, cocoa powder and salt.

In a stand mixer fitted with the whisk, whisk the eggs, brown sugar and vanilla for about 10 minutes on medium speed until pale, light and airy. Using a spatula, gently fold in the chocolate mixture, in three batches. Be careful to fold very gently so you incorporate the chocolate without losing aeration in the egg mix. Mix until just combined, making sure you scrape the bottom of the bowl.

Sprinkle half the dry ingredients over the surface of the egg and chocolate mixture, and use a spatula to gently fold them through. (Sprinkling the dry ingredients over the mixture means you don't lose too much of the air.) Repeat with the remaining dry ingredients and mix until just combined, ensuring that you scrape the bottom of the bowl to incorporate everything fully. The mixture should be quite runny.

Gently fold in the walnuts until just combined, then pour the mixture into the baking tray. Gently spread it out evenly in the tray using the tip of the spatula.

Bake for 20 minutes, then turn the tray and bake for another 5 minutes. The top should be shiny and smooth, with perhaps one or two cracks appearing. Cool the brownie in the tray for 30 minutes, then transfer to a wire rack to cool completely and sprinkle with sea salt. This will give you nice gooey edges in contrast to the crisp top. Cut the brownies once completely cool, or as needed (they will keep longer uncut). The brownies will last for 5 days in an airtight container at room temperature, or a week in the fridge. (I personally like them straight from the fridge, cold and fudgy.)

SEASONAL

There are a few occasions each year that people like to celebrate with delicious baked goods. This means we always have something to work towards and look forward to, and the different flavours and aromas make it all worthwhile. We like to infuse some local ingredients into the mix and make something a little bit different, whether that means adding macadamias to our Christmas pudding or turning the traditional lamington into a doughnut.

Most of our Christmas items are made months in advance. It is a little odd prepping for Christmas early in the year, but the longer you leave your fruit to soak, the better the result. I would even recommend making a bigger batch up and working a few years ahead. The flavours will be exceptional, and well worth the effort.

We tweaked our hot cross buns for three years until we were finally happy with the balance of the dough, spice and fruit. We were even lucky enough to have Dan Lepard visit us one Easter, and help us refine the recipe. The aroma of gently fragrant spices and citrus during baking is amazing, and will bring your neighbours knocking.

Lamington doughnuts

Makes 10

Ingredients

Coconut coating
200 g (7½ oz) shredded coconut

Chocolate ganache
100 g (3½ oz) dark chocolate, at
    least 70% cocoa solids, roughly
    chopped
280 g (10 oz) whipping cream,
    35% fat
15 g (½ oz) glucose syrup

200 g (7 oz) raspberry jam (see
    page 278)
1 quantity doughnuts (see page 188)

Bakery notes

For a more traditional lamington, the jam, chocolate ganache and coconut crust could also be used on squares of sponge cake.

When coating the doughnuts, use one hand to roll in the chocolate ganache and the other to roll in the coconut. This avoids a messy finish.

These were created as a fun alternative to a traditional lamington. We serve them at the bakery around Australia Day, and for other special Australian occasions.

There's much debate between Australians as to whether a lamington should contain jam or not. My preference is based on taste, not tradition, and I have to say I love the combination of tart raspberry jam, chocolate and coconut.

To prepare the coconut, preheat the oven to 160°C (320°F). Spread the coconut out over a tray lined with baking paper. Bake for 3–4 minutes, until lightly toasted, and set aside to cool.

To make the chocolate ganache, place the chocolate in a medium sized metal bowl. Bring the cream and glucose syrup to a simmer in a heavy based saucepan over medium heat, stirring to combine. Pour the cream over the chocolate and leave to stand for a few minutes so the chocolate can melt, then mix thoroughly, stirring well to ensure there are no lumps of chocolate left.

Put the jam in a piping (icing) bag, make a slit in the side of a doughnut and insert the tip of the piping bag into it. Fill generously, but not so much that it's oozing out of the top.

Holding the doughnut over the bowl, use one hand to cover it in ganache, making sure you coat the entire surface well with chocolate. Repeat for the remaining doughnuts, putting them on a clean tray lined with baking paper as you go.

With clean hands (or clean gloves, if you prefer), roll each doughnut in the coconut, making sure the entire surface is coated. To keep things tidy, it's a good idea to place the doughnuts into patty pans once coated – this will stop the doughnuts rolling around, and gives people something to hold their doughnut in while they eat it.

Anzac biscuits

Makes 12

Ingredients
200 g (7 oz) soft brown sugar
150 g (5½ oz) whole-wheat flour
120 g (4½ oz) rolled oats
50 g (1¾ oz) desiccated (shredded)
   coconut
125 g (4½ oz) butter
50 g (1¾ oz) golden syrup (use honey
   or maple syrup if unavailable)
20 g (¾ oz) water
½ teaspoon bicarbonate of soda
   (baking soda)

Bakery notes
I use whole-wheat flour for more flavour and wholesomeness. For variation, I also like to add 100 g (3½ oz) of currants in with the wet ingredients, just before adding the bicarbonate of soda (baking soda). It can no longer be called an Anzac biscuit if you do that, of course, but it does taste good.

When mixing this dough it is handy to cover your hands with a little oil or water to stop it from sticking to your fingers and make it easier to work with. When measuring the golden syrup, coat the spoon with a little mild-flavoured vegetable oil to get an accurate measurement and avoid a sticky mess.

You can freeze these biscuits to bake later – you'll just need to let them defrost first. The bake time in the recipe produces a chewy biscuit; if you prefer them a little crunchy, leave them to bake for a few more minutes.

Australians grow up hearing about the legendary heroics of the Anzacs during the First World War. This chewy, wholesome biscuit is eaten with delight to commemorate the landing in Gallipoli on 25 April 1915. These biscuits were baked at home and posted to the troops on the frontline. That version notably omitted egg, not just to keep the biscuits from spoiling during the journey, but also because there was an egg shortage at the time, as most of the poultry farmers had enlisted.

I like to eat my Anzac biscuits for a mid-morning snack, with a strong cup of tea.

Preheat the oven to 160°C (320°F). Put the sugar, flour, oats and coconut in a medium sized bowl, and mix to combine.

Combine the butter, golden syrup and water in a medium sized saucepan over low heat, and stir until the butter has melted and the mixture is nice and syrupy. Add the bicarbonate of soda and mix well. The mixture will fizz up a little on reacting with the soda. Pour the syrup over the dry ingredients and mix with your hands until well combined.

Line two trays with baking paper and divide the dough into 12 even balls. Gently flatten each ball with the palm of your hand until you have discs 2 cm (¾ in) high. Space them out evenly on the trays – the cookies will expand a little during baking, so make sure you leave enough space around each one.

Bake for 10 minutes, then turn the trays and bake for another 5 minutes, until lightly golden brown. I like my biscuits a little chewy, but if you prefer a crispier finish leave them in the oven for another couple of minutes. Place the biscuits on a wire rack to cool, then store at room temperature in an airtight container.

Hot cross buns

Easter is our crazy time at the bakery and by far the busiest week of the year. People travel from all over Melbourne to stand in line for our hot cross buns, and have even asked us to post them interstate! We bake around the clock from the Thursday before Good Friday until Easter Sunday, and it's still not enough – Pippa and I usually end up having a hot cross bun-free Easter, as there are never any to spare.

This recipe is precise as we like the exact ratio of spices, but feel free to adjust them to your taste.

Makes 12 buns

Ingredients

Brown sugar glaze
100 g (3½ oz) soft brown sugar
100 g (3½ oz) water
1 cinnamon stick
1 star anise
5 cloves

Dough
200 g (7 oz) full-cream (whole) milk
1 medium orange
500 g + 50 g (1 lb 2 oz + 1¾ oz)
    bakers flour
40 g (1½ oz) soft brown sugar
10 g salt
6 g ground cinnamon
1 g ground allspice
3 g nutmeg, freshly grated
1 g ground clove
1 medium egg, at room temperature
35 g (1¼ oz) fresh yeast
50 g (1¾ oz) butter, ideally cultured,
    softened
130 g (4½ oz) sourdough dough
    (optional) (see page 26)
85 g (3 oz) currants, soaked in water
    overnight
85 g (3 oz) sultanas, soaked in water
    overnight
85 g (3 oz) raisins, soaked in water
    overnight
70 g (2½ oz) mixed peel (mixed
    candied citrus peel) (see page 274)

Cross
50 g (1¾ oz) plain (all-purpose) flour
25 g (1 oz) self-raising flour
pinch salt
pinch sugar
65 g (2¼ oz) water
15 g (½ oz) oil

Egg wash
1 egg
splash full-cream (whole) milk
pinch salt

Bakery notes
There are several factors in making a great bun, starting as always with the ingredients. We always freshly grate the nutmeg, as we find it improves the final flavour. Already ground is fine for the other spices, just try to buy them from a shop with a high turnover to ensure they haven't been sitting around for years.

You need to use strong bakers flour with high protein content for this dough, so it will hold its structure when mixing.

If you can't find mixed peel and don't have time to make it, just use the zest of one lemon and one orange. The flavour lacks the bite of the mixed peel, but it's still good.

At the bakery we add 130 g (4½ oz) of sourdough dough to strengthen the dough and enhance the flavour. If you don't have any sourdough dough you can just leave it out – these will still be very delicious hot cross buns.

You will need to start a day ahead to soak the fruit; if it isn't soaked, the fruit has a tendency to burn on the crust. If you want to make these over two days, just refrigerate the dough overnight after the first fold and finish off the buns the following day. You can also make the glaze ahead of time.

To make the brown sugar glaze, combine the sugar, water and spices in a small saucepan over a low heat. Bring it slowly to the boil, stirring constantly until the sugar has dissolved, then reduce the heat and simmer gently for about 5 minutes to infuse the spices. It will reduce slightly, making a fragrant sticky glaze. Pour the glaze into a container and store it at room temperature.

To start the bun dough, slowly bring the milk to a simmer in a saucepan over a medium heat, being careful not to let it boil. Remove from the heat and set aside to cool.

Place the orange in a medium sized saucepan and cover well with water. Bring to the boil, reduce the heat slightly and continue to boil for about 1 hour, until a knife goes through it easily. Drain, and when cool enough to handle, quarter the orange and remove any pips. Place it in a blender and blend for a minute or two, until you have a smooth puree, then set aside to cool.

Combine 500 g (1 lb 2 oz) bakers flour with the sugar, salt and spices in the bowl of a stand mixer fitted with the dough hook, and stir to combine. In a separate bowl, lightly whisk together the milk, 70 g of the orange puree (you can freeze the rest), egg and yeast, and add to the dry ingredients. Mix for five minutes on

Hot cross buns

a medium speed. Stop the mixer and scrape down the sides and base of the bowl with a spatula to ensure that all of the dry mix is incorporated and that the mixture is forming one large ball of dough. Mix for another five minutes until the dough is smooth and strong, and comes away easily from the sides of the bowl.

With the mixer still running, incorporate the butter and sourdough dough, if using, a little at a time. Make sure they are being incorporated into the dough and not just coating the sides of the bowl – you may need to stop and scrape down the sides once or twice. Mix for 2–3 minutes, until the dough is firm and shiny, not sticky or wet. Use the windowpane test to check the dough. Take a small ball of dough and gently stretch it between your hands – you should be able to stretch it very thin without it breaking. If you find that it breaks easily, mix for a few more minutes to continue working the gluten in the flour, then test it again. If you are mixing by hand, this step will take a good 15 minutes of folding.

Drain the fruit and sprinkle the remaining 50 g (1¾ oz) of bakers flour over it. Add the fruit and the mixed peel to the dough in three batches, then mix for 2–3 minutes, until the fruit is evenly dispersed.

Turn the dough out onto a lightly floured bench, and knead it for about a minute, then place it in a lightly greased bowl and fold it by lifting it up and over itself a few times, turning the bowl 90 degrees between each fold. Leave the dough to rest in the bowl, covered with a damp tea towel, for an hour. If you want to spread the workload over a couple of days, the dough will be fine if left in the fridge overnight at this point.

Knead the dough in the bowl for about 1 minute, then fold the dough by lifting it up and over onto itself a few times, turning the bowl 90 degrees between each fold. Leave it to rest, covered with the damp tea towel for up to 2 hours, or until risen by half. Gently press the dough; it's ready if your finger leaves a dent in the surface. If the dough springs all the way, leave it longer, and then test again.

Turn the dough out onto a lightly floured bench and cut it into 12 equal pieces. Take each piece and gently flatten the dough, then bring the edges together in the middle so it forms a rough ball. Turn it over so the seam is at the bottom, then cup your hand over the dough and roll it on the bench using firm pressure until it forms a nice tight round ball with a smooth, even surface. Cover the buns again with the damp tea towel, and leave them to rest for 15–20 minutes.

Preheat the oven to 200°C (390°F). Line two trays with baking paper. On a lightly floured bench, take each bun and knock it flat, fold the edges into the middle, and then turn it over so the seam is at the bottom. Using firm pressure, roll it in your hand on the bench again. Putting pressure on the bun strengthens the dough; you want a round, firm ball that sits up on the bench rather than a saggy form.

Place the buns on the lined trays, evenly spaced out to allow for the eventual rise (if you prefer the look of clustered hot cross buns, place them side by side). Cover with a damp tea towel and leave to rise for around 2 hours, until risen by half (the timing will depend on the weather). Test the buns again by gently pressing the surface – if your finger leaves a dent, you're ready to bake; if the dough springs back it still needs more time.

To prepare the cross mix, combine all the ingredients in a medium-sized bowl and whisk until it forms a smooth paste. Put this into a piping (icing) bag with a plain nozzle and set aside.

Make the egg wash by lightly whisking the egg, milk and salt in a small mixing bowl, then brush it evenly over the buns. Pipe a cross onto each bun.

Put the trays in the oven, reduce the temperature to 180°C (360°F) and bake for 10 minutes. Turn the tray and bake for a further 3–5 minutes, until golden brown. While the buns are baking, warm the brown sugar glaze in a small saucepan. Once they are baked, use a pastry brush to coat the buns lightly in syrup. Cool slightly on a wire rack, but not for too long. They are best eaten when still warm, though they're also excellent the next day, toasted, with lashings of butter.

MURRAY VIEW ORGANICS

Frank and Pene Porter run Murray View Organics at Koraleigh,
in the central Murray region of New South Wales. Nestled in the
shade of majestic Murray River red gums, the 15 hectare certified
organic farm produces a variety of fresh and dried fruit products.

Tell us about the variety of fruit that you grow?
We grow organic sultanas, raisins, currants and apricots for drying. We also grow
Australian blood limes and sunrise limes. Biodiversity provides eco-cultural balance.
Over time, appropriate species selection has identified varieties suited to our land.
Our plantings create a unique ecosystem, sustaining insects and predators in the way
that nature intended.

What's the overriding philosophy driving your farming practices?
We are sun and soil lovers, second-generation farmers, and passionate advocates
of organic food. Only natural ingredients are used to help the plants overcome the
challenges that nature sends their way. This enhances the flavour and nutrition of the
food that is produced here. The farm size and scope allows individual attention to be
paid to the vigour of vines, trees or plants, which is complemented by a balanced dietary
intake, derived from the soil's pantry of biological microbes, minerals and nutrients.
Our smallness is a strength, providing us with a capacity for meaningful integrity.

Why did you choose to grow organically?
We believe in healthier living through healthier choices. Natural ingredients from organic
sources are essential when creating highly nutritious food and true taste.

How do your drying methods differ from other methods?
We dry fruit outside under the sun, on large racks laid with chicken wire. When the fruit
has dried a little, the racks are vigorously shaken so the fruit drops down onto mats laid
underneath. It is then dried further on the mats, then we rake over the fruit to remove the
branches before it is packed. It's a very simple, age-old method. We don't use any sulphur
or chemical additives. It's just great fruit dried by the sun.

Gingerbread

Makes 24

Ingredients

Gingerbread

585 g (1 lb 5 oz) plain (all-purpose)
   flour
pinch ground clove
⅓ nutmeg, freshly grated
1 teaspoon ground cinnamon
2 teaspoons ground ginger
1 teaspoon bicarbonate of soda
   (baking soda)
½ teaspoon salt
215 g (7½ oz) unsalted butter,
   softened
225 g (8 oz) soft brown sugar
185 g (6½ oz) golden syrup (use honey
   or maple syrup if unavailable)
3 egg yolks, at room temperature

Icing (frosting)

1 egg white
250 g (9 oz) icing (confectioners')
   sugar, sifted
½ teaspoon lemon juice

Here's something for everyone to enjoy at Christmas.
This gingerbread has
enough warm spice to
make a sophisticated treat
for the grown-ups, but
not enough to turn the
kids off. The kids can get
involved in making them,
too; cutting out the shapes
and icing them can be a lot
of fun. The gingerbread
will last up to five days in
an airtight container, so it
makes an excellent gift in
the lead-up to Christmas.

To make the gingerbread, sift together the flour, spices, bicarbonate of
soda and salt in a medium sized bowl. In a stand mixer fitted with the paddle
attachment, cream the butter, sugar and golden syrup until pale but not
too aerated.

With the mixer still running, add the egg yolks one a time, beating between each
addition until just combined. Add the dry ingredients and mix gently on a low
speed, until just combined.

Divide the dough into two pieces and roll each piece out into a disc roughly 2
cm (¾ in) thick. Wrap each disc in plastic wrap and refrigerate for 1 hour, to rest.

Remove the dough from the fridge and roll each disc out between two sheets
of baking paper into a sheet 5 mm (¼ in) thick. Leave them between the
sheets of baking paper and return them to the fridge for an hour, to set firm.

Preheat the oven to 170°C (340°F). Remove the biscuit dough from the fridge
and lay the sheets out on the bench. Line three trays with baking paper, and cut
your shapes out of the dough with cookie cutters, laying them out evenly on the
trays and leaving 2 cm (¾ in) between each biscuit to ensure an even bake. Bake
for 6 minutes, then turn the trays around and bake for another 4–6 minutes,
until the biscuits are golden brown. Set aside to cool completely before icing.

To make the icing, place the egg white in a medium sized bowl and add the
icing sugar one spoonful at a time, whisking lightly to fully incorporate the sugar
between each addition. Whisk through the lemon juice, then transfer the icing
to a piping (icing) bag fitted with a fine nozzle and decorate your biscuits as you
like. The gingerbread is ready to eat once the icing has set.

Pistachio and sour cherry nougat

Makes one 24 cm (9½ in) square tin

Ingredients
6 rice paper sheets
1725 g (3 lb 13 oz) caster (superfine)
    sugar
570 g (1 lb 4 oz) glucose syrup
570 g (1 lb 4 oz) honey
250 g (9 oz) water
300 g (10½ oz) white chocolate,
    roughly chopped
600 g (1 lb 5 oz) whole raw pistachios
420 g (15 oz) dried sour cherries
270 g (9½ oz) egg white (approx.
    9 egg whites), at room temperature

Bakery notes
Timing is very important with this recipe. You need to have the sugar at the correct temperature just as the egg whites come to a meringue, as well as having the chocolate already melted, and the pistachios and cherries warm. It's important to have the nuts and cherries warm so they don't solidify the nougat before you have time to mix them through properly at the end. Read through the method thoroughly before you start making the nougat – it will make the process smoother. Make the nougat the day before you need it, to allow it to set overnight.

SEASONAL—221

The dark red cherries and green pistachios set into snow-white nougat make this treat the very image of Christmas. It's so pretty and festive looking, cut into small pieces for your Christmas table, and it makes a beautiful gift simply wrapped in clear cellophane. The sour cherries are a nice counter to the sweetness of the nougat, and the pistachios add texture and nuttiness.

Lightly grease the sides and base of the tin, then lay the rice paper over the base, shiny side down, so that the sheets are slightly overlapping (cut to fit if needed). Preheat the oven to 170°C (340°F).

In a large stockpot, mix together the sugar, glucose syrup, honey and water. Place over a high heat and bring it up to 140°C (280°F) on a sugar thermometer. This will take about 20 minutes.

Meanwhile, half-fill a saucepan with water and bring to a simmer, then place a metal mixing bowl over it, ensuring that the bowl doesn't touch the water. Put the white chocolate into the bowl and melt, stirring occasionally to remove any lumps. Be careful not to overheat the white chocolate. Turn off the heat and leave until ready to use. If it starts to set, gently reheat it using the same method.

Spread the pistachios out on a baking tray and bake in the oven for 4 minutes, until lightly toasted. Add the cherries to the tray and return it to the oven, then turn the oven off and leave the door slightly ajar. This will help keep the pistachios and cherries warm until you're ready to use them.

Place the egg whites in the bowl of a stand mixer fitted with the whisk attachment. Once the sugar syrup reaches 140°C (280°F), start whisking the egg whites on a medium–high speed until a soft, loose meringue starts to form. By this time your syrup should be at 145°C (290°F). Take it off the heat and, with the whisk still running, pour the syrup slowly into the egg whites in a thin, steady stream, being very careful not to get splattered by the molten sugar. The mixture will increase in volume and become very thick. Turn the mixer down to a low speed and leave it to mix and cool for a few more minutes.

Remove the whisk attachment and add the paddle attachment to the mixer. Mixing on a slow speed, slowly add the melted white chocolate in a thin stream, until totally incorporated. Turn the mixer off, add the nuts and cherries, then turn it back onto a low speed. Mix just until the nuts and cherries are evenly distributed – be careful not to mix for any longer, or the cherries will bruise.

Wearing gloves (this bit gets messy), use a scraper to scoop the nougat out of the bowl into your prepared tray. With wet hands, press the nougat into all the corners of the tin and flatten out the top. Place another layer of rice paper over the top, with the shiny side up, pressing gently to flatten it over the top for a nice even finish. Leave the nougat in a cool dry place to set overnight.

Run a knife around the edge of the tin to loosen the nougat, then invert it over a chopping board, gently pressing the base to release the nougat (it might need a bit of a wiggle). Use a large cook's knife to trim the edges and cut into your desired portions. The nougat will keep for several months at room temperature in an airtight container. Don't store it in the fridge, or anywhere too warm.

Mince pies

Mince pies were one of the earliest written British recipes, first documented in the Middle Ages. They originally contained minced meat, offal and suet, made tasty with generous spicing. They have since evolved into a spiced fruit pie traditionally eaten at Christmas time.

At Tivoli Road we make about 140 kg (300 lb) of fruit mince for our pies, starting in March. We macerate the dried fruit for a couple of weeks, and then when the apple season starts we prepare and add those. Once a month for the next nine months, we give it a good stir and add some Pedro Ximenez. By Christmas we've got a rich, heady mix of plump fruit, liquor and spices. Pedro Ximenez isn't traditionally used, but it adds a lovely rich flavour to the mince. To appease the traditionalists, we also use brandy and apple cider, rounding the flavour out nicely. When the first batch of pies comes out of the oven everyone around the bakery knows that Christmas is coming.

Makes 24 pies

Ingredients

Fruit mince
300 g (10½ oz) currants
300 g (10½ oz) raisins
60 g (2 oz) mixed peel (see Candied mixed peel, page 274)
100 ml (3½ fl oz) brandy
330 ml (11 fl oz) apple cider
60 g (2 oz) soft brown sugar
2 medium cooking apples, peeled and cored and chopped in 1 cm (½ in) dice
25 g (1 oz) unsalted butter
80 g (2¾ oz) raw almonds, roughly chopped
juice and zest of 1 lemon
1 teaspoon ground cinnamon
½ teaspoon freshly grated nutmeg
½ teaspoon ground clove
100 ml (3½ fl oz) Pedro Ximenez

Pastry
800 g (1 lb 12 oz) plain (all-purpose) flour, sifted
25 g (1 oz) table salt
600 g (1 lb 5 oz) unsalted butter, softened
300 g (10½ oz) icing (confectioners') sugar, sifted
105 g (3½ oz) egg yolk (approx. 6 yolks)

Egg wash
1 egg
pinch salt
splash full-cream (whole) milk

100 g (3½ oz) caster (superfine) sugar
10 g (¼ oz) ground cinnamon

Bakery notes
Start this recipe at least one month before you want to eat your mince pies. The longer you leave it, the more flavour the mince will have. Our head baker, Emily, also makes mince pies at home. She creates a suet-based mince mix each year, leaving some for the next year, and some for two years. The complexity of flavour in the two-year aged mince is incredible.

Feel free to adjust the fruit, spices and alcohol to create a mince that suits your tastes. Write down your changes each year to develop your own family recipe.

The pastry will keep in the fridge for a week, and 3 months in the freezer, wrapped well in plastic wrap or in a container.

We use 6.5 cm (2½ in) individual sized foil pie cases for our mince pies. You could use small shallow muffin tins instead, though you may need to adjust the sizes and quantities to suit.

Fruit mince

Place the currants, raisins and mixed peel in a large container with a lid, and stir to combine. Pour the brandy and cider over the fruit and stir it through. Leave the fruit to macerate in the alcohol at room temperature for at least a week or up to three weeks, stirring occasionally for the first few days to thoroughly distribute the liquid – you want it soaked through the fruit, not settled at the bottom of the container.

Once your dried fruit has been soaking for a good week or three, prepare the rest of your filling. First place a colander over a large bowl, then heat a large frying pan over medium heat and sprinkle the brown sugar evenly into the pan. Leave it to melt, and when it starts to bubble, stir the sugar and add the diced apples. Continue stirring until the apples are well coated in caramel, then add the butter and stir for another 30 seconds to make sure that it's melted and fully incorporated into the caramel.

Transfer the apples to the colander to drain the liquid, and set aside to cool. The reserved liquid can either be discarded or kept to use as a delicious caramel sauce – it's great over ice cream or apple crumble. It will keep in the fridge for up to one week.

Once the apples have cooled completely, add them to the macerated fruit mix. Add the almonds, lemon juice and zest, spices and Pedro Ximenez, and mix well with a spoon. Leave the fruit mince to mature at room temperature for at least one month before assembling your mince pies. If keeping aside for longer, mix the fruit once a month, and add Pedro Ximenez or brandy to your liking each time.

Mince pies

Pastry

To make the pastry, place the flour and salt in a medium sized bowl and whisk to combine, and to remove any lumps. Gently cream the butter in a stand mixer fitted with the paddle attachment, until smooth. Add the icing sugar and cream the butter and sugar together to form a paste, mixing on a slow speed to avoid incorporating air into the pastry.

With the mixer still running, add the egg yolks one a time, beating between each addition until just combined. Add the dry ingredients in three batches, mixing slowly between each addition until just combined.

Divide the dough into two pieces and flatten each out into a disc roughly 2 cm (¾ in) thick. Wrap the pastry in plastic wrap and refrigerate for at least 1 hour.

Assembly

Preheat the oven to 170°C (340°F). To make your egg wash, whisk together the egg, salt and milk. In a separate bowl, mix together the caster sugar and cinnamon. Lightly grease twenty-four 6.5 cm (2½ in) foil pie cases with a little butter.

Lay your pastry discs out on a lightly floured bench, and roll each out into a sheet 2 mm (⅒ in) thick. Cut out 24 discs of pastry with a diameter 2 cm (¾ in) larger than the bottom of the pie cases, to form the bases. Next, cut out 24 discs of pastry the same diameter as the cases – these will be the tops of the pies.

Lay the pastry bases over the pie cases, and use your thumb to press the pastry into the corners all the way around. Divide the fruit mince into 24 portions, and fill each case with mince.

Lightly brush the rim of each case with the egg wash, place the pastry lid on top and gently press the two pieces of pastry together to seal the edges. Brush the top of each mince pie with egg wash and sprinkle with a little cinnamon sugar. The assembled pies can be refrigerated for up to five days before baking, or frozen for up to three months. Bake from frozen until the pastry is nicely golden all over.

Place your mince pies onto baking trays and put them on the middle rack in the oven. Reduce the temperature to 160°C (320°F) and bake for 15 minutes, until the pastry is nicely golden. Gently lift one mince pie out of its case and check the pastry on the bottom, to ensure it is cooked through evenly. The pastry should be nice and golden both top and bottom.

Transfer your mince pies to a wire rack and leave to cool slightly before eating. The mince pies will last for 3–5 days in an airtight container at room temperature, although the pastry will start to soften after a day or two.

Christmas cake

Makes one 13 cm (5 in) round cake

Ingredients

Fruit soak
20 g (¾ oz) water
20 g (¾ oz) caster (superfine) sugar
40 g (1½ oz) sultanas
35 g (1¼ oz) currants
70 g (2½ oz) raisins
60 g (2 oz) dried figs, quartered
35 g (1¼ oz) prunes, pitted and
    quartered
35 g (1¼ oz) dates, pitted and halved
25 g (1 oz) mixed peel (see Candied
    mixed peel, page 274)
35 ml (1¼ fl oz) brandy
35 ml (1¼ fl oz) sherry

Cake
65 g (2¼ oz) unsalted butter
55 g (2 oz) soft brown sugar
20 g (¾ oz) treacle (use honey if
    unavailable)
1 tablespoon honey
2 eggs, lightly beaten, at room
    temperature
1 tablespoon marmalade
    (see page 276)
55 g (2 oz) plain (all-purpose) flour
1 tablespoon almond meal

15 g (½ oz) pistachios
15 g (½ oz) almonds
1 teaspoon ground cinnamon
pinch freshly grated nutmeg
pinch ground allspice
pinch ground clove
pinch ground ginger
40 g (1½ oz) dark chocolate
    (70% cocoa solids), roughly
    chopped
brandy

Bakery notes
*You can use almost any nut in this recipe
if you don't have the ones suggested. Make
sure you use good quality chocolate that's
at least 70% cocoa solids.*

*Start soaking the fruit any time from
March, in order to have your cake ready
for Christmas – the longer it soaks, the
better the flavour. We've timed the recipe as
if you're making the cake in early October.
If you're making it closer to Christmas, just
feed it twice a week, and stop feeding it a
week before Christmas so all the alcohol
can settle before you cut into the cake.
The cake will last for months at room
temperature, well wrapped in baking paper
and foil and placed in an airtight container.*

When I worked at Bourke Street Bakery we made a beautiful Christmas cake. I've adapted it slightly after being given the recipe by then-Bourke Street pastry chef, Nadine Ingram. Nadine now owns Flour & Stone in Sydney, a lovely bakery turning out excellent pastries, cakes and savoury food. At Tivoli Road we include pistachios and chocolate, and use our homemade marmalade. This cake has a beautiful marzipan flavour that develops over time, and the bitter dark chocolate brings the nuts and fruit together without being overpowering or too sweet. We cook this cake several months in advance and feed it with brandy weekly until Christmas, producing a rich, boozy cake.

To make the fruit soak, heat the water and sugar in a small saucepan over medium heat, stirring constantly until the sugar has dissolved. Combine all the other ingredients in a large container with a lid, then pour over the sugar syrup and stir well until all the ingredients are thoroughly combined. Leave the fruit to soak, covered, at room temperature for at least a week and up to two months. Stir the mixture through occasionally for the first few days to thoroughly distribute the liquid – you want it soaked through the fruit, not settled at the bottom of the container. The longer you leave it, the more the flavour will develop.

To make the cake, preheat the oven to 140°C (280°F). Lightly grease a 13 cm (5 in) round cake tin and line it with baking paper.

In a stand mixer fitted with the paddle attachment, gently cream the butter and sugar together until smooth. Add the treacle and honey, and continue to beat for another 2–3 minutes, until fully incorporated.

Gradually add the eggs in three batches, ensuring that each addition is fully incorporated before adding the next. Work very slowly to ensure that the mixture doesn't curdle at this stage; if you notice it starting to split, add a small amount of plain (all-purpose) flour to bring it back together. Continue to beat for about 10 minutes, until pale and light.

Take the bowl off the stand mixer and use a spatula to fold the fruit soak and marmalade through the mixture. Add the plain flour, almond meal, pistachios, almonds, spices and chocolate and mix until combined and evenly distributed. It will become a thick, heavy cake batter.

Pour the batter into the tin, then wet your hands and gently flatten the top for a nice finish and an even bake. Bake uncovered for 40 minutes, then loosely cover the top with a piece of foil and bake for another 30 minutes, until the cake is firm to touch and a skewer inserted into the middle comes out clean. Leave to cool in the tin for 30 minutes, then invert the cake onto a wire rack to cool completely.

Once cool, wrap the cake in baking paper and then in a layer of foil. Place it in a sealed container and store it in a cool, dark place. After a week, unwrap the cake and use a skewer to make about 20 holes in the top, about two-thirds of the depth of the cake. Brush the top generously with brandy, so that it soaks into the holes and well into the cake – this is called feeding the cake. Feed the cake weekly for 10 weeks, ensuring it is well wrapped in baking paper and foil after each feed. After the last feed, leave the cake for at least a week before eating, although it will last for several months well wrapped in an airtight container, and will continue to mature with age.

Christmas pudding

I love Christmas pudding, although it is a bit strange eating it during the Australian summer. I usually keep one or two aside to warm up on a particularly foul winter's day. Here we've kept the traditional flavours of Christmas pudding and added some local touches with macadamias and candied cumquats. Macadamias have an almost meaty texture, and I really like them through this pudding. Melbourne is full of cumquats in late winter and our customers bring them into the bakery, picked off their trees, for us to candy.

There are a lot of ingredients to gather for this recipe, but it's actually very simple to make, and the result is extremely satisfying come Christmas Day.

Makes one 1.2 litre (41 fl oz) pudding

Ingredients
125 g (4½ oz) raisins
100 g (3½ oz) sultanas
200 g (7 oz) currants
65 g (2¼ oz) prunes, pitted and chopped
65 g (2¼ oz) dates, pitted and chopped
75 g (2¾ oz) cooking apple, peeled and cored, in 1 cm (½ in) dice
60 g (2 oz) coarse sourdough breadcrumbs (or any kind of coarse breadcrumb)
50 g (1¾ oz) self-raising flour
125 g (4½ oz) dark brown sugar
25 g (1 oz) candied cumquats (see page 274), roughly chopped
2 tablespoons slivered almonds, lightly toasted
15 g (½ oz) almonds, lightly toasted and roughly chopped
15 g (½ oz) macadamia nuts, lightly toasted and roughly chopped
75 g (2¾ oz) suet, coarsely grated (ask your butcher for this)
1 teaspoon ground cinnamon
1 nutmeg, freshly grated
pinch ground allspice
pinch ground ginger
pinch ground clove
2 large eggs
zest and juice of 1 orange
zest and juice of 1 lemon
15 g (½ oz) treacle (use honey if unavailable)
25 ml (¾ fl oz) Pedro Ximenez
75 ml (2½ fl oz) stout
30 ml (1 fl oz) Armagnac

50 ml (1¾ fl oz) brandy, to flambé when serving (optional)

Bakery notes
In keeping with the heady indulgence of yuletide festivities this pudding is laden with alcohol – and for good reason. Pedro Ximenez is a sweet sherry with rich raisin and currant flavours that perfectly complement the spiced fruit. Stout brings a richness and deep chocolatey notes, and Armagnac lends a boozy Christmas cheer to the finished pudding. You can alter the fruits, nuts and alcohol to your taste – just keep the quantities the same to achieve a nice consistency.

Combine the raisins, sultanas, currants, prunes, dates, apple, breadcrumbs, flour, sugar, cumquats, slivered and chopped almonds, macadamias, suet and spices in a large mixing bowl and stir well until thoroughly combined.

In a separate bowl, combine the eggs, orange zest and juice, lemon zest and juice, treacle, Pedro Ximenez, stout and Armagnac and mix well.

Pour the egg mixture over the fruit mixture and use a large spoon to stir it all through, ensuring all the fruit and nuts are well combined and the liquid and spices are evenly distributed. You will have a wet, sloppy mixture. Cover with plastic wrap and leave at room temperature, overnight. The breadcrumbs, flour and fruit will soak up the liquids, so by the following day your mixture should be firmer, with only a little free liquid left in the bowl.

Preheat the oven to 160°C (320°F). Cut two discs of baking paper – one the diameter of the base of the bowl, and one the diameter of the top. Lightly grease a 1.2 litre (41 fl oz) pudding bowl and place the small disc of baking paper in the bottom.

Give the pudding mixture a good stir, then pour it into your prepared basin. Place the large disc of baking paper over the top, then cover the top of the pudding bowl in several layers of foil, tying it tightly in place with a piece of string.

Fill and boil the kettle. Place the pudding bowl in a large, deep saucepan that will contain the bowl. Pour boiling water around the bowl, up to three-quarters of the height of the bowl. Put the lid on the pan or cover well with foil, and cook in the oven for 4 hours. Check the water from time to time, and top up if necessary to ensure the water level is maintained.

Remove the pudding from the oven, leaving the bowl in the larger pot. Set aside until completely cool.

Wrap the bowl well in plastic wrap and store it in a cool, dark place for up to a year. Every couple of months, unwrap the pudding and sprinkle a little brandy or Armagnac over the top. Re-wrap it before storing again. This will keep the pudding moist and add to the final flavour.

On Christmas Day, remove the plastic wrap then cover the top with several layers of foil and tie it with string, as you did when it was first cooked. Gently steam the pudding in a steamer basket or saucepan, immersed in boiling water again, for 1 hour, until warmed through.

Turn the pudding onto a plate, pour over the brandy and set the pudding alight. Serve with your favourite accompaniment: custard, clotted cream or brandy butter.

BRITISH BAKES

The Cornish are fiercely proud of their traditional foods. One of the joys a visitor to the county might experience is a proper Cornish ice cream, clotted cream on a scone, or a traditional pasty (the 'a' is pronounced as in 'has', not 'par-sty').

Cornish people never refer to their pasties as being Cornish. The pasty was historically known as a 'tiddy oggy', 'tiddy' being the local word for 'proper' and 'oggy' being a west-country name for 'pasty'. Proper is a very common word in the local vernacular, and means 'satisfactory'; it is used a lot in phrases like 'proper job', 'proper answer' or 'proper pasty'.

Traditional Cornish pasty

I grew up eating traditional pasties made by my Gran – good skirt steak with onion, potato, swede and nothing else except generous seasoning. The pasty is unique in that the filling and the pastry are assembled raw, and everything bakes at the same time. The meat must be cut, never minced. Vegetables must be sliced or chipped, never cubed. And definitely no peas! When times were lean, the steak was replaced with extra potato and butter to aid the gravy. The pastry acts as a pressure cooker and, once baked, it's left so the filling can stew inside and finish cooking. A pasty is a meal in itself, with no room for more food, just a nice cup of tea.

These days when I go home, our first excursion from Penzance is usually the 16-kilometre (10-mile) drive to Ann's Pasty Shop down at Lizard Point. We buy our pasties, wander down to the lighthouse and eat them, and I know I'm home.

Makes 8

Ingredients

Pasty pastry
700 g (1 lb 9 oz/4⅔ cups) plain (all-purpose) flour
½ teaspoon salt
130 g (4½ oz) lard or beef dripping, in small chunks, chilled
130 g (4½ oz) unsalted butter, in 1 cm (½ in) dice, chilled
360 g (12½ oz) water, chilled

Filling
400 g (14 oz) brown onion (approx. 2 large onions)
280 g (10 oz) swede (approx. 1 medium swede)
280 g (10 oz) old floury potato (approx. 2–3 potatoes), such as desiree, sebago, maris piper or king edward
800 g (1 lb 12 oz) skirt or chuck steak, diced into 1 cm (½ in) pieces

20 g (¾ oz) fine sea salt
white pepper, to taste

Assembly
1 egg, lightly beaten

Bakery notes
Make the pastry in advance so you have it rested from the fridge. The pastry will also freeze well for up to a month.

In Cornwall the vegetables are traditionally 'chipped' – this means cutting them into random pieces using a small sharp knife while holding the vegetable in the other hand. At the bakery we find it more efficient to roughly chop them on a board – just don't leave them in large chunks, or they won't cook properly. Use good quality braising steak such as skirt or chuck, and old potatoes, so they soften and soak up the delicious juices.

To make the pastry, combine the flour and salt in a large mixing bowl. Add the lard and rub it into the flour with your hands until well combined.

Add the well chilled butter and rub it into the flour until it has broken up but there are still pea-sized lumps of butter visible. Pour in the chilled water and continue to mix by hand until you have a smooth and soft dough. You still want to see some streaks of butter, so be careful not to overmix. Wrap the pastry in plastic wrap and refrigerate for at least 1 hour, or preferably overnight.

Peel and roughly chop the onions, swede and potato into roughly 1 cm (½ in) sized, randomly shaped, pieces.

Combine the beef and vegetables in a large bowl, but don't season the mix until you have the pastry ready and you're about to assemble the pasties. This is to avoid the salt drawing water out and creating a wet mess – you want that moisture to come out during cooking, to create a gravy inside the pasty.

Preheat the oven to 190°C (370°F). Generously flour the bench; this allows the pastry to relax as you roll it. Take the pastry out of the fridge and divide it into 8 equal pieces, then roll each piece into circles about 4 mm (¼ in) thick.

Season the filling generously with the salt and white pepper, and mix through thoroughly. Divide the mix between the pastry rounds, placing the filling over the top half of the pastry and leaving a 2 cm (¾ in) margin around the top edge for crimping.

Brush the margin with the lightly beaten egg, then fold the bottom half of the pastry over the mix so the edges meet. Cup your hands around the pasty to bring it all together tightly, then crimp (or tuck) the edges together with your thumb and forefinger to form a seam along the side of the pasty. You can patch any holes with a little dampened, rolled out pastry.

As you finish the pasties place them onto trays lined with baking paper, leaving 5 cm (2 in) between each so they bake evenly. Make a small slit in the top to allow steam to escape while baking, and brush the tops with the egg.

Bake for 10 minutes, then lower the oven temperature to 160°C (320°F) and bake for a further 50 minutes. The pastry will turn a lovely golden brown and the filling will be super hot. Leave them to rest for at least 10 minutes before eating, so they can finish cooking.

Eccles cakes

Makes 8

Ingredients
65 g (2¼ oz) unsalted butter
115 g (4 oz/½ cup) soft brown sugar
275 g (9½ oz) currants
1¼ teaspoons ground allspice
1¼ teaspoons freshly grated nutmeg
¼ teaspoon ground clove
zest of 1 lemon
juice of ½ lemon
25 g (1 oz) Pedro Ximenez
½ quantity puff pastry (see page 252)
1 egg, separated, both white and yolk
     lightly whisked
2 tablespoons raw (demerara) sugar,
     for dusting

Bakery notes
The fruit mix for this recipe can be made well in advance, and it will mature with age, developing wonderfully complex flavours. It will keep for months in a container in the fridge – just stir it through every couple of days for the first week or so, to ensure the liquid is evenly distributed through the fruit, not settled at the bottom.

Pedro Ximenez is a sweet, sticky Spanish sherry. If you don't have any you could use brandy, sherry or red wine instead. The result will have a slightly different flavour, but will be equally delicious.

Years ago our friend Suzanne started a competition on Twitter to find the best Eccles cake in Melbourne. We had to make an Eccles cake as well as something to go with it, so I made potted Stilton to accompany mine – and won! Since then our Eccles cakes have become a bit of a cult item, and sell especially well at the farmers' markets. They're part of my culinary upbringing; we'd have them with tea as an afternoon treat.

These pastries originate from the town of Eccles in Lancashire and are traditionally served alongside hard Lancashire cheese. They are also excellent with a good strong cheddar or Stilton. The strong sharp or pungent cheese and sweet spiced fruit are a match made in heaven.

To prepare the fruit, melt the butter and sugar in a small heavy based saucepan over a high heat, stirring until you have a smooth paste. Reduce the heat to medium and continue to cook slowly for about 5 minutes, stirring occasionally, until the sugar has completely dissolved in the butter. Take the pan off the heat.

In a medium bowl, combine the currants, allspice, nutmeg and clove. Add the spiced fruit to the butter mix, and mix well with a wooden spoon to ensure that the spices, sugar and butter are evenly distributed. Add the lemon juice and zest and the Pedro Ximenez and give it all a good mix, then leave it covered in the fridge for 6 hours or overnight.

Preheat the oven to 190°C (370°F) and line a tray with baking paper. Take the fruit mix out of the fridge and divide it into 8 balls – they should be roughly 60 g (2 oz) each.

Roll the puff pastry to 3 mm (⅛ in) thick. Cut 8 discs of pastry roughly 13 cm (5 in) in diameter, and brush the edges all the way around with the lightly beaten egg yolk. Place a ball of fruit mix in the middle of each disc then bring the edges into the middle and pinch them together so the fruit mix is sealed inside.

Turn the Eccles cakes over so that the sealed pastry edges are on the bottom, and score the top lightly three times (be careful not to cut all the way through the pastry, or the Eccles cakes will split open during baking). Dip the top of each Eccles cake in the egg white and space them out evenly on your pre-prepared baking tray. Sprinkle the tops with the raw sugar.

Bake in the oven for 10 minutes, then reduce the temperature to 175°C (350°F) and bake for another 10 minutes, until the pastry is golden and flaky on the top and bottom. Leave on a cooling rack to cool for 30 minutes, then serve with the cheese of your choice, or on their own, enjoyed with a cup of tea.

Saffron buns

Makes 12 buns

Ingredients

225 g (8 oz) full-cream (whole) milk
1 teaspoon saffron threads
125 g (4½ oz) sultanas, soaked
  in water overnight
125 g (4½ oz) currants, soaked
  in water overnight
500 g + 50 g (1 lb 2 oz + 1¾ oz)
  bakers flour
50 g (1¾ oz) soft brown sugar
10 g salt
5 g (¼ oz) cinnamon
2 g freshly grated nutmeg
zest of 1 orange
1 large egg, at room temperature
35 g (1¼ oz) fresh yeast
50 g (1¾ oz) cultured butter, in
  1 cm (½ in) dice, softened

Egg wash

1 egg
splash of full-cream (whole) milk
pinch salt

Bakery notes

Scalding the milk with the saffron denatures the protein in the milk, which creates a lighter crumb. Infusing the saffron in the milk better distributes the flavour into the buns, too.

You will need to start this recipe the day before to make the saffron milk infusion and soak the fruit.

I grew up in Cornwall eating saffron buns. They're still very common in Cornwall, but nowadays many contain food colouring instead of the real deal. Saffron buns are similar to a hot cross bun in that they're a light bun with fruit, cinnamon and nutmeg, the difference being the subtle note of saffron above all the other spices (and the absence of the cross). They make a lovely morning or afternoon tea served with clotted cream or butter. Some say they're even better the next day, toasted. A large version, saffron cake, is also very popular, and easier to make.

Warm the milk and saffron in a small saucepan over medium heat, until the mixture simmers. Turn it off and leave it in the fridge to cool and infuse for a few hours, or preferably overnight.

Drain the soaked fruit and squeeze out any excess moisture. In a stand mixer fitted with the dough hook, combine 500 g (1 lb 2 oz) of the bakers flour, the brown sugar, salt, cinnamon, nutmeg and orange zest. In a separate bowl whisk the saffron-infused milk, egg and yeast together until the yeast has dissolved.

Pour the egg mix into the bowl with the dry ingredients and mix for five minutes on a medium speed. Stop the mixer and scrape down the sides and base of the bowl with a spatula to ensure that all the dry mix is incorporated and the mixture is forming one large ball of dough. Mix for another five minutes until the dough is smooth and strong, and comes away easily from the sides of the bowl.

With the mixer still running, incorporate the butter slowly, a couple of cubes at a time. Make sure the butter is being incorporated and not just coating the bowl – you may need to stop and scrape down the sides once or twice. Mix for 2–3 minutes, until the dough is firm and shiny, not sticky or wet. Use the windowpane test to check the dough – take a small ball of dough and gently stretch it between your hands. You should be able to stretch it very thin without it breaking. If you find that it breaks easily, continue to mix for a few more minutes to work the gluten in the flour, then test it again.

Sprinkle the remaining 50 g (1¾ oz) of bakers flour over the fruit. With the mixer running, incorporate the dried fruit into the dough in three batches, and mix for 2–3 minutes after each addition, until the fruit is evenly dispersed.

Knead the dough in the bowl for about a minute, then fold the dough by lifting it up and over onto itself a few times, turning the bowl 90 degrees between each fold. Leave the dough to rest in the bowl, covered with a damp tea towel, for an hour. (If you want to spread the work over a couple of days, you can leave the dough in the fridge overnight at this stage – it will be fine.) Once again fold the dough by lifting it up and over onto itself a few times, turning the bowl 90 degrees between each fold. Leave it to rest, covered with the damp tea towel for 2 hours or until risen by half, and gently pressing it leaves a dent (if it is still springy, leave it for a bit longer then test it again).

Turn the dough out onto a lightly floured bench and cut it into 12 equal pieces. Take each piece and gently flatten the dough. Bring the edges together in the

→

middle so it forms a rough ball, then turn it over so the seam is at the bottom. Cup your hand over the dough and roll it on the bench using firm pressure until it forms a nice tight round ball with a smooth, even surface. Cover the buns again with the damp tea towel, and leave them to rest for 15–20 minutes.

Line two trays with baking paper. Take each bun and knock it flat, fold the edges into the middle, then turn it over so the seam is at the bottom. Cup your hands over the bun and roll it in your hand on the bench again, using firm pressure, to make tight round balls that sit up on the bench. Putting pressure on the bun strengthens the dough so it will rise well.

Place the buns on the lined trays, evenly spaced to allow for the eventual rise. Cover with a damp tea towel and leave to rise for 2–3 hours, until risen by half. Test the buns by gently pressing the surface – if it leaves a dent, you're ready to bake; if it springs back it still needs more time.

Preheat the oven to 200°C (390°F). Lightly whisk the egg, milk and salt in a small mixing bowl to make the egg wash, and brush it evenly over the buns. Put the trays in the oven, reduce the temperature to 180°C (360°F) and bake for 10 minutes. Turn the tray and bake for a further 3–5 minutes, until golden brown. Cool slightly on a wire rack. They are delicious still warm from the oven, with clotted cream.

Sultana, buttermilk and lemon zest scones

Makes 12

Ingredients
100 g (3½ oz) sultanas
400 g (14 oz/2⅔ cups) plain
 (all-purpose) flour
100 g (3½ oz) whole-wheat flour
15 g (½ oz) baking powder
2 g salt
70 g (2½ oz) soft brown sugar
zest of 1 lemon, finely grated
220 g (8 oz) butter, in 1 cm (½ in) dice,
 chilled
300 g (10½ oz) buttermilk
1 whole egg
pinch salt

Bakery notes
I use a little bit of whole-wheat flour in these scones because I like them to taste wholesome and homely. You could use just plain flour if you prefer. The dough keeps well in the freezer and can be baked from frozen as required.

My Gran made excellent scones when I was a kid. The Cornish are sticklers for the way scones are served – we always put the jam on first, followed by the cream. It seems the only proper way. Buttermilk, zest and sultanas make these scones really flavoursome. They are an excellent stage for cream and jam, which need to be applied lavishly.

Cover the sultanas with water and leave to soak for an hour.

Sift together the flours, baking powder and salt in a large mixing bowl, then mix in the sugar and lemon zest.

Tip the dry ingredients out onto the bench and scatter over the cubed butter. Use a rolling pin to break the butter into the flour, gathering the flour in as you go until you have a crumbly textured mixture with pea-sized lumps of butter still visible. Having small chunks of butter helps the scones rise, so be careful not to overmix at this stage.

Drain the sultanas and squeeze out any excess liquid, then make a well in the dry ingredients and pour the buttermilk and sultanas into the middle. Use a spoon to gently 'cut' the flour into the wet mix. You want to bring it together into a dough, handling it as little as possible so you don't melt the butter or work the gluten in the flour. Tip it onto a lightly floured bench and gently push the ingredients together into a slab about 4 cm (1½ in) high.

Cut out the scones using a 6½ cm (2½ in) round cookie cutter and place them on a tray lined with baking paper, evenly spaced. Refrigerate the scones for a couple of hours to set the butter back into the dough.

Preheat the oven to 200°C (390°F). Lightly whisk the egg and salt, and brush this mixture onto the top of each scone (any leftover buttermilk would also work well for this). Place the tray in the oven and turn the heat down to 180°C (360°F). Bake for 15 minutes, then turn the tray around and bake for another 5 minutes. These are best eaten fresh on the day they're baked, preferably still warm with lashings of jam and cream, and a nice cup of tea.

Treacle and vanilla salt tart

Makes one 23 cm (9 in) tart (serves 8)

Ingredients
½ quantity sweet pastry, chilled (see page 255)

Treacle filling
90 g (3 oz) eggs (approx. 2 small eggs)
40 g (1½ oz) thick cream
1 teaspoon table salt
454 g (1 lb) golden syrup (1 tin) (use honey or maple syrup if unavailable)
90 g (3 oz) butter
85 g (3 oz) sourdough breadcrumbs
zest of 1½ lemons
juice of 1 lemon

Vanilla salt
½ vanilla pod, seeds scraped
1 teaspoon sea salt

clotted cream or crème fraîche, to serve

Bakery notes
Start this recipe at least a day before you want to eat the tart. Once mixed, the filling needs to be rested overnight to allow the breadcrumbs to absorb the syrup properly. If you choose to age the syrup, you'll need to start this recipe three days ahead. To save time on the day, you could also blind bake the pastry case and mix the vanilla salt the day before.

We make breadcrumbs from our spelt and honey sourdough because its nuttiness and honey notes add to the richness and complexity of this tart. Plain sourdough crumbs, or any coarse breadcrumbs, will also work well.

We use Tate & Lyle golden syrup as it has the best flavour of any that we've tried. We 'age' the syrup in the oven over two nights at a very low temperature to develop the flavour. This gives it a rich caramel, toffee flavour. It will keep in the tin once aged for years, so you could do a few tins at a time if you're a treacle tart lover.

To age the golden syrup, start three days ahead. Preheat the oven to 80°C (180°F) and place the tin, still sealed, on the centre rack. Leave overnight, then remove and leave at room temperature for the day. Repeat the following night.

On a lightly floured bench, roll the pastry out into a large disc, 5 mm (¼ in) thick. Lightly grease a 23 cm (9 in) round tart tin with butter, and gently lay the pastry over it. Press the pastry firmly into the base of the tin. Trim the excess with a knife, then place the tart shell in the fridge to rest for an hour.

Preheat the oven to 160°C (320°F). To make the filling, whisk together the eggs, cream and salt in a large mixing bowl and set aside. Warm the tin of golden syrup in the oven for a few minutes. This makes the syrup more viscous, so it's easier to get out.

Brown the butter in a saucepan over medium heat. Once melted, leave it until it starts to brown – you will know it's ready when it stops spitting and bubbling, and produces a wonderful nutty aroma. This means the water has evaporated and it's close to burning. Strain through a fine sieve to remove the solids, and weigh 60 g (2 oz) into a medium sized bowl.

Add the warmed golden syrup to the butter and mix to combine. Stir this into the egg mixture, then add the breadcrumbs, followed by the lemon zest and juice, stirring well between each addition. Chill the mixture in the fridge overnight to allow the breadcrumbs to absorb all the liquid.

The next day, to blind bake the tart shell, line the rested pastry case with baking paper and fill with dried beans, rice or baking weights. Bake for 20 minutes, then remove the paper and beans and bake the tart shell for a further 10 minutes, until lightly golden. Set aside to cool in the tin.

To make the vanilla salt, rub the vanilla seeds and sea salt together. You will have more than you need, but it keeps for ages in a small jar, so you can save it for later.

Preheat the oven to 155°C (310°F). Take the breadcrumb mix out of the fridge. It will have separated slightly, so mix it with a spoon until it comes back together then pour it into a jug.

Place the tart shell on a flat tray lined with baking paper. Place the tray in the oven, then gently pour in the treacle mixture. Fill the pastry case to just below the rim, as it will expand a bit in the oven. Bake for 45–50 minutes, until just set. The filling should be just firm on the edges and have a bit of wobble in the centre, like a jelly.

Place the tart on a wire rack to cool, then remove the tart from the tin and transfer onto a serving dish. Sprinkle the top with the vanilla salt, and serve with a dollop of clotted cream or crème fraîche, if desired.

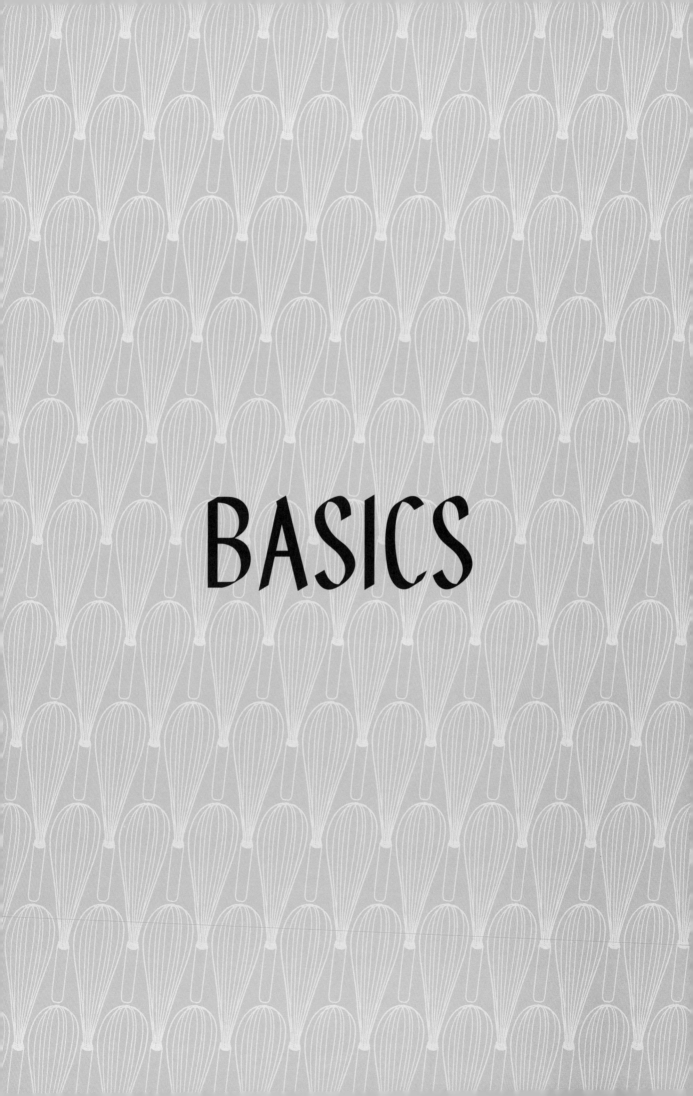

BASICS

Here are the building blocks for many of our recipes. Some of them, like the puff and choux pastry, take time and practice. Others are simple to achieve. All of these pastry recipes will freeze well. I like to make them in large batches so I can pull them out when inspiration strikes.

If you're interested in learning to make croissant pastry, making puff pastry is a good place to start. It's a bit simpler and much more forgiving, as it doesn't contain yeast. This is a great way to learn to roll pastry at home, laminating your butter into the dough for beautiful flaky layers.

We're not reinventing the wheel here, but are confident in these recipes as foolproof baking basics. Take the time to learn them and you will end up with much better quality pastry than anything you could buy from a supermarket or shop, and your baking will ultimately be much more satisfying.

Puff pastry

Makes 830 g (1 lb 13 oz) dough

Ingredients
70 g (2½ oz) unsalted butter, chilled
150 g (5½ oz) water
10 g white vinegar
340 g (12 oz) plain (all-purpose)
  flour, sifted
10 g salt
250 g (9 oz) unsalted butter, at room
  temperature

Bakery notes
Start this recipe two days before you need it. Make the dough and prepare the butter on the first day, then on the second day laminate the dough and let it rest overnight again before using it. It will last well for up to a month in the freezer.

Unless you have great air conditioning in your kitchen, don't attempt puff pastry on a hot day – the butter will melt into the pastry rather than laminate properly. If you find the dough is getting too soft, put it in the fridge after each fold rather than after every second fold. We suggest refrigerating for an hour between folds, but you can leave it longer – just take it out of the fridge 15 minutes before you roll it to avoid breaking the butter.

Flaky pie lids, delicious sausage rolls ... so many wonderful foods rely on a great puff pastry. This recipe requires time and dedication, but the resulting buttery, flaky pastry is more than worth the effort.

Most of the recipes in this book that use puff pastry use a half quantity, but you will find it easier to block in a larger amount of butter. And as you're going to the effort of making your own puff, it is nice to have any leftover pastry on hand in the freezer for next time.

Take the 70 g (2½ oz) of butter out of the fridge, dice into cubes, then leave for 10 minutes to soften slightly before you start – you want it to be cold, but pliable.

Combine the water and vinegar in a jug. Put the flour, salt and diced butter into the bowl of a stand mixer fitted with the paddle attachment. Beat the butter into the flour, mixing until you have pea-sized lumps of butter. With the mixer still running, pour in the combined water and vinegar and mix until the dough just comes together. You don't want any dry pieces, but you need to be careful not to overwork it.

If you are mixing the dough by hand, combine the flour and salt in a medium sized bowl and toss through the diced butter. Use your fingertips to rub the butter into the flour, as above, then pour the combined water and vinegar evenly over the top. Mix to combine and then tip the dough out onto a lightly floured bench. Knead the dough until it is smooth. Again, you want to make sure there are no dry pieces but also avoid overworking the dough.

Flatten the dough into a rectangle about 1 cm (½ in) thick. Wrap it in plastic wrap and rest it in the fridge overnight.

To prepare the butter block for laminating, place it between two sheets of greaseproof paper and roll it out into a square about 1 cm (½ in) thick. Refrigerate it overnight.

The next day, remove the rolled-out butter and the dough from the fridge about half an hour before you laminate the pastry. You want them both to be of similar consistency, and the butter to be malleable but not soft (this helps to maintain the dough and butter as separate layers as you laminate).

At this stage the dough may be sticky, so keep your work surface well dusted with flour while you roll and fold the dough. If the dough sticks to the bench it will be harder to roll out a nice, even rectangle and may cause the dough to tear.

Roll out the dough into a rectangle 12 × 24 cm (4¾ × 9½ in), with the long edge towards you. Place the butter block in the centre of the dough and fold in each free side of the dough so they meet in the middle like a book. The dough should join together along the seam.

Roll the dough away from you to form another rectangle 12 × 24 cm (4¾ × 9½ in). You want the open edges, where the butter is visible, to measure 12 cm (4¾ in). Rotate 90 degrees, and fold one third of the pastry into the middle, then the other third over the top of that, as if folding a letter.

Roll the dough away from you again to form another rectangle 12 × 24 cm (4¾ × 9½ in). Rotate 90 degrees, and do another letter fold. Rotating the block each time you fold it will give a more even lamination, and should make it easier to roll out.

Wrap the dough in plastic wrap and refrigerate it for at least an hour. Chilling your pastry between folds helps to keep the layers separate and allows the dough to relax a bit, which will make it easier to roll out and prevent it from shrinking back.

Take your pastry block out of the fridge and, starting with the 'hinge' (the closed edge of the letter fold) on the left-hand side, roll into a rectangle 12 × 24 cm (4¾ × 9½ in). Rotate the block 90 degrees, do another letter fold and then repeat the rolling and folding once more, so that all up you have performed four letter folds (two before chilling, and two more just now). A good trick for keeping track of how many folds you've done is to make an indent in the top surface with your finger after each fold.

Once done, wrap your block of puff pastry again and let it rest in the fridge for at least an hour, preferably overnight, to stop it shrinking. Then it's ready to use!

Sable pastry

A wonderfully light and biscuity pastry, this sable makes an excellent base for freeform tarts made with curds or custards, and piled high with fresh fruit. Easy to prepare, these are a fantastic option for an impromptu dinner celebration or last-minute party invite.

We use this pastry for our Strawberry and chamomile tart (see page 164) and our Raspberry and goat's milk tart (see page 168).

Makes 1 kg (2 lb 3 oz)

Ingredients
285 g (10 oz) unsalted butter, diced and softened
110 g (4 oz) icing (confectioners') sugar, sifted
½ vanilla pod, seeds scraped (or ½ teaspoon vanilla bean paste)
285 g (10 oz) plain (all-purpose) flour
¼ teaspoon table salt

In a stand mixer fitted with the paddle attachment, gently cream together the butter, icing sugar and vanilla until you have a smooth paste, mixing slowly to avoid incorporating air into the mixture.

In a medium sized bowl, whisk together the flour and salt then add to the creamed butter mixture in three increments, beating slowly with the paddle between each addition. After the third addition, mix until just combined.

If you are mixing by hand, place the butter, icing sugar and vanilla in a medium sized bowl and beat with a wooden spoon for several minutes, until smooth. Add the flour and salt a little at a time, ensuring that each addition is fully incorporated before adding the next. Mix until just combined – there should be no flour visible.

Tip the pastry out onto a lightly floured bench, then divide it into two pieces and flatten each out into a disc 2 cm (¾ in) thick. Wrap them in plastic wrap and rest it in the fridge for at least one hour, then use as desired. Sable pastry will keep in the fridge for a week and in the freezer for up to three weeks, wrapped well in plastic wrap or in a container.

Choux pastry

You need to use strong flour with a high protein content for this pastry, so it can hold the structure when baking. This will produce a lovely crisp bite, and an airy centre.

We use this pastry for our Chocolate and wattleseed éclairs (see page 174). It can be used for any recipe calling for choux pastry, such as profiteroles or gougères.

Makes 1.2 kg (2 lb 10 oz)

Ingredients
220 g (8 oz) bakers flour
350 g (12½ oz) eggs, at room temperature (approx. 7 eggs)
400 g (14 oz) water
185 g (6½ oz) unsalted butter, roughly chopped
7 g (¼ oz) salt
7 g (¼ oz) caster (superfine) sugar
30 g (1 oz) whole milk powder

Bakery notes
It's best to use this pastry straight from the fridge, so it's easier to handle. If you are still practising your piping skills, you can manipulate the piped pastry with wet hands to fix any messy bits.

Like a croissant or a soufflé, there will be a marked initial rise in the oven. This is dependent on maintaining a steady heat to allow for good lift. It's important not to open the door during baking, or you will end up with an inferior rise.

Sift the flour into a medium sized bowl. In a separate bowl, gently beat the eggs together.

Combine the water, butter, salt and sugar in a saucepan and bring to a simmer over a medium heat. Add the milk powder and whisk to dissolve.

Take the pan off the heat, add the sifted flour and whisk to combine, then return the saucepan to the stove and cook out the flour over a low heat for 2–3 minutes, stirring constantly until the dough starts to pull away from the sides of the pan.

Transfer the dough to the bowl of a stand mixer and beat on low speed for two minutes, using the paddle attachment, to cool slightly. Gradually beat in the eggs, in four additions, ensuring that each is fully incorporated into the dough before the next is added.

Pour the pastry into a clean bowl, and cover the surface with plastic wrap to avoid a skin forming. Rest the pastry in the fridge for at least half an hour before using.

Sweet pastry

This is a reliably versatile pastry that's perfect for the range of tarts we make in the bakery (think fresh fruit, lemon meringue and cherry pie).

This is the pastry we use for our baked custard (see page 163) and treacle tarts (see page 244).

Makes 1 kg (2 lb 3 oz)

Ingredients
200 g (7 oz) unsalted butter, diced and softened
200 g (7 oz) caster (superfine) sugar
110 g (4 oz) eggs (approx. 2 large eggs)
500 g (1 lb 2 oz/3⅓ cups) plain (all-purpose) flour
½ teaspoon salt

Bakery notes
There is no water in this recipe, which means you'll have minimal shrinking. It holds its shape well and produces a beautiful crisp crust.

In a stand mixer fitted with the paddle attachment, gently cream the butter and sugar just until smooth, mixing slowly to avoid incorporating too much air as you beat it. Add the eggs one at a time until just combined, then add the flour and salt in two additions. Mix very gently for 10 seconds, until the pastry just comes together.

If you are mixing by hand, place the butter and caster sugar in a medium sized bowl and beat with a wooden spoon for several minutes, until smooth. Add the eggs one at a time, ensuring the first is fully incorporated before adding the next. Use a wooden spoon to fold through the flour and salt, until just combined.

Tip the pastry out onto a lightly floured bench, then divide it into two pieces and flatten each out into a disc 2 cm (¾ in) thick. Wrap them in plastic wrap and rest in the fridge for at least 1 hour, then use as desired. Sweet pastry will keep in the fridge for a week and in the freezer for up to three weeks, wrapped well in plastic wrap or in a container.

Savoury shortcrust pastry

Shortcrust is the workhorse of the pastry world, providing a firm base for pies, quiches and savoury tarts. Luckily, it is an easy dough to master. Nothing you can buy will ever taste like the shortcrust you make at home.

Makes 540 g (1 lb 3 oz)

Ingredients
90 g (3 oz) water
10 g white vinegar
320 g (11½ oz) plain (all-purpose) flour
10 g table salt
110 g (4 oz) unsalted butter, cold, cut into 1 cm (½ in) dice

Bakery notes
This dough will set hard as it contains lots of butter, so take it out of the fridge at least an hour before using, so it's easy to roll. You want the pastry to be malleable without being too soft. Having a few streaks of butter visible in the finished dough will result in a flaky texture once baked.

Combine the water and vinegar in a jug. Put the flour, salt and butter in the bowl of a stand mixer fitted with the paddle attachment and beat the butter into the flour, mixing until you have pea-sized lumps of butter. With the mixer still running, slowly pour in the combined water and vinegar, and mix until the dough just comes together. You don't want any dry pieces, but you need to be careful not to overwork it. You can add a bit more water if you have any dry clumps, but don't let the dough get sticky.

If you are mixing the dough by hand, combine the flour and salt in a medium sized bowl and toss through the chilled butter. Use your fingertips to rub the butter into the flour until just combined and you still have pea-sized lumps of butter visible. Tip the mixture out onto the bench. Slowly pour the combined water and vinegar over the top, using the heel of your hand to work the mixture into a dough. Push it away from your body and then gather it together with both hands. Repeat this a few times until it all comes together and no flour is visible.

Wrap the dough in plastic wrap, and refrigerate for at least an hour before using. If it's wrapped well, savoury shortcrust will keep for a week in the fridge, or up to three months in the freezer.

GRAZING PADDOCKS

Michelle Ellis and Di Stannard used to live on the same street as the bakery. They moved to a property near Mount Macedon in 2015, with the dream of raising heritage-breed chickens for egg laying.

How did you come to be where you are?

As children, we were both fortunate to have families involved in farming in Western Australia. After moving from Perth to Melbourne, our interest in fair food and sustainability came to the fore. We routinely shopped at farmers' markets and tried where possible to minimise supermarket purchases. Along this journey, we met many inspirational farmers who became firm friends. This also reinforced our desire to own a farm and be part of the fair food movement.

As a result, we decided to stop being passengers and to do something. The journey to find our farm took two and a half years. After several unsuccessful offers on other farms, the day after we sold our inner city Melbourne property we chanced upon Spring Hill. The next week our new farm was listed, and within a fortnight, we had placed a successful offer on it. We moved to the farm in January 2015.

Why did you decide to raise heritage-breed chickens?

Joel Salatin (American holistic farmer) inspired us to raise chickens alongside cattle as part of a system for natural soil regeneration. Not being fans of the super fast-growing Cobb/Ross chickens that are slaughtered at 6–8 weeks old, we decided to go back to basics and raise dual purpose (meat and eggs) heritage-breed chickens. They are hardy birds, look beautiful and are what our grandparents and generations before them would have had.

Being involved in heritage breeds is our way of being part of the slow-food movement by being able to grow animals that are true to breed, that grow at a natural rate, live their lives as naturally as possible and are free to safely roam our grazing paddocks.

What's the egg yield per chicken of your flock?
We have found egg yield varies based on age and weather conditions. Most new layers produce an egg daily. This shifts at around one year of age to an egg every two or so days. Warmer weather can impact our yield, as it can make the hens go 'broody', which is when they decide to try and hatch eggs even if there are no eggs under them and they stop laying. Moulting is also a period where egg production drops or ceases.

How does this yield differ from conventional egg farming?
Conventional hybrid hens such as Isa Browns, Bond and Lohmann Browns are genetically modified to lay at unnaturally high levels: 300+ eggs a year. This high output comes at the expense of their longevity. Most egg producers turn over their stock after a year or two, selling hens or processing them as 'spent hens'.

Heritage-breed chickens haven't been genetically modified, and possess all the natural behaviours a chicken should. They take regular breaks from laying, lay at different times during the day and live longer. On average they lay 200–250 eggs a year.

How do you manage the land raising free-range birds?
Alongside our chickens, we also raise Dexter cattle. Our cattle and our chickens work together. We strip/cell graze our cattle in paddocks, and once the grass length is suitable for the chickens, we move them in. The chickens are all free to roam safely within electrified poultry nets during daylight hours. They get to fly, scratch, forage, eat bugs and worms (and the occasional frog), stretch their wings and sleep safely at night in their handmade chicken tractors.

What is your vision for the future of your business?
We're gradually increasing our flock size to approximately 250–300 heritage hens. We're also looking at offering a limited and exclusive quantity of pastured heritage meat birds, as well as increasing our Dexter herd size and offering grass-fed Dexter beef in the future. Dexter meat is lean, and of excellent quality and flavour with good marbling.

We have planted a small heritage orchard on the farm, which includes apples, pears, quince, cherries, nectarines and figs. Once they're producing, we plan on offering preserves and relishes. We also plan on running open farm days and workshops, which will enable us to engage with the public. We look forward to sharing our farm, story and produce with others.

Vanilla custard

This is a light custard and not too sweet, making it the perfect filling for our doughnuts and fresh fruit tarts, and for finishing our Viennoiserie. This is the custard you want to eat with poached fruit and crumble after dinner on a cold evening, or with fresh berries in a tart case for a quick delicious dessert during summer. Rather than dominating with a rich, sugary custard, it lets other flavours shine through and plays a supporting role.

Makes approx. 600 ml (20½ fl oz)

Ingredients
500 g (1 lb 2 oz) full-cream (whole) milk
1 vanilla pod, seeds scraped or 1 teaspoon vanilla bean paste
6 egg yolks
60 g (2 oz) caster (superfine) sugar
40 g (1½ oz) plain (all-purpose) flour

Bakery notes
If you like your custard very thick, just cook it out for a bit longer than specified. Stir it continuously and be careful not to leave it unattended, to avoid it sticking and burning.

You can use this recipe as a vehicle for other flavours by infusing the milk as you warm it. Fig leaves, lemon verbena, cinnamon and citrus rind are all excellent options.

Combine the milk and vanilla (seeds and pod) in a heavy based saucepan, and bring to a simmer over a medium heat. Remove the vanilla pod.

While the milk comes to a simmer, whisk together the egg yolks and sugar in a medium sized bowl, until slightly pale. Add the flour and whisk to combine.

Pour the milk over the egg mixture, whisking constantly as you go to avoid scrambling the eggs.

Return the custard to the saucepan and cook over a low heat for around 5 minutes, stirring constantly to avoid burning. Alternate between using a whisk and a spatula, as described in the bakery notes below. The custard will become thick, and just start to bubble. As soon as this happens, remove it from the heat and strain the custard through a fine sieve into a clean bowl. Lay a piece of plastic wrap over the surface to avoid a skin forming, then refrigerate the custard to cool it completely. This custard will keep for 3–5 days in the fridge.

Pastry cream

This recipe makes a more traditional pastry cream that holds its shape when baked. It has more flour for added strength, and uses cornflour to help make a thicker custard that's perfect for holding fruit on our Danishes, or for any recipe where the vanilla custard isn't strong enough.

Makes approx. 500 ml (17 fl oz/2 cups)

Ingredients
325 g (11½ oz) full-cream (whole) milk
35 g (1¼ oz) unsalted butter
½ vanilla pod, seeds scraped
4 egg yolks
90 g (3 oz) caster (superfine) sugar
15 g (½ oz) plain (all-purpose) flour
20 g (¾ oz) cornflour (cornstarch)

Bakery notes
When cooking out the custard, I like to use a whisk and a spatula, alternating between the two. The whisk helps to mix everything together thoroughly and to get rid of any lumps as they appear. I use the spatula to scrape the sides and base of the pan, to stop any spots catching while it's cooking. This results in a smooth, consistent custard with no risk of scorching.

Combine the milk, butter and vanilla (seeds and pod) in a heavy based saucepan, and bring to a simmer over medium heat. Remove the vanilla pod.

While the milk is coming to a simmer, whisk together the egg yolks and sugar in a medium sized bowl, until slightly pale. Add the plain flour and then the cornflour, whisking to combine after each addition.

Gradually pour the milk over the egg mixture, whisking constantly as you go to avoid scrambling the eggs.

Return the custard to the saucepan and cook for about 5 minutes over a low heat, stirring constantly to avoid burning. Alternate between using a whisk and a spatula, as described above. The pastry cream will become very thick and will just start to bubble. It should be nice and shiny, with no lumps. Remove it from the heat and strain the pastry cream through a fine sieve into a clean bowl. Lay a piece of plastic wrap over the surface to avoid a skin forming, then refrigerate to cool it completely. The pastry cream will keep for 3–5 days in the fridge.

LARDER

A well-stocked larder brings great comfort. Just a small amount of these intensely flavoured preserves makes simple food truly delicious.

I became interested in fermentation through making bread, and my curiosity about old methods of producing food continues to expand. Our larder range started with chutneys, which we made for our sandwiches. Customers started asking if they could buy them to take home, so we jarred them up and put them on the shelves. We now make batches of different jams, pickles and preserves each week to keep up with demand. The tomato chilli jam is perfect with our beef cheek, stout and treacle pie, and is never out of production.

Fermenting, pickling, candying and preserving have been done for centuries in many cultures. They are a great way to deal with seasonal gluts and extend availability of fruits and vegetables beyond their seasons.

Make them in large batches in advance – that way, when you are short of time, you can just open a jar and have a snack or create a meal. Most of these recipes keep well and age even better; they also make great handmade gifts.

TIVOLI&BAKERY

BREAD & BUTTER PICKLES
LEBANESE CUCUMBERS,
SHALLOTS, APPLE CIDER
VINEGAR, SUGAR,
SEA SALT, SPICES.

TIVOLI&BAKERY

RED ONION CHUTNEY
RED ONIONS, APPLES,
RAISINS, FRESH GINGER,
RED WINE VINEGAR,
DARK BROWN SUGAR,
SPICES.

TIVOLI&BAKERY

BREAD & BUTTER PICKLES
LEBANESE CUCUMBERS,
SHALLOTS, APPLE CIDER
VINEGAR, SUGAR,
SEA SALT, SPICES.

Bread and butter pickles

**Makes two 1-litre
(34 fl oz/4 cup) jars**

Ingredients
900 g (2 lb) Lebanese cucumbers,
   sliced into ½ cm (¼ in) thick
   round slices
330 g (11½ oz) shallots, peeled and
   sliced to ½ cm (¼ in) thick
40 g (1½ oz) sea salt
330 ml (11 fl oz) apple-cider vinegar

365 g (13 oz) caster (superfine) sugar
1 tablespoon yellow mustard seeds
1 tablespoon cumin seeds
½ teaspoon turmeric
½ teaspoon cayenne pepper

Pickles are tasty on just about anything, and will liven up any snack or sandwich. These ones have the zing of vinegar and a mellow note from the cumin and turmeric. We use them on sandwiches with pastrami and gruyère for a variation on a Reuben sandwich.

People are always asking why these are called bread and butter pickles. The story goes that a couple of cucumber farmers in Illinois survived the Depression years by making these pickles and bartering them for staples such as bread and butter.

Combine the cucumbers, shallots and salt in a large mixing bowl, and toss gently to coat the vegetables in the salt. Cover the bowl with plastic wrap and refrigerate overnight to brine.

The next day, rinse the cucumbers and shallots in a colander under cold water to remove all the salt, then pack them tightly into a sterilised jar (see page 279).

Place the vinegar, sugar and spices in a heavy based saucepan and bring to a simmer over a medium heat, stirring, until the sugar has dissolved. Pour the liquid into the jar, making sure it completely covers the cucumbers and shallots, and seal it immediately.

Your pickles will be ready to eat the next day, but we prefer to leave them for a week to further develop the flavour. You can store the jar at room temperature for up to two months, unopened. Once opened, the pickles will last in the fridge for a couple of weeks.

Sauerkraut

It should come as no surprise that we love to ferment things. In sauerkraut, fermentation transforms the texture and flavour of cabbage, providing a slightly sour taste that brings everything alive. Sauerkraut works well with rich meat dishes; we use it at the bakery on a pastrami sandwich, and I love to keep a jar in the fridge at home to serve with roasted meats or to use in cheese toasties.

Makes one 500 ml (17 fl oz/2 cup) jar

Ingredients
675 g (1½ lb) white cabbage
¾ tablespoon table salt
¼ teaspoon caraway seeds, lightly toasted

Remove the stem of the cabbage, then roughly chop the leaves into 1 cm (½ in) thick strips. Place the cabbage in a large bowl then sprinkle over the salt. Mix the salt through, massaging it into the cabbage for around 10 minutes. The cabbage will start to turn pale and release some liquid. Add the caraway seeds and toss them through to thoroughly combine.

Drain the cabbage, reserving the liquid. Pack the cabbage into sterilised jars (see page 279), pressing down so it's very tightly packed. Pour over the released liquid, ensuring it covers the cabbage – any cabbage not covered will spoil. If you don't have enough juice, add water to cover.

Seal the jar and leave to ferment at room temperature. After three days, remove the lid and push the cabbage down to compress it further and ensure it's still covered with liquid. Leave it for another 2–4 days, depending on the weather. It will ferment faster in a warmer environment; a total of five days would be fine in summer, and up to seven days in winter. After this initial fermentation, store the sauerkraut in the fridge to slow down the process. It is now ready to eat, but will last for several months in the fridge, developing a stronger flavour the longer it's stored.

Mayonnaise

Mayonnaise is very easy to make, as long as you are patient and add the oil very slowly. You're creating an emulsion, so you can't pour it in too slowly, but if you add it too fast it will split. Mayonnaise can be made by hand, using a whisk, although the time taken to pour in the oil means you'll need to have strong arms and determination! An easier option is to make it in a food processor or stand mixer fitted with the whisk attachment.

Makes 300 g (10½ oz)

Ingredients
2 large egg yolks
1 tablespoon dijon mustard
1 tablespoon lemon juice
1 tablespoon white-wine vinegar
sea salt, to taste
250 g (9 oz) extra virgin olive oil

Bakery notes
If you find extra virgin olive oil too strong in mayonnaise, use half vegetable oil to soften the flavour. Ensure all of your ingredients are at room temperature before you start.

To make mustard mayonnaise for the roasted pork sandwich on page 118, add 55 g (2 oz) seeded mustard to your finished mayonnaise and mix well to combine. To make aioli, add a clove of minced garlic to your finished mayonnaise and mix well to combine.

If you like a creamier consistency, add a couple of tablespoons of water halfway through the emulsifying process, then continue whisking.

Whisk together the yolks, mustard, lemon juice, vinegar and a pinch of salt until the mixture forms a smooth paste.

Continue mixing at high speed, and very slowly pour in the oil. The mixture will start to emulsify. Once you are happy that this is under control you can slightly increase the speed of pouring.

Once the oil is incorporated and you have a smooth emulsion, season to taste and set aside until you're ready to use. Mayonnaise will last for a couple of weeks in the fridge in a sealed container or sterilised jar (see page 279).

Tomato chilli jam

**Makes approx. 1 litre
(34 fl oz/4 cups)**

Ingredients
500 g (1 lb 2 oz) ripe tomatoes,
  roughly chopped
4 red chillies, roughly chopped
4 cloves garlic, peeled and roughly
  chopped
50 g (1¾ oz) fresh ginger, peeled
  and grated
300 g (10½ oz) raw (demerara) sugar
100 g (3½ oz) red-wine vinegar

Bakery notes
*If making jam to give away as gifts, or
to store for some months, always be
meticulous about sterilising your jars first.
Jam will last for months in sterilised jars.*

*Use the 'plate test' to check consistency
before jarring (see page 279).*

This hot and sweet condiment is delicious with pies and sausage rolls, and great on a bacon and egg roll for breakfast. You could also stir a spoonful into a casserole to add some warmth, or loosen it with a little lime juice and fish sauce and use it as a dipping sauce for spring rolls.

Put half the tomatoes in a blender along with the chillies, garlic and ginger. Blitz them for a minute or two until well broken down, then transfer to a heavy based saucepan. Add the sugar and vinegar and bring to the boil over high heat.

Cook at a rapid boil for 10 minutes, then add the rest of the chopped tomatoes and stir them through. Keep the pan on the heat until it reaches 105°C (220°F) on a sugar thermometer, then use the 'plate test' to check the consistency (see page 279).

Leave your jam to cool for 10 minutes in the pan, stirring from time to time to keep the solids from dropping to the bottom. Pour the jam into sterilised jars and seal immediately (see page 279).

Red onion chutney

Makes two 1-litre (34 fl oz/4 cup) jars

Ingredients

1 kg (2 lb 3 oz) red onions, thickly sliced

600 g (1 lb 5 oz) granny smith apples, cut into 1 cm (½ in) dice

100 g (3½ oz) raisins

1 teaspoon ground cinnamon

20 g (¾ oz) brown mustard seeds

½ teaspoon mustard powder

½ teaspoon ground ginger

25 g (1 oz) fresh ginger, peeled and grated

500 g (1 lb 2 oz) red-wine vinegar

300 g (10½ oz) dark brown sugar

Bakery notes

If making chutney to give away as gifts, or to store for some months, always be meticulous about sterilising your jars first (see page 279).

This is a recipe from my days working with Tom Aikens. I had been baking in Sydney for a couple of years before returning to London to work with Tom on the opening of Tom's Kitchen in Chelsea. It was the first kitchen I worked in that exposed me to the ancient craft of preserving food in season to last until the next harvest. This is one of the first chutneys I made there.

Combine all the ingredients in a large saucepan or stockpot over medium heat. Bring the mixture slowly to the boil, then reduce the heat slightly. Simmer for 45 minutes to an hour, stirring occasionally so the chutney doesn't stick and burn at the bottom. It's ready when most of the moisture has cooked out and you have a nice thick chutney.

Once you are happy with the consistency, spoon the chutney into sterilised jars. Seal the jars immediately and store at room temperature for up to a year. Once opened, store your chutney in the fridge and use within six months.

Piccalilli

**Makes two 750 ml
(25½ fl oz/3 cup) jars**

Ingredients
375 g (13 oz) cauliflower, cut into
  small florets
150 g (5½ oz) zucchini (courgettes),
  cut into 1 cm (½ in) dice
150 g (5½ oz) red onion, sliced thickly
150 g (5½ oz) fennel, thickly sliced
150 g (5½ oz) celery, thickly sliced
½ red chilli, thinly sliced
75 g (2¾ oz) sea salt
1½ litres (51 fl oz/6 cups) cold water
25 ml (¾ fl oz) vegetable oil
10 g brown mustard seeds
5 g cumin seeds
5 g fennel seeds
2 teaspoons ground turmeric
25 g (1 oz) dijon mustard
⅓ nutmeg, grated
30 g (1 oz) cornflour (cornstarch)

Pickling liquor
425 g (15 oz) apple-cider vinegar
185 g (6½ oz) caster (superfine) sugar
3 sprigs thyme
2 bay leaves
30 g (1 oz) fresh horseradish, roughly
  chopped
2 cloves garlic, crushed

Bakery notes
*If you are making the piccalilli to give away
as gifts, or to store for some months, always
be meticulous about sterilising your jars
first (see page 279).*

This English pickle is so tasty, we always have a jar in the fridge at home for quick sandwiches and picnics. The vibrant yellow mixture looks as good as it tastes, and the chunky vegetables have a delightful crunch. It will keep for months in sterilised jars, and the flavour will only improve with age.

We use this at the bakery in a ham, cheddar and piccalilli sandwich, which always goes down well.

Combine the cauliflower, zucchini, red onion, fennel, celery, chilli and sea salt in a large mixing bowl, and toss to combine. Add the water and fill the bowl until the vegetables are just covered, then refrigerate overnight.

Combine all the ingredients for the pickling liquor in a medium sized saucepan and bring to a simmer over medium heat, stirring constantly until the sugar is dissolved. Refrigerate overnight to infuse.

The next day, place the vegetables in a colander over the sink. Rinse under cold water a few minutes to remove excess salt.

Pass the pickling liquor through a fine sieve and discard all the solids.

Heat the oil in a large saucepan over low heat, then add the brown mustard seeds, cumin seeds and fennel seeds. Toast for a couple of minutes, until fragrant. Add the drained and rinsed vegetables, and the turmeric, dijon mustard and nutmeg, and mix through until the vegetables are thoroughly coated in the spices.

Pour the pickling liquor over the vegetables and bring to a simmer over low heat. Mix the cornflour with a little water to form a loose paste, and stir this into the mixture while it's simmering, to thicken slightly. The liquid should be thick enough to bind the vegetables, not too runny or wet. Once you are happy with the consistency, spoon the vegetables into sterilised jars and pour over the liquid. Seal the jars immediately and store at room temperature for up to a year.

Candied mixed peel

We use mixed peel in our Christmas pudding, Christmas cakes and our hot cross buns. It's also lovely dipped in dark chocolate, for a simple homemade gift. This peel will keep for four to six months at room temperature.

Makes approx. 300 g (10½ oz)

Ingredients
5 medium-sized citrus fruits (such as oranges, limes, lemons, bergamot, grapefruit)
1 kg (2 lb 3 oz) white sugar

Slice each piece of fruit into eight wedges, then slice the flesh out of each wedge to leave the peel with a little pith still on. Set aside the flesh for another purpose, and slice the peel into 4–5-mm (¼ in-) wide strips. Put the peel in a heavy based saucepan pan, cover well with cold water and place the pan over high heat. Bring to the boil and then reduce the heat to simmer for 5 minutes.

Drain the peel and return it to the pan. Cover again with cold water, bring to the boil, then reduce the heat to simmer for 30 minutes. Drain the liquid, reserving the water this time.

Preheat the oven to its lowest temperature (about 60°C/140°F). Return the reserved water to the saucepan, making a note of its weight. Add an equal weight of sugar to the pan, reserving the remaining sugar, and place it over medium heat. Bring the mixture to the boil, stirring constantly until the sugar has dissolved. Add the peel and reduce to a simmer for 30 minutes, until the peel has softened and turned translucent. Leave the peel to cool slightly in the liquid for about 10 minutes.

Line a tray with baking paper, and use a large slotted spoon to transfer the peel onto the tray. Discard the sugar syrup, or reserve it for another use. Spread the peel evenly over the tray in a single layer and bake for 30–40 minutes to remove any excess moisture. The texture of the peel will be quite leathery at this stage.

Remove the peel from the oven. Place the remaining sugar in a medium sized bowl, then gently toss the peel in the sugar a few pieces at a time until completely coated. Put the peel back on the tray, evenly spread in a single layer, and leave to dry at room temperature for several hours, preferably overnight.

Candied cumquats

Cumquats grow abundantly in Melbourne, and this is a great way to preserve them for use in baking, or just to spread on toast. Cumquats are very tart and quite bitter, and are commonly cooked or preserved before eating. We use them in our Christmas pudding recipe (see page 228); they add beautiful moisture and small bursts of intense citrus flavour.

Makes 500 g (1 lb 2 oz)

Ingredients
400 g (14 oz) water
300 g (10 1/2 oz) sugar
20 g (¾ oz) glucose syrup
500 g (1 lb 2 oz) cumquats, halved and deseeded
2 cloves
2 star anise
1 vanilla pod, seeds scraped (or 1 teaspoon vanilla bean paste)

Bakery notes
Cumquats are a small fruit, so removing the seeds can be fiddly work. Use the tip of a sharp knife to dig them out when the fruit is still raw – it becomes quite a messy job once the fruit has been cooked down in the syrup.

You can use this method to candy other fruit, such as quince, cherries, sour cherries, or even sliced pineapple. Just use the same weight of fruit, and adjust the spices to your taste.

The glucose syrup is added to keep the candy from crystallising during storage. If you prefer, you could substitute with the juice of one lemon.

Bring the water, sugar, spices and glucose syrup to a simmer in a heavy based saucepan, stirring constantly until the sugar has dissolved.

Add the cumquats and bring the mixture to the boil, then reduce the heat and simmer for 20–30 minutes, until the fruit is translucent.

Remove from the heat and set aside to cool completely. Spoon the cumquats into hot sterilised jars (see page 279), and pour over the syrup to cover. Seal the jars immediately and store at room temperature for up to a year. Once opened, store in the fridge and use within two months.

Blood plum and bay leaf jam

Makes 1.6 kg (3½ lb)

Ingredients

1 kg (2 lb 3 oz) blood plums, washed, destoned and roughly chopped

40 ml (1¼ fl oz) lemon juice

750 g (1 lb 11 oz) caster (superfine) sugar

8 g (¼ oz) apple pectin

2 bay leaves

Bakery notes

If making jam to give away as gifts, or to store for some months, always be meticulous about sterilising your jars first. Jam will last for months in sterilised jars (see page 279).

Because plums are low in pectin, we use a little apple pectin here to produce a fairly firm-set jam. If you're happy with a runny jam you can leave it out. Pectin is usually made from apple skins, not artificial additive.

The bay leaves bring a more fragrant, savoury note to the jam.

Combine the plums and lemon juice in a saucepan over low heat. Slowly stew them for a couple of minutes, until the plums start to break down a bit. In a separate bowl, combine the sugar and pectin, then add the mixture to the saucepan in four batches, stirring to completely dissolve each addition before adding the next.

Once the sugar is fully incorporated, turn up the heat and boil the mixture rapidly for 10–15 minutes, stirring frequently so it doesn't stick on the bottom of the pan. As it boils, a light foam will form on the surface; just skim this off with a spoon as it appears.

As soon as your jam reaches 105°C (220°F) on a sugar thermometer, turn off the heat and use the plate test to check the consistency (see page 279). Add the bay leaves, then set the jam aside to cool and infuse for 10 minutes in the pan. Stir the mixture occasionally to keep the fruit from dropping to the bottom. Pour the jam into hot sterilised jars and seal immediately.

Seville orange marmalade

Makes 1.5 kg (3 lb 5 oz)

Ingredients
450 g (1 lb) unwaxed Seville oranges
1125 ml (38 fl oz) water
juice of 1 lemon
900 g (2 lb) caster (superfine) sugar

Bakery notes
If making jam to give away as gifts, or to store for some months, always be meticulous about sterilising your jars first. Jam will last for months in sterilised jars (see page 279).

The Seville orange season is very short, so we buy as many as we can and make a big batch of this very popular marmalade. We sell it in jars and use it in sweet treats, always reserving some for our Christmas cakes.

Seville oranges are lovely and tart, producing a better marmalade flavour than sweeter varieties.

Make thin incisions to mark quarters in the oranges, then peel off the rind in petals, leaving the orange intact with the pith still attached. Slice the rind into thin strips, and set aside.

Cut the oranges in half and put them in a blender. Liquefy the oranges, then strain the juice through a sieve into a saucepan, pressing the pulp into the sieve to extract as much juice as possible. Tie the remaining pulp, pith and seeds in a muslin cloth and add this to the pan. Add the water and lemon juice, together with the strips of rind.

Bring the mixture up to a simmer over medium heat. Simmer for an hour, until the rind softens completely. Remove the muslin bag and squeeze it tightly, pouring the juice back into the pan.

Gradually add the sugar in three batches, stirring until each addition has dissolved before adding the next.

Once the sugar is fully incorporated, turn up the heat and boil the mixture rapidly for 10–15 minutes, stirring frequently so it doesn't stick on the bottom of the pan. As it boils, a light foam will form on the surface; just skim this off with a spoon as it appears.

As soon as your marmalade reaches 105°C (220°F) on a sugar thermometer, turn off the heat and use the plate test to check the consistency (see page 279). Leave the marmalade to cool for 10 minutes in the pan, stirring from time to time to keep the fruit from dropping to the bottom. Pour into hot sterilised jars and seal immediately.

Raspberry jam

Makes 1.6 kg (3½ lb)

Ingredients
1 kg (2 lb 3 oz) raspberries, rinsed
50 ml (1¾ fl oz) lemon juice
850 g (1 lb 14 oz) caster (superfine)
  sugar

Bakery notes
*If making jam to give away as gifts, or
to store for some months, always be
meticulous about sterilising your jars first
(see page 279).*

We always have this jam
available at Tivoli Road.
It's our house staple,
served with toast and
croissants, or used to fill
doughnuts for the pastry
cabinet. We use the same
recipe to make blackberry
and strawberry jams.
Combination berry jams
are also delicious – use
the recipe as a base and
use whatever berries
you have to hand.

Combine the raspberries and lemon juice in a saucepan over low heat. Slowly
stew them for a couple of minutes, until the berries start to break down a little.
Add the sugar in four batches, stirring to completely dissolve each addition
before adding the next.

Once the sugar is fully incorporated, turn up the heat and boil the mixture
rapidly for 10–15 minutes, stirring frequently so it doesn't stick on the bottom
of the pan. As it boils, a light foam will form on the surface; just skim this off with
a spoon as it appears.

As soon as your jam reaches 105°C (220°F) on a sugar thermometer, turn off
the heat and use the plate test to check the consistency (see page 279). Leave
the jam to cool for 10 minutes in the pan, stirring from time to time to keep
the fruit from dropping to the bottom. Pour the jam into hot sterilised jars and
seal immediately.

Variations

Some fruits have a higher pectin level than others, so using a combination of different fruits is nice way to get variation while still achieving a good consistency. For example, raspberries and peaches are wonderful together, and when made into a jam the high pectin level in the berries compensates for the peaches having less, leaving you with a delicious and nicely set jam.

If you're using fruit with low pectin levels, you could add pectin powder (available from most supermarkets), as in the blood plum and bay leaf jam recipe, or grate an apple into a muslin bag and add this to the saucepan with the fruit. Pectin is naturally occurring; we use an apple pectin made of powdered dehydrated apple skins.

High-pectin fruits	Low-pectin fruits
· raspberries	· figs
· blackberries	· blueberries
· gooseberries	· peaches
· boysenberries	· nectarines
· citrus	· plums
· quince	· apricots
· apples	
· rhubarb	
· pears	

Infused jams

We also like to infuse our jams with different herbs or warm spices. Place a handful of your chosen herb or spice in a muslin bag, and once setting point has been reached, add it to the pan to infuse for the final 10 minutes. Remove the muslin bag before jarring your jam. Some lovely flavour combinations include pear and vanilla, raspberry and rose geranium, apricot and amaretto seed, blackberry and lemon verbena, or blueberry and star anise. Your options are only limited by your tastes and your imagination.

A note on texture

If you prefer a chunky jam, macerate the fruit with the sugar and lemon juice overnight before applying any heat. As they're already well combined, they won't need as long on the heat, giving them less time to 'cook down' and lose their structure.

Setting point

Use the 'plate test' to check the consistency of your jams before jarring them. To do this, put a small plate in the freezer before you start making your jam. Once the jam reaches 105°C (220°F) on your sugar thermometer and starts to make large bubbles rather than small foamy ones, turn off the heat and take the plate out of the freezer. Drop a little jam onto the plate and put it in the fridge for 1 minute, then check the consistency by running your finger through the jam. If the jam spreads over the plate where your finger was, it needs more time. If you are left with a clear line, it has reached the correct setting point and is ready for jarring.

Sterilising jars

We always sterilise jars used to store pickles, jams and chutneys. Your preserves will last almost indefinitely in containers that are sterilised before use. To sterilise your jars, wash them in hot soapy water and rinse thoroughly, then place the clean jars on a baking tray and transfer to a low oven set between 100–120°C (230–430°F) for 20 minutes. Make sure your jars are completely dry and still warm when you fill them.

Acknowledgements

Creating this book has been a very collaborative process, and there are many people to thank. So thank you to ...

- Pippa, who is always there for me and makes everything worthwhile. Thank you for bringing this book together.

- Our beautiful daughter, Clover, who was so patient during the whole process of us writing this book.

- Jane, Andrea and the team at Hardie Grant. Thank you for believing in us, it's been amazing to work with you.

- Alan Benson and Bonnie Savage, two amazing photographers. We were so lucky to work with you.

- Emily Hart, for being the best head baker we could hope for. You kept it all together during the writing of this book, and contributed to recipes and testing on top of everything else.

- Charlie Duffy, for your ideas, creations, styling and constant drive for perfection.

- Krista Corbett, for your dedication to our customers and team, and your absolute precision in everything you do.

- Darren Purchese & Cath Claringbold, for giving us the nudge to get this project moving. Your positivity and support is endless and we are so grateful.

- Dave McGuinness and Paul Allam from Bourke Street Bakery. Thank you for lighting the fire and for teaching me so much.

- Dan Lepard, an endless inspiration. I picked up *Baker & Spice* as a young chef in London, and it inspired me to get into baking. You are always so generous with your time and knowledge.

- Chad Robertson, for inspiring a generation of bakers and being so generous to me.

- Ben Shewry, for showing the Aussies what's on their doorstep, and your support and friendship.

- Tom Aikens, my first mentor. You pushed me so hard and taught me to strive for the best in everything I do.

- Ian Lowe for being a great friend, sharing your encyclopedic knowledge and bringing the grain community together in our part of the world.

- Emily Salkeld & John Reid.

- Bruce Pascoe, for sharing your knowledge of Indigenous grains and bread.

- Len Harrison, from the Walter and Eliza Hall Institute.

- Our suppliers, who give us such beautiful produce to work with. And especially to Craig & Renée, Ben & Bianca, Richie, Frank & Pene, Mish & Di and Moss & Andrew. Thank you for giving us your time and generosity.

- Katie Falkiner, this book would not exist without you.

- To our recipe testers: Anna Augustine, Suzanne Farrell, Malissa Gough, Roslyn Grundy, Jenny Watling, Julian Smith, Kelly Piola, Lili Foster, Liesa Latham, Kim Wiggins and Pamela Anderson.

- Geoffrey Smith, the best grandpa ever to Clover. Thank you for babysitting whenever we need it!

- And of course to our amazingly supportive customers. Thank you for creating such a warm community around us.

About the authors

Michael James grew up in Penzance, West Cornwall. He moved to London at the age of 18 and worked at the five-star Selsdon Park Hotel before joining Tom Aikens at the two-Michelin star restaurant Pied-à-Terre. It was here he met his Australian wife Pippa. After moving to Sydney in 2004, he had the opportunity to work and learn with Dave McGuinness and Paul Allam at Bourke Street Bakery. This job was the start of his baking career, and he has never looked back.

Originally from Canberra, Pippa James worked for Janet Jeffs before moving to London, on a mission to get some experience in fine-dining restaurants. She worked at Pied-à-Terre and The Greenhouse, before returning to Australia as restaurant manager at Flying Fish in Sydney, and then HR manager at Vue de monde in Melbourne. Pippa was general manager of the Andrew McConnell restaurants Cutler & Co. and Golden Fields, before opening Tivoli Road Bakery with Michael.

Index

This edition published in 2019 by Hardie Grant Books,
an imprint of Hardie Grant Publishing
First published in 2017

Hardie Grant Books (Melbourne)
Building 1, 658 Church Street
Richmond, Victoria 3121

Hardie Grant Books (London)
5th & 6th Floors
52–54 Southwark Street
London SE1 1UN

hardiegrantbooks.com

 A catalogue record for this
book is available from the
National Library of Australia

The Tivoli Road Baker
ISBN 978 1 74379 590 3

10 9 8 7 6 5 4 3 2 1

Publishing Director: Jane Willson
Managing Editor: Marg Bowman
Project Editor: Andrea O'Connor
Editor: Vanessa Lanaway
Design Manager: Jessica Lowe
Designer: Mark Campbell
Illustrator: Alice Oehr
Photographers: Bonnie Savage and Alan Benson
Stylist: Lee Blaylock
Production Manager: Todd Rechner
Production Coordinator: Rebecca Bryson

Colour reproduction by Splitting Image Colour Studio
Printed in China by Leo Paper Products LTD.

Notes on the recipes

This book uses 15 ml (½ fl oz)
tablespoons; cooks with 20 ml
(¾ fl oz) tablespoons should be scant
with their tablespoon measurements.

Oven temperatures are for a fan
assisted oven.